DIRECTORY OF
COLLECTIONS

THE UNIVERSITY OF
EDINBURGH

THE UNIVERSITY
of EDINBURGH

Third Millennium
Publishing

Previous page: Joannes Ruckers, double-manual harpsichord, 1638

First published in Great Britain in 2016 by
Third Millennium Publishing, an imprint of Profile Books Ltd

3 Holford Yard
Bevin Way
London WC1X 9HD
United Kingdom
www.tmiltd.com

Main author: Joseph Marshall
Cover image: Robert Barker, *Panorama of Edinburgh*, 1792
Endpapers: Collection of legal theses with decorated paper wrappers (detail)

All images were created by the University of Edinburgh's Digital Imaging Unit
and are copyright of the University of Edinburgh, unless otherwise stated.

A CIP catalogue record for this book is available from The British Library.

ISBN: 978 1 908990 85 3 (hardback edition)
ISBN: 978 1 908990 89 1 (paperback edition)

Project Editor: Hannah Bowen
Design: Susan Pugsley
Production: Simon Shelmerdine

Reprographics by Studio Fasoli, Verona, Italy
Printed and bound in China by 1010 Printing International Ltd

Contents

Foreword

The University of Edinburgh has one of the world's great collections, which
has been growing ever since the University's foundation in 1582. The collections
include rare books, archives and manuscripts, art, historical musical instruments
and a wide range of other museum objects from geological specimens to anatomical
models. They are curated by specialist staff across 45 different sites within the
University and are used for teaching, research and by the wider public community.
In total we have some 60 kilometres of heritage material, from 1st-century Greek
papyrus fragments to new works of sculpture. The scale and diversity of the collections
is one of the reasons why the University of Edinburgh is truly exceptional. It also
makes it a challenge to describe the collections clearly – which is what this new
directory does for the first time.

   This Directory of Collections outlines all the main collections across the
University, divided into six sections for ease of navigation. It starts with the iconic
items for which the Special Collections are known, such as the Celtic Psalter. The
remaining sections present the collections in rare books, archives and manuscripts,
musical instruments, art and museums, arranged in A–Z order by the name of the
collection. Our collections are usually named after the individual who created them
or gave them to the University. We thereby recognise and honour all our generous
donors, dating back to Clement Litill whose bequest of 276 books in 1580 brought
Edinburgh University Library into existence.

   The collections continue to grow and it is important that this directory
includes collections which have arrived in the last five years, such as the Heiskell
Darwin collection and the Paolozzi mosaics. We look forward to new collections
arriving to complement new areas of work for the University, which will meet
the needs of our students and the immediate Scottish community as well as our
growing international audience. This book captures the collections at one moment
in time in the University's story. Future collections will of course be made available
digitally – and increasingly the collections themselves will be born digital, giving
curators the exciting challenge of preserving them for the centuries to come.

   It is my hope that the Directory will be of immediate benefit to our students and
scholars, as well as a lasting record of the University of Edinburgh's rich holdings
as they stand in the early 21st century.

Professor Sir Timothy O'Shea

Principal

Introduction

This book presents a guide to the main named heritage collections of the University of Edinburgh. It is not a treasures book, although it does highlight some of the items we think of as 'iconic'. Nor is it trying to give a comprehensive description of the thousands of discrete collections that fill some 60 kilometres of shelving. Instead, this offers a way in to the collections arranged in A–Z format, primarily by the name of the person who created or assembled the material. From the Aberdeen Breviary to Zoology, we aim to give an overview of the breadth and variety of the unique strengths of the cultural assets which the University of Edinburgh holds.

Raphael Holinshed, *Chronicles*, 1587

The collections

The story of the collections at the University of Edinburgh would require a separate book. From its foundation the University of Edinburgh was voracious for knowledge – not just in the traditional areas of medicine, law and theology but also in new areas such as modern literature. The early collections of books and manuscripts reflect the wide interests and international reach of the young College. From an early date there were also collections of art – particularly portraits – and objects. The earliest remaining item from these first museum collections is the skull of the Scottish writer and tutor of King James VI, George Buchanan (1506–1582). The University's growth in the 17th and 18th centuries was spectacular, leading it to develop the international reputation it maintains today, and spurring the rapid growth of collections to support and record its teaching and research. During the Enlightenment the Library held the privilege of legal deposit, meaning it could claim a copy of every book printed in Great Britain and Ireland – one reason why we have 400,000 rare books today. New areas of University activity led to explosions of collecting, as can be seen in anatomy and natural history. Generous donors such as General John Reid and David Laing trusted the University with their own money and/or their own holdings of manuscripts or art works. Throughout this activity the University generated records of its own doings, which form what are now the University Archives.

New College, University of Edinburgh

boys are children forever in neverland

The modern period

By the 20th century the collections were already world-class, and they continued to grow with the University. Major collections arrived such as Lothian Health Services Archive, which the University curates on behalf of NHS Lothian. The musical instruments have become a collection of international importance, particularly with the gifts of the Nicholas Shackleton woodwinds and the Raymond Russell collection of early keyboards. The buildings and the professional care of the materials progressed with the opening of the new Main Library in 1967 and its refurbishment in 2006–2012. The Main Library now houses the Centre for Research Collections, which acts as the hub for all the heritage collections. The story of the buildings of the University is told elsewhere, but the spaces are a key part of the collections landscape, such as St Cecilia's Hall, newly refurbished to its former glory and open as our new public museum and our home for the musical instruments, as of spring 2017. The University of Edinburgh's merger with Edinburgh College of Art in 2011 brought a major boost to the art collections, which are now seen on display across the campus. Equally the merger with the Roslin Institute in 2008 has enriched the collections on science and veterinary medicine; the records of the story of the cloning of Dolly the sheep are now attracting research in their own right. As the areas of informatics and computing science develop, new objects and digital records are already starting to be created. This book captures the collections as they stand in 2016, but these collections are alive, constantly growing and changing.

Lending collection, Main Library

How to use this book

We hope you will use this book as a route map through the collections. Whether you are researching specific topics, looking for images for a publication or simply wanting ideas, this book can help. The descriptions are not presented in a uniform way; these different materials are curated in different ways, and in this book they are described in ways to suit their particular needs. So you may find that we describe an archive collection differently to an art collection. The book is not a catalogue, and underpinning the content is a range of ever-developing online finding aids. However, everything that is described in this book is available to be consulted, by anyone who wishes.

We have divided the book into six main sections, according to collection type. Several collectors (such as James Corson, the Walter Scott devotee) accumulated material of several different types – this

Giovanni Battista
Piranesi, *Vedute
di Roma*, 1778

is indicated by cross-references where appropriate. The categories are broad, but essentially are as follows.

- 'Iconic special collections' are individual rare books and manuscripts recognised as having exceptional importance. What is classed as 'iconic' is inevitably subjective and changing.
- 'Archives and manuscripts' are documents produced by hand or in typescript, and therefore by definition unique.
- 'Rare books' are volumes printed and published before 1900, or classed as rare because they were owned and marked by someone significant.
- 'Musical instrument collections' range from large keyboard instruments to small woodwind pieces, many still playable and used for performance.
- 'Art collections' are primarily visual materials including paintings, works on paper, sculptures and increasingly digital installations.
- 'Museum collections' encompass objects ranging from geological specimens to artefacts from ancient human history.

There are many rich holdings that do not fit into this A–Z scheme, and several books would be needed to do justice to these curiosities alone. Individual items range from an 11-inch sebaceous horn cut from a woman's head in 1671, to the coffee pot presented to Professor Adam Ferguson by exiled Jacobite George Keith. There is even a table which the Emperor Napoleon had in his study on St Helena. We have countless items that have not yet been explored or which have yet to release their potential – and most excitingly, we know that future years will see the arrival of collections we cannot presently even imagine.

Jeremy Upton

Jeremy Upton
Director of Library and University Collections

Joseph Marshall
Head of Special Collections

Joseph Marshall

Selected further reading

Anderson, Robert David, Michael Lynch and Nicholas Phillipson.
The University of Edinburgh: An Illustrated History. Edinburgh
University Press, 2003.

Bownes, Mary, and Jean Grier. *Private Giving, Public Good:
The Impact of Philanthropy at the University of Edinburgh*.
Edinburgh University Press, 2014.

Fraser, Andrew. *The Building of Old College: Adam, Playfair & the
University of Edinburgh*. Edinburgh University Press, 1989.

Guild, Jean R, and Alexander Law. *Edinburgh University Library
1580–1980: A Collection of Historical Essays.* Edinburgh University
Press, 1982.

http://collections.ed.ac.uk

Exhibition Gallery,
Edinburgh University
Library

13

Edinburgh University Library, George Square

of inr h̃ cu ꝝ ecu

onfitebor domin

qͫ ineth.num

(faded)

bati immaculi

lant inlege d

bati qui cur

mll ə intoto co

ec hrim qui oph

inuir etur ambu

umundaꝗ pchꝭ

tuam dnigari

adcurꝺdibioa

i. Iconic Special Collections

Among the thousands of precious objects in the
collections of the University of Edinburgh are a
few that are important enough to be designated
'iconic'. Whether because of their extreme rarity,
their beauty or because they define some key moment
in the University's history, they are the most prized
individual items in our care.

Celtic Psalter

Aberdeen Breviary

*Breuiarij Aberdone[n]sis ad percelebris eccl[es]ie Scotor[um]
potissimu[m] vsum et consuetudine[m]* [**The Aberdeen
Breviary, according to the principal use and custom of the
most famous church of the Scots**] [**Edinburgh: Printed by
Andrew Myllar and Walter Chepman, 1509–1510**].

Scotland's first substantial printed book

This is the finest surviving copy of this book. It was commissioned by
William Elphinstone, Bishop of Aberdeen, in order to give Scotland
its own distinctive liturgy, including prayers to Scottish saints such as
St Kentigern and St Ninian. Elphinstone had it printed in what is now
Edinburgh's Cowgate. Printed in red and black, with handsome woodcuts,
it was meant to signal a great cultural and religious renaissance. The Battle
of Flodden in 1513 and the troubled years that followed ensured that
Elphinstone's vision was never fulfilled, and the Breviary rapidly fell into
disuse. This copy was acquired through student contributions in 1635.
De.1 / 1.53-54

Aberdeen Breviary,
1509–1510

The religious leader Bihafarid, from Al-Bîrûnî's *Chronology of Ancient Nations*

Al-Bîrûnî's *Chronology of Ancient Nations*

Al-Bîrûnî, *al-Athar al-baqiya (The Chronology of Ancient Nations)*, **Arabic, Tabriz, Iran, 706 AH (AD 1307).**

A pinnacle of early Persian art and historiography

This important work by the Persian polymath al-Bîrûnî was written originally in circa 390 AH (AD 1000). The manuscript has a distinct multi-ethnic and multiconfessional flavour. Al-Bîrûnî, who calculated that the world was round on the basis of measurements he took in the Punjab plain, describes the systems of calculating time used by the known races of the world, and their associated festivals. Its text and 26 illustrations (painted in AD 1307) breathe a spirit of tolerance and open-eyed curiosity about the world at large. Here, Christian scenes (the Baptism and the Annunciation) complement Islamic images, as well as others of Zoroastrian, pre-Islamic Arabian, Jewish and Hindu

origin, and even one of the birth of Julius Caesar. The manuscript
was donated by Robert Munro Blair Binning (1814–1891) of the
Madras Civil Service, in 1877.

Or.MS.161

Anglo-Saxon charter

Our earliest English manuscript

We have a fine collection of more than 3,000 charters (official
documents recording land transactions) bequeathed by the great
collector David Laing in 1878. The earliest is this Anglo-Saxon document
dated AD 854, in which King Ethelwulf of Wessex grants 20 hides
of land to the monks of St Peter at Winchester. It is probably an
11th-century copy, on vellum, and is among our earliest manuscripts.

Laing charters 18 (box 1)

Anglo-Saxon charter,
AD 854

Robert Barker,
Panorama of Edinburgh,
1792

The 'Barker Panorama' of Edinburgh

Edinburgh from the Calton Hill, Robert Barker, 1792.

Edinburgh, birthplace of the panorama

Robert Barker (1739–1806) invented the word 'panorama' along with
the art form that it originally described and which he patented in 1787.

Barker was an Irish itinerant portrait painter. He moved to Edinburgh
in the early 1780s. The story goes that he was out walking on Calton Hill
with the whole vista of the city of Edinburgh laid out before him, and
he seized upon the idea of capturing the scene in the round. In 1787 he
opened an exhibition in Edinburgh which was to have a major impact
on the 19th- and 20th-century entertainment industries. It featured
a panoramic view of the city painted around the inner wall of a rotunda
which, when viewed from the centre of the room, gave the spectator the
illusion of reality. Viewers were admitted via a spiral staircase to a central
gallery. Special note was made that the viewer should not see the top or
bottom of the painting to improve the illusion 'of being on the very spot'.

Barker took his invention to London where it was an immediate
success. Housed in specially built circular buildings, Panoramas
subsequently became a very popular form of visual entertainment,
in some ways heralding the cinema. Unfortunately none of Barker's
large-scale Panoramas survive. This small, watercolour version of
Barker's first full Panorama is dated 1792 and follows from a set
of engravings published two years earlier.

Coll-1709

....

Black, Joseph

The invention of the thermometer

Joseph Black (1728–1799), one of the founders of modern
chemistry, made major discoveries regarding the different gases

in the atmosphere and invented a way to obtain accurate measurements of heat. From 1766 until 1799, he was Professor of Chemistry at the University of Edinburgh. His lectures circulated in manuscripts drawn up by his students. The image here shows a drawing of a thermometer made by one such student in 1784. Now a familiar image, at the time it was a revolutionary device that transformed systematic research.

Dc.2.41

....

Lecture notes on Joseph Black

Bohemian Protest

Our first star exhibit

This is the last surviving copy of the famous protest of the Bohemian nobles against the burning of the religious reformer Jan Hus in 1415. A magnificent vellum document surrounded by the seals of the Bohemian nobility, it was acquired by Aberdonian theologian William Guild (1586–1657) while he was on the continent during the British civil wars. It was for many years on display at the University of Edinburgh and came to be seen as an icon of religious freedom – anticipating the Protestant Reformation. It is considered to be the first star exhibit at the University.

Coll-1698

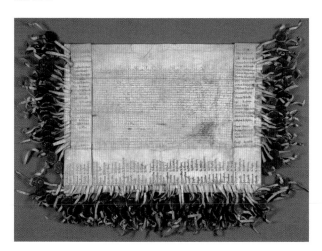

Bohemian Protest, 1415

Burns, Robert

The national bard's 'Address to Edinburgh'

This collection of poems in the hand of Robert Burns is among the greatest literary treasures of the David Laing collection. As well as a number of famous poems it includes letters and ephemera connected to the national bard.

It contains manuscripts of the following major poems:

- 'Address to Edinburgh'
- 'Holy Willie's Prayer'
- 'The Inventory'
- 'The Kirk of Scotland's Alarm'
- 'Lament for James Earl of Glencairn'
- 'Love and Liberty: A Cantata'
- 'A New Psalm for the Chapel of Kilmarnock'
- 'Ode, Sacred to the Memory of Mrs. Oswald of Auchencruive'
- 'Ode to the Memory of the Regency Bill 1789'
- 'On Seeing a Fellow Wound a Hare with a Shot'
- 'Passion's Cry' (fragments)
- 'To Robert Graham of Fintry, Esquire'
- 'Verses Intended to be Written below a Noble Earl's Picture'
- 'Written in Friars' Carse Hermitage' (two versions).

La. III. 586

Robert Burns,
'Address to Edinburgh'

Celtic Psalter

The oldest known Scottish book still in Scotland

Perhaps the Library's greatest treasure is this pocket-size Psalter, with extraordinary illuminations in vivid green, red, purple and gold. It has been dated to the 11th century and is almost certainly the oldest Scottish book still in Scotland. The Irish minuscule script is bold and clear and it gives a text of the Psalms in Latin that can still be read today. Although the original binding is lost, it was probably commissioned for a figure of some importance, such as St Margaret, Queen of Scotland, to whose reign it can be dated. The fact that some of the decoration was enhanced in the English 'Winchester' style may indicate a connection with St Margaret, who descended from the Anglo-Saxon royal family.

Celtic Psalter

How the book was acquired by the University is unclear; it quietly appears in a manuscript catalogue of 1636. Other notes in the volume indicate that it was previously in Aberdeen and it is entirely possible that it was written at a Scottish monastery. Its survival in almost pristine internal condition strongly suggests that it was valued for an association now lost to us. This is the oldest of some 275 Western medieval manuscripts in our collection. *MS.56*

Copernicus, *De revolutionibus*

Copernicus, Nicolaus. *De revolutionibus orbium cœlestium.*
Norimbergæ: Apud Ioh. Petreium, 1543.

The earth goes round the sun

When Copernicus, the Polish astronomer, found he had clear evidence that the earth revolves around the sun, he was very cautious about how he announced his discovery. This book did not appear until after

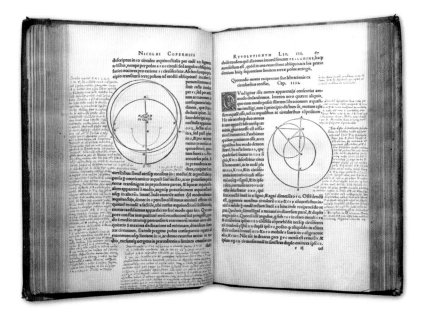

Nicolaus Copernicus,
De Revolutionibus, 1543

his death, when he was beyond the reach of those angered at the way he had shattered the geocentric universe. This is an outstanding copy, bound in contemporary continental vellum, of one of the defining books of the scientific renaissance. It was owned by an astronomer, who filled the pages with scholarly annotations, and subsequently by the Scottish economist Adam Smith.

Smith.1630

....

Darwin, Charles

Charles Darwin, six University of Edinburgh class cards and one matriculation card, signed.

Origin of evolutionary theory

Darwin's medical studies at the University of Edinburgh were a formative influence on his scientific career. These class cards show the courses he signed up for in 1825. Edinburgh professors in the 1820s received little or no salary from the University. The only payment they received came directly from class fees paid by students. The more popular their courses, the higher their incomes became. As a result there were no entrance requirements and every man and his fee were welcome. These class cards were presented to the University of Edinburgh by the late Sir Francis Darwin in 1909.

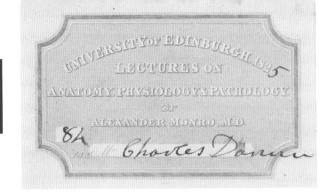

In 2012 the University received an outstanding collection of first
editions of Darwin's numerous works, including two copies of the first
edition of *On the Origin of Species* (1859). This collection was presented by
the Heiskell Bibliographical Foundation to the University of Edinburgh USA
Development Trust, and is on loan to the Library. We also have a fragment
of the manuscript of *Origin* in the Bright correspondence, Coll-344.
EUA CA6

Derricke's Image of Ireland

**John Derricke, *The Image of Irelande*. London:
By [J. Kingston for] Jhon Daie, 1581.**

Unique pictures of Irish life

Only one complete copy survives of this controversial work, which
defends England's subjugation of Ireland in verse. In the 1570s English
troops under Lord Deputy Sir Henry Sidney, father of the poet Philip
Sidney, were engaged in a brutal struggle against native Irish forces. John

John Derricke, *The
Image of Irelande*, 1581

Derricke was a Protestant English engraver who accompanied Sidney and produced this illustrated account to justify and glorify the English actions. The 12 remarkable woodcuts are intended to depict the native Irish as savages and the English forces as heroic conquerors. Ironically, the images give us a powerful insight into life in Ireland, as Derricke was despite his prejudices an eye-witness and a skilled observer.

De. 3.76

....

Doyle, Sir Arthur Conan: medical thesis

Arthur Conan Doyle, *An Essay Upon the Vasomotor Changes in Tabes Dorsalis***, MD, Edinburgh, 1885.**

His first case

Doyle (1859–1930) is famed as the creator of Sherlock Holmes and for developing the genre of crime fiction, which continues to have a distinctively Scottish slant in writers such as Ian Rankin. However, he was trained and initially practised as a doctor. His medical dissertation of 1885 discusses syphilis from a literary as well as a medical perspective. This is certainly the most famous item in the University's vast thesis collection, which records the primary research of many who became eminent scholars.

Arthur Conan Doyle, MD Thesis, 1885

MS 2600

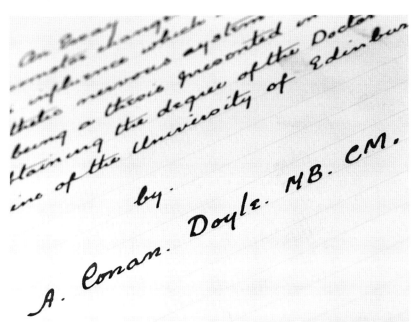

Earliest Donations Book

The first gifts

Donations – of money, books, objects and works of art – have helped keep the collections growing ever since the foundation of the University. William Henderson, one of the greatest University librarians, started this first register of donations in the 17th century, and it ran from 1667 until 1755, recording some great treasures.

EUA IN1/ADS/LIB/2/Da.1.31

Earliest Donations Book

. . . .

Earliest Laureation Album

The first students

This volume records the first group of students to graduate from the University of Edinburgh.

It begins with the Scots Confession of Faith of 1580, to which the students subscribed, and to which professors and students would continue to subscribe for many years. The entries for laureations (or graduations) begin in August 1587, when Robert Rollock, the first Principal, presided over the first graduation ceremony. This first class consisted of 47 students, all of whom signed their names.

Earliest Laureation Album

The Register records all graduates up to 1712, and medical graduates from 1710 to 1809, and thus played a central role in the life of the institution for more than 200 years.

Many of the signatures in the volume are of key figures in the life of the University, and include those of William Drummond of Hawthornden, the poet and benefactor to the University, and Hugh Blair, holder of the world's first chair of what is now called English Literature.

EUA IN1 / ADS / STA / 1 / 1

Earliest Library Catalogue

The first books

The early records of the University Library are complex and highly detailed and show a rapidly growing collection. Edinburgh was Britain's first post-Reformation university and the first secular, municipal foundation. This is reflected in the breadth of the collections from a very early date – not just law and divinity but also modern literature, radical philosophy and foreign books from as far away as America and China.

EUA IN1 / ADS / LIB / 1 / Da.1.1

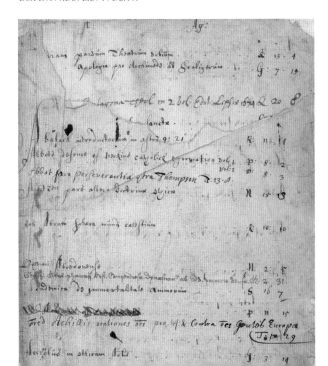

Earliest Library
Catalogue

First University Court Minutes

Independence for the University

The University Court was established under the
Universities (Scotland) Act of 1858, which saw
the University of Edinburgh reconstituted as
an autonomous, self-governing organisation. It
was convened the following year, originally with
a restricted remit but subsequently becoming
the senior governing committee following the
Universities (Scotland) Act of 1889.

EUA IN1 / GOV / CRT / 1 / 1 (previously Da.23)

First Court Minutes

Fleming, Alexander: penicillin mould

Mould is beautiful

Alexander Fleming (1881–1955) was born in Ayrshire, and was one
of the great figures of 20th-century medicine. Not only did he discover
the antibiotic powers of penicillin, for which he shared the Nobel Prize
in 1945, but he was the first to use anti-typhoid vaccines on human
beings and pioneered the use of Salvarsan for syphilis. This sample

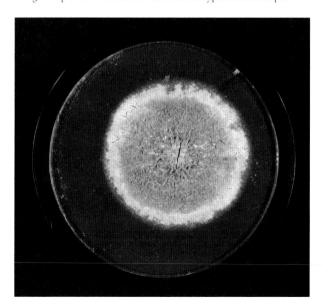

Alexander Fleming,
penicillin mould

of the mould that makes penicillin was presented to the University by Fleming to commemorate his time as Rector. To many viewers it is a beautiful object, simple and ethereal, which transcends the mere fact of it being mould.

Medals.110

Gaelic Liturgy

Foirm na nurrnuidheadh agas freasdal na sacramuinteadh, agas foirceadul an chreidimh Christuidhe andso sios

Foirm na nurrnuidheadh, 1567

[Edinburgh: Printed by Robert Lekprevik, 1567].

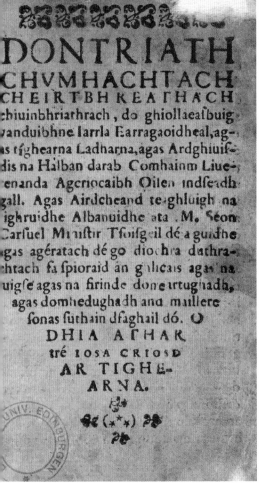

The first book printed in any of the Gaelic languages

This unassuming little book, the opening of whose title translates 'The form of the prayers', is of the greatest national importance. It is the only copy in Scotland of the first book printed in Gaelic. After the Reformation there was a strong impetus, sponsored primarily by the Campbell Earls of Argyll, to evangelise the Highlands and Islands, where Gaelic rather than Scots was spoken. John Carswell, Bishop of the Isles, adapted John Knox's *Book of Common Order* into Scottish Gaelic. It was a hugely ambitious undertaking, particularly considering it would be another two centuries before the New Testament was finally published in vernacular Gaelic. This copy has clearly been well used.

Dd.10.44

Hill and Adamson photographs

**Calotype photographs by Scottish pioneers
David Octavius Hill (1802–1870) and Robert Adamson
(1821–1848).**

Birth of photography

Hill and Adamson photographed a wide range of subject matter:
portraits of well-known characters of the time, ordinary working
people, local landscapes and urban scenes. The prints in our
collection exemplify their innovative and sensitive approach
to composition and demonstrate how Hill brought his own
experience as an artist to bear on the new medium of photography.

Mrs Elizabeth Hall
(Johnstone), calotype
photograph by Hill
and Adamson

The calotype process was invented by William Henry Fox Talbot
in 1839, and Hill and Adamson were perhaps its greatest exponents.
During their four-year partnership they made more than 3,000
photographs including portraits, landscapes and architectural studies.
Their study of Newhaven fishwives and men is among the earliest
examples of social documentary photography.

Coll-1073

....

Indian Primer

John Eliot, *The Indian Primer*. Cambridge [Mass.], 1669.

Unique copy of one of the first American books

This tiny book contains Christian instruction, mainly in the indigenous
American Algonquian language. Printing began in America in 1640
and was used by missionary John
Eliot, who translated the Bible
and many other works into the
indigenous language for the first
time. Amazingly, this copy is still
in its original American wooden
binding. It was gifted to the
University Library in 1675 by
James Kirkton, a church minister
and Edinburgh graduate.

Df.7.98

John Eliot, *The Indian
Primer*, 1669

Kirk, Robert: *The Secret Commonwealth*

Away with the fairies

Robert Kirk (1644–1692) was a minister and Gaelic scholar who is best known for this manuscript on fairy superstitions and the second sight. As well as pioneering the translation of the Bible into Scottish Gaelic, Kirk collected traditions of elves, ghosts and witchcraft. *The Secret Commonwealth* was eventually published by Sir Walter Scott in 1815. After Kirk's death it was rumoured that he had been taken by fairies in revenge for revealing their secrets.

La.III.551

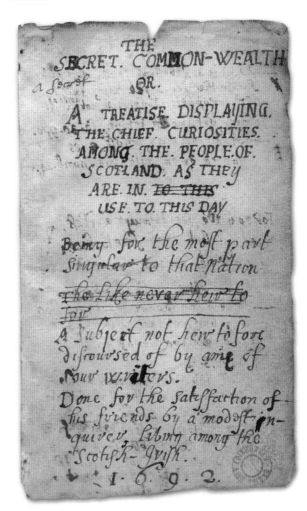

Robert Kirk, *The Secret Commonwealth*, 1692

Litill, Clement

Clement Litill's bequest charter, 1580

This large vellum document records the foundation of Edinburgh
University Library — before the college itself had come into being.
Clement Litill (c.1527–1580) was an advocate and commissary of

Clement Litill,
Bequest charter, 1580

Edinburgh. The younger son of an Edinburgh merchant and burgess, he was educated at the University of St Andrews and at Louvain, eventually returning to Edinburgh in 1550 to practise as a lawyer. He had first met the opinions of the Reformers at St Andrews, and eventually embraced the reformed kirk. His bequest of 276 volumes, mainly theological, to the town and kirk of Edinburgh, founded the Library. The collection, in which Catholic and Lutheran treatises are both well represented, was handed over by the Town Council to what was then called the Tounis College in 1584, the year after the first students were admitted. Each book is stamped with a circular seal showing the arms and initials of Maister Clement Litill and another stamp that states:

I AM GEVIN TO EDINBURGH & KIRK OF
GOD BE MAISTER CLEMENT LITIL
THAIR TO REMAN. 1580

The books listed here remain today at the core of the University's collections.

Dd.3.16

··

Mahabharata

The longest of them all

The Mahabharata is one of the two major ancient Sanskrit epics of India, the other being the Ramayana. Traditionally ascribed to Vyasa, it is the longest literary epic poem in the world. Besides being hailed as one of the greatest literary accomplishments of humanity, it is also of immense religious and philosophical importance in India.

This lavishly illustrated scroll manuscript is written on a continuous silk strip, approximately 75 metres long, and mounted on rollers to enable convenient consultation. It is dated AD 1795. Its provenance is unknown, but it was presented to Edinburgh University Library in the early 19th century. There are 77 elaborate miniatures in the late Mughal or Kangra style. All the miniatures have gold backgrounds with red and white flowers,

green leaves, blue diamond shapes and gold flowers in orange cartouches.

Or.MS.510

....

McBeath Gaelic medical manuscript

Medicine from the Highlands

Gaelic history and culture is strongly represented in the University of Edinburgh's collections and this is an extremely important early book. Dating from the 16th century, it is a medical manuscript in Gaelic and Latin. It was owned by the family of McBeath (also known as Bethunes or Beatons) who were for many generations physicians of repute in the West Highlands, particularly in Mull and Islay. On pages 189 and 190 there is a carefully prepared family tree. In the Gaelic world basic medical texts were available in the vernacular, whereas Latin remained the language of medical learning in the rest of Scotland. This manuscript shows close ties with Irish book-making traditions, particularly in the decoration. One of the more elaborate treatises details the colour of urine as an indication and symptom of disease.

David Laing bought the book in Edinburgh in 1835 and bequeathed it to the University in 1878.

McBeath medical
manuscript

La.III.21

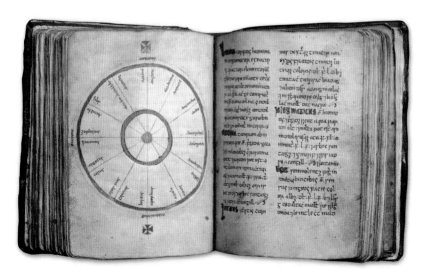

Rashid al-Din's History of the World

Rashid al-Din, *Jāmi' al-tawārīkh* (The Collection of Histories), Arabic, Tabriz, Iran, 714 AH (AD 1314).

Mahmud ibn Sebuktegin, from Rashid al-Din's History of the World, 1314

Our greatest oriental treasure

This work, the greatest oriental treasure of Edinburgh University Library, was collected by Colonel John Baillie (1772–1833) and donated in 1876. One of the supreme masterpieces of Persian book painting, it is one of the most important medieval manuscripts from either West or East. Written by the historian and vizier to the Ilkhanid court, Rashid al-Din, and copied in Tabriz by the author's own scribes and illustrators, the manuscript's importance as the first world history was quickly recognised. Encompassing the known world from China in the east to Ireland in the west, it represents an intellectual enterprise of the first order and one unique in the history of the medieval world.

Or. MS. 20

Carlo Ruini, *Anatomia del Cavallo*, 1618

Ruini's *Anatomia del Cavallo*

Carlo Ruini, *Anatomia del Cavallo* [Anatomy of the Horse]. Venetia: Fioravante Prati, 1618.

Opening up the horse

Edinburgh was a centre for veterinary studies, particularly farriery, from the early 19th century, and this has resulted in outstanding collections of books and manuscripts. Ruini (1530–1598) was a pioneering anatomist who applied to the horse the kind of rigorous approach that had been applied to human anatomy by the likes of Andreas Vesalius. This copy of his splendidly illustrated work was formerly in the Veterinary Library.

RB.F.45

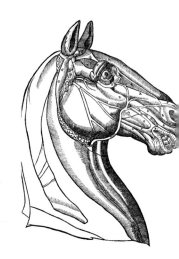

Sarum Breviary

Breviarium ad usum sar[um]
[Rouen: Printed by Martin Morin
for John Richard, 1496].

One of the Library's first books

In 1580 Clement Litill, an advocate, gave
his library to the town and kirk of Edinburgh.
Among the books in this foundation bequest
is this magnificent breviary, which was printed
in Rouen in 1496. The woodcut of St George
and the dragon indicates that it was meant for
the devout English reader, but the annotations
on the title page indicate that it was used in
Scotland by priests before the Reformation.
No other complete copy of this particular
printing is known to survive.
Dd.1.24

Servetus, Michael

Michael Servetus, *Christianismi Restitutio* [The Restoration
of Christianity]. Viennæ Allobrogum, 1553.

The book that was meant to be burned with its author

The Spanish theologian Michael Servetus (1511–1553) was a
radical thinker who defied orthodox doctrine on the Trinity and
on baptism. In this book he dismissed the idea of predestination as
held by leading reformer John Calvin, whom he enraged further in
a series of letters. Servetus unwisely paid a visit to Calvin at Geneva,
who promptly had him seized and condemned to death. He was
burned alive at the stake with what was believed to be the last copy
of this book chained to his leg. This is one of only three surviving
copies, and appears to be the very one which Servetus had sent to

Michael Servetus,
Christianismi Restitutio,
1553

Calvin. The first few pages were torn out by Calvin in fury and have been replaced by manuscript.

This copy was presented in 1695 by Alexander Cunningham in memory of his late pupil Lord George Douglas of Queensberry.
Df.8.90

....

Shakespeare, William

Including the greatest love story in English

Edinburgh University Library has a fine collection of early editions of Shakespeare and of English drama generally. Three of the quartos are of such outstanding importance that we class them as 'iconic'.

A pleasant conceited comedie called, Loues labors lost. **London: Printed by W[illiam] W[hite] for Cutbert Burby, 1598.**

This is the original quarto edition of this play, and was the first of Shakespeare's published works to include his name on the title page. It is, however, termed 'newly corrected and augmented', suggesting that there may have been an earlier quarto which has been lost.

This work is one of several Shakespeare quartos which were given to the University Library by the poet William Drummond in 1626.
De.3.74

The most excellent and lamentable tragedie, of Romeo and Iuliet. **London: Printed by Thomas Creede, for Cuthbert Burby, 1599.**

This is Shakespeare's first great tragedy. When the Scottish poet William Drummond presented his library to the University of

Edinburgh in 1626, Shakespeare had been dead for only ten years and this book was an example of modern literature. Drummond wrote Shakespeare's name on the title page, just in case anyone was uncertain who the author was. *Romeo and Juliet* is now perhaps the most famous piece of Elizabethan drama, a genre which is well represented in our collections. This is a very nice copy of the first good quarto (or authentic text) of the play, published during Shakespeare's lifetime. *De.3.73*

The most lamentable Romaine Tragedie of Titus Andronicus. London: Printed by I. R. for Edward White, 1600.

This is one of two known copies of the second edition of *Titus Andronicus.* It was donated by William Hog in 1700. In the 1860s this copy was lent to Shakespeare scholar and collector James Orchard Halliwell-Phillipps so he could make a facsimile. This arrangement, brokered by David Laing, eventually led to Halliwell-Phillipps donating a vast collection of books and manuscripts to Edinburgh University Library. *De.5.111*

William Shakespeare, selection of quartos

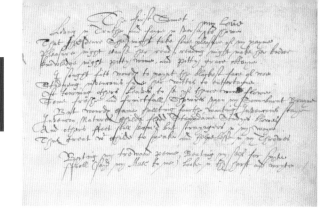

Philip Sidney,
Astrophil and Stella

Sidney's *Astrophil and Stella*

The English sonnet

This is the most important early manuscript of Sir Philip Sidney's
sonnet sequence, a defining work of Elizabethan English love poetry.
Sidney (1554–1586) wrote his original manuscript in the 1580s; this
copy was made by Sir Edward Dymoke, an associate of Sir William
Fowler, uncle of William Drummond, from whose collection it came
to Edinburgh University Library in the 1620s.

De.5.96

....

Traquair, Phoebe Anna

**Phoebe Anna Traquair, *Medallions for the Song School of
St Mary's Episcopal Cathedral*, Edinburgh, 1897.**

**Outstanding work by one of Scotland's first professional
woman artists**

Traquair (1852–1936) is best known for her murals which decorate
three buildings in Edinburgh, including the Song School attached to
St Mary's Episcopal Cathedral. This manuscript reproduces the Song
School medallions, painted in ink and watercolour on vellum. The
images can be compared to illuminated medieval manuscripts in their
use of colour, gold leaf and fine detail. They embody the spirit of the
Arts and Crafts movement, which sought to use traditional craft
skills to produce modern work of the highest quality. The volume
was bound in green calf by Thomas James Cobden-Sanderson at the
Doves Bindery.

Coll-518

Phoebe Anna Traquair,
*Medallions for the
Song School*

nd flowers covered
the earth

University Charter

This is the starting point of the University of Edinburgh. It is often described wrongly as the University's founding charter but is actually a charter of *novodamus*, or new giving, in which King James VI confirmed a previous gift of ecclesiastical revenues to the burgh of Edinburgh made by his mother, Mary Queen of Scots, and allowed the Town Council to use the resulting funds to build a college for the teaching of arts, theology, medicine, law or any other branch of the liberal arts.

EUA GD4

University of Edinburgh Charter (courtesy of Edinburgh City Council)

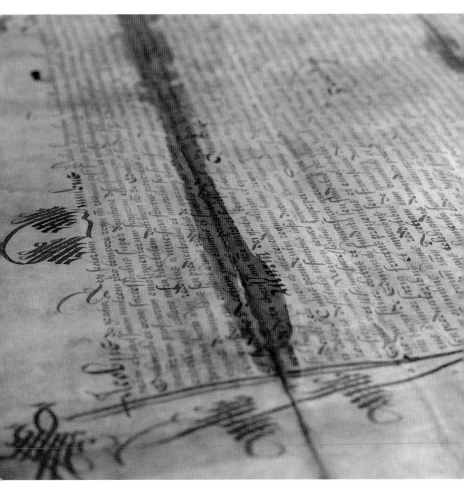

University of Edinburgh
Coat of Arms

University Coat of Arms

With a book at its heart

The University Arms were formally granted in 1789, after a period of high drama for the University:

> On the night betwixt the 29th/30th October 1787 the door of the Library was broken open by thieves and the University Mace was stolen from the press where it was usually deposited. The Magistrates offered a reward of ten Guineas for the discovery of the Delinquents.

So reads the inset entered between the College minutes for 11 September and 3 December 1787. The University would appear to have been without a mace until 1789. William Creech presented the College with a new one at the meeting of 2 October that year. At the same meeting it was reported that the University had been granted Arms by the Lord Lyon and that a new seal was to be made, the use of one of the city's seals being 'inconvenient and unsuitable to the dignity of the University'.

Van Meer Album Amicorum

Michael van Meer. Album Amicorum/Stam Boek
(c.1614–1630)

This exquisite manuscript of watercolour paintings gives a fascinating glimpse into the 17th century. Little is known of van Meer other than that he was a lieutenant in Hamburg who died on 13 October 1653. He clearly spent some time in London early in the century, as this album has numerous contemporary images of people and scenes in the capital city.

The *album amicorum* (book of friends) is a kind of autograph book collected by early modern students or scholars often from Germany or the Low Countries, as they moved about from university to university. A typical page will have a tag or set of verses in Latin or Greek (or sometimes Hebrew) at the top, and below, a formal greeting in Latin to the owner of the album. Perhaps as part of the greeting there will be a heraldic shield of the signator or a small picture, often emblematic in nature, and these are sometimes coloured.

This particular album bears the signatures of many celebrities: royalty, soldiers, statesmen and artists. It came to the Library as part of the Laing Bequest in 1878.

La.III.283

London Bridge,
from Van Meer Album
Amicorum

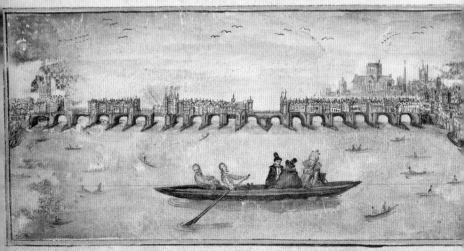

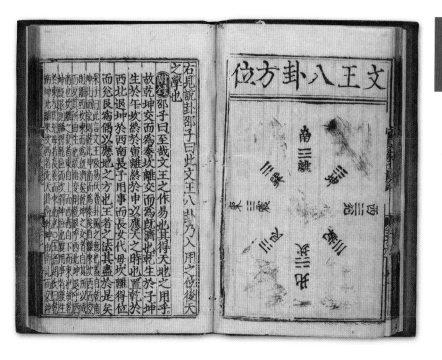

Zhouyi zhuanyi daquan
(*Book of Changes*), 1440

Zhouyi zhuanyi daquan (Book of Changes)

Our earliest printed book

The earliest printed book in Edinburgh University Library is an incomplete edition of the *Zhouyi zhuanyi daquan* [*Complete Commentaries on the Changes of Zhou*], which was published in 1440, during China's early Ming period. The *Book of Changes*, as it is generally known in English, remains one of the most important works of the Confucian tradition. This commentary was first published in 1415 and became the standard text of the Civil Service examinations, defining the way the classic was read for at least two centuries. This is a copy of the very rare 1440 edition, which was published in a popular edition in Jianyang county, northern Fujian. It is printed using woodblock technology, on thin paper made predominantly of bamboo. The book was given to Edinburgh University Library by a minister, Robert Ramsay, who graduated Master of Arts in July 1628 and probably donated the book to the Library to mark that occasion. How Ramsay might have acquired the volume, however, is not known.

Dd.7.106

ii. Archives and Manuscripts

We hold around 6 kilometres of unique handwritten
or typescript material. This includes literary, personal
and business papers; the archives of NHS Lothian; the
corporate archives of the University of Edinburgh and
merged institutions such as Edinburgh College of Art.
Our archives and manuscripts, dating back to the
1st century AD, provide documentary evidence
about life through the centuries and are essential
primary sources for research of many kinds.

Balneum, 1413

Abercrombie, David

Professor David Abercrombie (1909–1992) was one of the 20th century's greatest phoneticians, best known for his *Elements of General Phonetics* (1967). He joined the University of Edinburgh as a lecturer in 1948. In 1964 he was appointed to the Chair of Phonetics, remaining in post until 1980, when he was created Professor Emeritus.

The collection includes:
- personal material such as documents and diaries, etc.
- material relating to his involvement in university or departmental administration
- notes for lectures, tutorials and other academic purposes
- material relating to publications and broadcast talks.

There is also a substantial amount of correspondence, both personal and professional, including letters on spelling reform and basic English. In addition, there are some papers relating to the Abercrombie family.
Coll-66

Abercromby, Lord John

See main entry under Rare Books.
Coll-55

Aitken, Alexander Craig

Alexander Craig Aitken (1895–1967) was not only one of the greatest mathematicians of the 20th century but also an accomplished writer, composer and musician.

Born in Dunedin, New Zealand, Aitken served and was badly wounded in the First World War. Invalided home in 1917, he resumed his interrupted university career, graduating in mathematics at the University of Otago in 1920. Encouraged by R J T Bell, the Scots-born Professor of Mathematics at Otago, he gained a postgraduate scholarship which brought him to the University of Edinburgh in 1923. His thesis on statistics gained him the degree of DSc in 1925. In the same year he joined the University staff as a Lecturer in Statistics and Mathematical Economics. In 1937 he was promoted to Reader, and in 1946 was appointed to the Chair of Mathematics.

Aitken's publications include *The Theory of Canonical Matrices* (jointly with H W Turnbull, 1932) and a series of mathematical texts

A C Aitken

written jointly with D E Rutherford. He was also the author of two autobiographical works: *Gallipoli to the Somme: Recollections of a New Zealand Infantryman* (1963), a harrowing account of his wartime experiences and, posthumously, *To Catch the Spirit: The Memoir of A. C. Aitken* (1995). Aitken made many important contributions to the fields of numerical mathematics, statistics, and in particular the algebra of matrices. He was reputed to be one of the fastest mental calculators in the world.

While at school, Aitken learned to play the violin, and later in life he played both the violin and viola and composed pieces for performance by university groups.

The collection is composed of:

- war mementos and maps
- correspondence relating to Aitken's memoir *Gallipoli to the Somme*
- photographs
- commonplace books
- circa 60 musical scores
- personal and business correspondence
- letters and copies of letters from Aitken to Dr Robert Schlapp, 1933–1970
- legal documents and personal material.

A further significant collection of mathematical manuscripts, correspondence and photographs was acquired in 2013. *Coll-1068*

. . . .

Allinson, Thomas R

Thomas Richard Allinson (1858–1918) held very particular views on how best to restore the sick to health. He advocated hydrotherapy, abstention from tobacco and alcohol, fresh air, no medical drugs or vaccination, and a healthy vegetarian and wholemeal diet.

Born in Manchester, Allinson studied medicine at the Royal Colleges of Physicians and Surgeons in Edinburgh. After graduating in 1879, he assisted in a general practice in Hull, then spent some time in Paris. After returning to Britain, Allinson acted as police surgeon and parish doctor in Shoreditch, where he developed an opposition to stimulants such as alcohol and tobacco, advocating total abstention from alcohol consumption.

In 1887, he wrote an article strongly condemning medical drugs which he described as poisons, and opposing vaccination. After his arguments provoked lengthy public and professional debate, he was struck off the medical register. Undaunted, he continued to use the letters Ex-LRCP.Ed (ex-Licenciate of the Royal College of Physicians, Edinburgh) after his name. In 1890, Allinson opened the Hygienic Hospital in Willesden where patients were treated according to his principles of hygienic medicine. He wrote widely on the advantages of wholemeal bread and wholemeal and vegetarian cookery, and in 1892 he purchased a stone-grinding flour mill in London's Bethnal Green. This was established as the Natural Food Company Ltd. Allinson died in 1918 but created a lasting demand for wholemeal bread. The material known as the Allinson Papers was presented in June 1987 by Booker Health Foods Ltd, owners of the Allinson brand at that time.

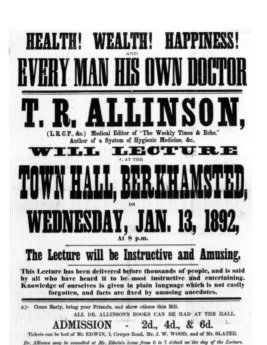

Poster for lecture by T R Allinson

The collection consists of:

- printed items and pamphlets, posters, photographs, and bundles of newspaper and magazine cuttings
- scrapbook albums containing mainly newspaper cuttings, dated from 1881 to 1918
- folders containing cuttings, handbills, and lecture posters from the 1880s to 1918.

Coll-39

Alston, Charles

The pioneering botanist Charles Alston (1685–1760) was instrumental in turning Edinburgh's medical school into one of Europe's greatest.

Alston was born at Eddlewood (now part of Hamilton) and was educated in Glasgow

with support from his patroness the Duchess of Hamilton. The Duchess subsequently funded a period of private study and, in 1715, used her influence to secure Alston an appointment as Superintendent of the Royal Botanic Garden in Edinburgh, a post he would hold for life. In 1718 he went to Leyden to further his medical studies under Hermann Boerhaave (1668–1738). There he met Alexander Monro *primus* (1697–1767), who would shortly become the University of Edinburgh's first Professor of Anatomy in 1720. On his return to Scotland, Alston graduated MD from Glasgow University

in 1719. Through Monro, Alston was invited to teach at the University of Edinburgh, where he was appointed Lecturer in Botany and Materia Medica. Alston's lecture course proved highly influential and was published after his death. Alston also published a number of medical papers and an index to the plants in the Botanic Garden in Edinburgh. In his most substantial work *Tirocinium Botanicum Edinburgense* (1753), he attacked the Linnaean system of classification.

The collection includes:
- writings on drugs, or materia medica
- lectures on materia medica and botany, 1736–1740.

Coll-1127 and elsewhere in Special Collections

Anderson, Robert Rowand

The architect Sir Robert Rowand Anderson (1834–1921) inaugurated a new era in Scottish architecture. He rejected the Scottish Baronial style in favour of functional and restrained buildings.

Anderson had four years of legal training in Edinburgh, then studied construction and design while serving with the Royal Engineers between 1854 and 1868. He subsequently entered the Architectural Section of the School of the Board of Manufactures, and spent a year in continental travel before setting up in practice in Edinburgh around 1875. His architectural practice proved highly successful and he worked on a large number of commissions. His original buildings include the New Medical School, Museum of Antiquities, and Montrose Memorial in the High Kirk of St Giles – all in Edinburgh – together with Central Station Hotel, Glasgow. His restorations at Iona Abbey (1874–1876), Dunblane Cathedral (1889–1893), Paisley Abbey (1898–1907) and Sweetheart Abbey, Dumfries (1911–1914) remain highly important. In 1892 he founded the School of Applied Art in Edinburgh to train architects and craftsmen, and in 1895 he instituted the national art survey of pre-1700 buildings. Anderson was knighted in 1902 and in 1916 became the first President of the Scottish Institute of Architects (a body which he was instrumental in creating). Some of the historic drawings from his firm came to Edinburgh University Library in 1976, where they complement other architectural collections including the papers of Sir Robert Lorimer who trained in Anderson's office.

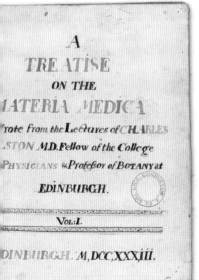

Charles Alston's 'A Treatise on Materia Medica', as taken down by one of his students

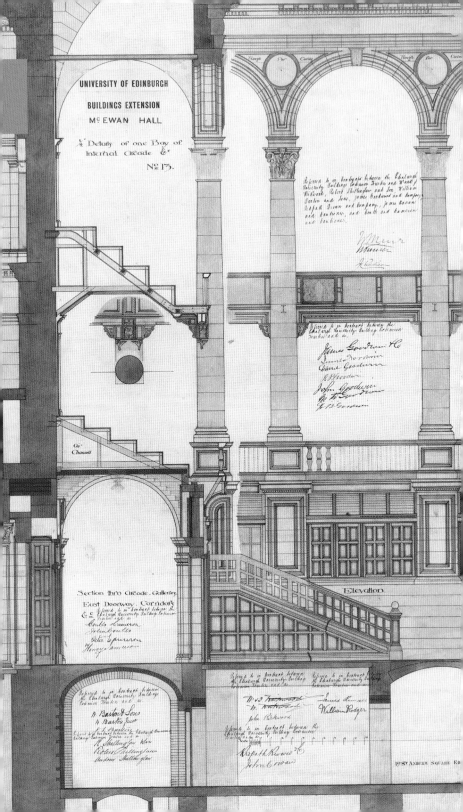

UNIVERSITY OF EDINBURGH

BUILDINGS EXTENSION

McEWAN HALL

½" Details of one Bay of
Internal Arcade &c.

No. 13.

Section thro' Arcade, Galleries.

East Doorway, Corridors
&c.

Elevation.

19 ST ANDREW SQUARE ED

The collection includes plans and elevations of the Medical School (1874) and the McEwan Hall (1890s) in Edinburgh, as well as drawings of many public and private buildings throughout the country: banks, barracks, libraries, institutions and mansions. There is further uncatalogued material from Anderson's successors.

Coll-31

Appleton, Edward

Sir Edward Victor Appleton (1892–1965) was Principal of the University of Edinburgh from 1949 until his death.

Born in Bradford, Appleton graduated from Cambridge University with a degree in Natural Sciences in 1914. His work as a signals officer with the Royal Engineers in the First World War introduced him to problems of radio-wave propagation caused by interference. Returning to Cambridge in 1919, he worked at the Cavendish Laboratory, then went on to occupy the Chairs of Physics at King's College London (1924–1936) and Natural Philosophy at Cambridge (1936–1939). He was knighted in 1941 and in 1947 was awarded the Nobel Prize in Physics for contributions to the knowledge of the ionosphere leading to the development of radar. The latter part of his career was devoted to university administration. As Principal and Vice-Chancellor of the University of Edinburgh, he proved an imaginative, diplomatic and responsive leader.

Detail of elevation of McEwan Hall by Robert Rowand Anderson

The printed Appleton Collection includes some 500 books and printed papers, particularly on physics. Scientific texts on electromagnetics and radio feature strongly. Many are copies of articles or publications presented to Professor Appleton. There are also general family books, including a significant number of religious works and some schoolbooks.

The manuscript collection is substantial and deals almost exclusively with Appleton's scientific work. There are diaries and engagement books and extensive folders of notes, research ideas, manuscript calculations and data from all periods of Appleton's career, as well as much additional data contributed by assistants or from observatories. The correspondence includes an extended exchange of letters with B van der Pol, 1921–1924, on oscillations and non-linearity, and long and frequent exchanges with friends and collaborators such as W J G Beynon, R Naismith and W R Piggott. Appleton's collection of reprints, preprints and limited circulation reports also includes some important items.

Coll-37

Arthur, John William

John William Arthur (1881–1952) was an important Church of Scotland medical missionary in Kenya.

Born in Glasgow, he was educated at Glasgow Academy and at Glasgow University, graduating MB ChB in 1903 and MD in 1906. He was appointed to the post of medical missionary at the

Kikuyu Mission, British East Africa (modern-day Kenya), in 1906. He opened the mission's first hospital and also became involved with its evangelical and educational work. Arthur became head of the mission in 1911 and, after his ordination in 1915, he concentrated increasingly on ministerial rather than medical practice. When he joined the mission staff there were no baptised Christians among the Kikuyu; by the time of his retirement there were nearly 11,000. Arthur came to be accepted as one of the foremost missionary spokesmen in East Africa and worked enthusiastically for inter-mission cooperation. He also worked with the colonial government, applying pressure from within for reforms. Arthur was particularly concerned with problems of education, land ownership and labour reforms, and was involved in debates over the practice of female circumcision, which he opposed. He retired from the missions in April 1937 and held a number of ministerial appointments in London and Scotland. He spent the last years of his life as chaplain to the Astley-Ainslie Hospital in Edinburgh. He returned to Kenya briefly in 1948 for the jubilee celebrations of the Church of Scotland mission. Arthur was a noted athlete and mountaineer. He was awarded the OBE in 1920.

The collection consists mainly of correspondence and papers (1907–1949) including:

- letters from Arthur to his mother
- circular letters and newsletters from the Kikuyu mission
- sections from Arthur's diaries and notes on his travels throughout East Africa
- reports on missionary conferences
- memoranda by Arthur and others on social problems
- minutes, memoranda and papers of the Kikuyu Association and the Kikuyu Mission Council
- papers relating to parliamentary commissions and court cases, and to Arthur's position as an unofficial member of the Kenyan Executive Council.

The collection also includes printed pamphlets, journals, articles and ordinances, press cuttings and photographs of Kenya.
Coll-207

Kikuyu Boys Brigade, 1912, photograph by John William Arthur

Auden, W H

See main entry under Rare Books.

Coll-45

....

Auerbach, Charlotte

Charlotte ('Lotte') Auerbach (1899–1994) was a leading geneticist whose work focused on the effects of radiation and chemicals on humans and animals, and who made a major contribution to founding the science of mutagenesis.

Charlotte Auerbach

Born in Krefeld, Germany, Auerbach studied biology and chemistry at the Universities of Würzburg, Freiburg and Berlin. After graduating, she taught science at secondary school level in Heidelberg (1924–1925) and briefly at the University of Frankfurt, a post from which she was dismissed, almost certainly on account of her Jewish roots. She started postgraduate research at the Kaiser Wilhelm Institute for Biology (Berlin-Dahlem) in 1928 but abandoned her project due to disagreements with her dictatorial (and pro-Nazi) supervisor Otto Mangold. She then taught biology at several schools in Berlin, before anti-Semitic legislation prevented her from working as a teacher. In 1933, she fled Germany for Edinburgh, graduating PhD at the Institute of Animal Genetics in 1935. She remained there for the rest of her career, becoming Honorary Director of the MRC Unit of Mutagenesis Research in 1959 and being awarded a personal chair at the University in 1967. Auerbach is best known for her 1940s work with J M Robson leading to the discovery that mustard gas causes often-lethal mutations in fruit flies. Besides her scientific work, she was a tireless political activist, strongly opposing apartheid and supporting the Campaign for Nuclear Disarmament.

The material includes:
- a copy of Auerbach's PhD thesis, with handwritten corrections
- Auerbach's degree and honorary degree certificates, as well as certificates relating to various medals and prizes
- correspondence with societies and organisations
- notebooks and a microscope belonging to Auerbach
- biographical papers relating to Auerbach collected by Geoffrey Beale in preparation for his biographical memoir of Auerbach for the Royal Society, including copies of some of Auerbach's publications, cassette tapes of interviews between Beale and Auerbach and original papers of Auerbach's dating from the 1940s.

Coll-1266

Baillie, John

John Baillie (1886–1960) was a leading
theologian and an outstanding figure in the
Christian ecumenical movement with a vast
network of correspondents.

Born in Gairloch, Wester Ross, he was
educated at Inverness Royal Academy and the
University of Edinburgh. He held assistant
lecturing positions at the University before
entering the church as an assistant in 1912,
being ordained in 1920. The First World War
saw Baillie play an active role in both the
YMCA and the British Expeditionary Force.
He then resumed his academic career holding
chairs at the Auburn and Union Theological
Seminaries, New York, and at Emmanuel
College, Toronto, before returning to
Edinburgh to become Professor of Divinity
at New College in 1934. The advent of
the Second World War saw Baillie use the
North American links he had maintained
to campaign for US entry into the conflict.
He was elected as Moderator of the General
Assembly of the Church of Scotland and
became Dean of the Faculty of Divinity at
Edinburgh in 1950, holding this position
for six years. As part of the ecumenical
movement, John Baillie was a member of
both the British Council of Churches and
the World Council of Churches; he became
a President of the latter.

The collection includes:
- personal and professional papers
  and correspondence
- school and university notes
- awards and achievements
- lectures, addresses and broadcasts
- sermons and prayers
- manuscripts of published works
- papers relating to the World Council
  of Churches, British Council of
  Churches, General Assembly
  of the Church of Scotland and
  other organisations.

The collection also includes family papers
of Baillie's wife Florence, as well as
papers relating to his father John Baillie,
mother Annie Baillie and brothers Donald
Macpherson Baillie and Peter Baillie.
Coll-104 / BAI

Barlow, Arthur Ruffell

Arthur Ruffell Barlow (1888–1965) was a
Church of Scotland missionary and linguist
with an intimate knowledge of the Kikuyu
language and culture.

Born in Edinburgh, Barlow was only
15 years old when he joined his missionary
uncle David Clement Ruffell Scott at
Kikuyu, British East Africa (Kenya) in
1903. He assisted with the mission's work
in an unofficial capacity until 1908 when
he was formally employed by the Church
of Scotland. His interest in and grasp of
the Kikuyu language and dialects meant
he was often employed as a translator and
his intimate knowledge of the Kikuyu people
made him a trusted counsellor. He was a
good friend of Jomo Kenyatta (c.1895–1978),
later president of Kenya, when both were
young. He was one of the founders of the
Kenya Missionary Council and acted as its
secretary for a number of years as well as
playing a prominent role in debates on
church and mission union.

'Building the first Hospital, Tumutumu, 1911', photograph by Arthur Ruffell Barlow

He prepared a Kikuyu grammar which became a standard and initiated a Bible translation. His knowledge of the language and culture and interest in questions such as land reform and the rights of Africans meant that he was often consulted on African matters by government. After he retired from the missions in 1941 he continued his linguistic and translation studies. He published *Studies in Kikuyu Grammar and Idiom* in 1951. He returned to Kenya during the Mau Mau Uprising and in 1953 took the role of Officer in Charge of the Translation Bureau of the African Information Services. Barlow devoted a large amount of time in his later years to the production of a Kikuyu-English dictionary, finally published in 1964.

The collection consists of material about the Church of Scotland mission in Kenya, about the Kikuyu language and culture, and about the interests and concerns of Africans and their relation to the colonial government.

In particular it includes:

- Barlow's notes on Kikuyu language, songs, music, customs and idioms
- minutes and constitution of the United Kikuyu Language Committee (1908–1917)
- letters from Barlow to his father (1904–1905)
- correspondence and other items relating to the missions including correspondence from the Church of Scotland's Foreign Missionary Council
- notes on the history of the mission in East Africa
- papers on the Kenyan Mission Council
- papers concerning the Mau Mau Uprising
- photographs (1904–1915) relating to Kenya.

Coll-208

. . . .

Beale, Geoffrey

Geoffrey Herbert Beale (1913–2009) is known as the founder of malaria genetics.

Born in Wandsworth, London, Beale studied at Imperial College London where he developed a keen interest in botany. After

Geoffrey Beale

graduating with first-class honours in 1935, he pursued doctoral studies at the John Innes Horticultural Institute and was awarded a PhD in 1938. During the Second World War, he served in the Intelligence Corps (Field Security) and was posted to Archangel and Murmansk in Russia. He returned to academia after the war, initially pursuing research at the Cold Spring Harbor Laboratory at New York, and working with geneticist Tracy Sonneborn at Bloomington, Indiana, where he developed his lifelong interest in the protozoan *Paramecium*. A Rockefeller Fellowship brought him back to the UK in 1947, and in 1948 he was offered a lectureship at the Institute of Animal Genetics in Edinburgh.

Here Beale continued to work on *Paramecium* for some 25 years, making a range of fundamental discoveries and, in 1965, establishing the Protozoan Genetics Unit. This work led to several research projects focused on discovering the genes that determine malaria's resistance to drug treatment. Beale was appointed a Royal Society Research Professor in 1963, a position he held until his retirement.

The collection contains Beale's original data notebooks, manuscript lecture notes and correspondence files as well as collections of offprints and papers relating to different aspects of his work. He wrote a biographical memoir for the Royal Society of the American biologist Tracy Sonneborn, who was Beale's former colleague and lifelong friend, and the research papers for this are included in the archive. Beale's library of printed books on genetics has also been donated.

Coll-1255

Beatty, Richard Alan

Alan Beatty (1915–2005) worked as a research fellow within the ARC Group at the Institute of Animal Genetics from 1957 until his retirement in 1980. He achieved the first successful non-surgical transfer of mammalian eggs.

Beatty was born in Belfast and moved with his family to London in 1922. He was educated at St Paul's School and St John's College, Cambridge, graduating in the Natural Sciences Tripos in 1938, and remaining in Cambridge as a PhD student in the Departments of Zoology and Biochemistry. During the Second World War he served in the Royal Artillery, Royal Army Service Corps, and finally in the War Department as an Analyst. Following demobilisation, he was appointed Senior (later Principal) Scientific Officer at the Genetics Laboratory of the Animal Breeding and Genetics Research Organisation (ABRO) in Edinburgh, moving in 1957 to the Agricultural Research Council Unit of Animal Genetics, based within the Institute of Animal Genetics. The following year he was awarded the title of Research Fellow.

Beatty's research over much of his career was concerned, in his own words, with 'where reproductive biology and genetics overlap'. He developed a particular interest in the genetics of the gamete (i.e. the environmental and genetic factors that determine a germ line cell to develop its particular characteristics). From the late 1960s onwards, Beatty advocated for a Centre for Reproductive Biology to be established in Edinburgh. This concept

Richard Alan Beatty

to emphasise the importance of quantitative measurements in chemistry. Finally, he invented the calorimenter, the first accurate method of measuring heat, thus laying the foundations of modern thermal science.

Black was born in Bordeaux, France, the son of a Scots-Irish wine merchant. He was educated in Belfast and then studied medicine and natural sciences at the University of Glasgow where his chemistry instructor was William Cullen (1710–1790), later to be a luminary of the University of Edinburgh's Medical School. In 1751 Black decided to further his medical studies at

was eventually realised in the late 1970s, with the Centre opening in 1980, after Beatty's retirement. Beatty also supervised the PhD of Robert G. Edwards, who in 2010 received the Nobel Prize in Physiology or Medicine for his pioneering work on *in vitro* fertilisation.

The collection, which covers the dates 1937–1993, includes papers relating to Beatty's experiments and research, lectures, conferences and visits, press clippings, grant applications and materials on the planning of the Centre for Reproductive Biology. *Coll-1364*

Black, Joseph

Joseph Black (1728–1799) made several major contributions to chemical science.

He discovered that 'fixed air', or carbon dioxide as we now know it, is produced by respiration, by the burning of charcoal, and by fermentation, and that it is found in the atmosphere. He was one of the first scientists

Specimens of printed cloth sent to Joseph Black by George Macintosh, 1782

61

the University of Edinburgh, writing a doctoral thesis on the treatment of kidney stones with the salt magnesium carbonate. In 1756 he succeeded Cullen as Lecturer in Chemistry at the University of Glasgow and was subsequently appointed Professor of Anatomy, later transferring to the Chair of Medicine. While in Glasgow, through his investigation of the heating of magnesium carbonate, Black discovered the existence of the gas carbon dioxide as distinct from common air. An account of his studies was published as 'Experiments upon Magnesia Alba, Quicklime, and Some Other Alcaline Substances' in *Essays and Observations, Physical and Literary* (1756).

In 1766, Black was appointed Professor of Chemistry at the University of Edinburgh, a post which he held until his death in 1799. In 1767 he was made a Fellow of the Royal College of Physicians, Edinburgh, serving as its President in 1788. His lecture notes, supplemented by those of his pupils, were written up and published posthumously by John Robison (1739–1805) as *Lectures on the Elements of Chemistry*, *Delivered at the University of Edinburgh* (1803).

The collection includes correspondence between Black and a number of individuals (including James Watt, Prince Paul Dashkov and John Robison) on a variety of subjects, such as linen bleaching, the use of lime water, assays of ores, civic water supply, mineralogical specimens and the absorption of heat. There are also family letters between Black, his father and his brothers Samuel, George and Thomas.

Coll-16

Blackie, John Stuart

See main entry under Rare Books.

Blair, Hugh

The minister and literary critic Hugh Blair (1718–1800) held the world's first Chair of English Literature.

Blair was born in Edinburgh and studied at the University of Edinburgh, where he defended his MA thesis entitled 'De fundamentis et obligatione legis naturae' in 1739. In 1741, Blair was licensed to preach and appointed as minister to Collessie parish in Fife. In 1743, he moved to Edinburgh as Minister of Canongate Kirk, and was subsequently elected to two other charges in the city, Lady Yester's Church (1754) and St Giles, which he held from 1758 to his death in 1800.

In 1759 Blair started giving lectures on composition at the University of Edinburgh and in 1760 was made Professor of Rhetoric, a post which was expanded to a Professorship of Rhetoric and Belles Lettres in April 1762. This marked the birth of English Literature as an academic discipline. Blair was part of Edinburgh's distinguished literary circle of the day, and was a contemporary of David Hume, Adam Ferguson and Adam Smith. He championed the publishing of the Ossian fragments by James Macpherson (1736–1796). Blair's own lectures and sermons were widely translated and read abroad.

The papers consist principally of correspondence. There are also manuscript notes of his sermons and lectures on rhetoric. *Coll-1405 and elsewhere in Special Collections*

Hugh Blair (1775)
David Martin
© The University of Edinburgh

Booth, Joseph

Joseph Booth (1851–1932) was a missionary in Malawi, Lesotho and South Africa, known for his radical religious views and egalitarian politics.

Born in Derby, Booth emigrated to New Zealand in 1880, where he became a farmer, then in 1887 moved to Australia, where he established himself as a successful small businessman. While in Australia, Booth joined the Baptist Church and became convinced that it was his vocation to be a missionary in Africa. In 1891, following the death of his first wife, he left Australia with his two young children. Arriving in Nyasaland (modern-day Malawi) in 1892, he established the Zambezi Industrial Mission (ZIM), which he hoped would develop into a network of self-supporting communities in which there

would be no colour bar. Booth's involvement with the ZIM was followed by association with other industrial missions and schemes with similar aims. He was variously affiliated to the Baptists, Seventh Day Baptists, the Watch Tower movement and Seventh-day Adventists.

Booth aroused the hostility of other missionaries and colonial authorities by advocating higher wages and more political power for Africans. He spent time in Nyasaland, South Africa, Basutholand (Lesotho), Britain and the United States trying to raise support for his many pro-African schemes. His activities led to him being accused of contributing to an uprising in Malawi, and he and his second wife Annie were deported from Basutholand to England in 1915. Poor and unable to find work, partly due to his pacifist convictions, the Booths struggled to make a life for themselves. After the First World War they went to South Africa where their daughter provided accommodation for them and where Annie died in 1921. Booth and his third wife Lillian were eventually forced to return to England where he died. Booth's fundamentalism and his apparently radical political and social

'A native baptism, Chiyenga'; Joseph Booth papers

views have led to varying assessments of his life and effect on African Christianity. The papers include:

- correspondence of members of the Booth family, mainly letters from Joseph Booth to his daughters Emily and Mary
- correspondence between George Shepperson and the Booth family
- publications by and about Booth (1897–1983) including copies of Booth's *Africa for the African* (1897) and Emily Booth Langworthy's *This Africa Was Mine* (1952)
- photographs of Booth and family.

Coll-210

Brewster, David

David Brewster (1781–1868) was one of the major figures in science and academia in 19th-century Scotland. Best known as the inventor of the kaleidoscope, he was the first Principal of the University of Edinburgh not to belong to the Church of Scotland.

Brewster was born in Jedburgh, Roxburghshire in 1781, and educated at the University of Edinburgh, graduating MA in 1800. Although initially a successful preacher in the Church of Scotland, fear of public speaking put an end to his ecclesiastical career. It also hampered his subsequent attempts to find an academic post. An income was provided when in 1808 he was invited to edit the *Edinburgh Encyclopaedia*, a project finally completed in 1830, and to which Brewster contributed a large number of entries himself. He later became joint editor of the *Edinburgh Philosophical Journal* and sole editor of the *Edinburgh Journal of Science*, besides contributing to other learned journals. The income from his journalistic work permitted Brewster to pursue significant scientific research. A pioneer in the science of optics, Brewster made significant discoveries about polarisation of light and absorption spectra, invented the kaleidoscope, and developed the stereoscope. He showed a keen interest in photography from its infancy and received a medal from the Photographic Society of Paris in 1865. He was one of the founder members of the British Association for the Advancement of Science in 1831.

The latter part of Brewster's life was devoted to university administration. In 1837 he was appointed Principal of the United Colleges of St Salvator and St Leonard in St Andrews. In 1859 he was elected Principal of the University of Edinburgh, a post he held until his death in 1868, and in which he oversaw the reforms brought in by the

David Brewster, photograph by D O Hill and Robert Adamson

Universities (Scotland) Act 1858. He was the first layman to occupy this post since Patrick Sands in 1622, and, as a Free Churchman (like the majority of the Town Council), the first postholder who was not a member of the Church of Scotland.

In a collection of miscellaneous correspondence we hold some 54 letters to or from Brewster.

Coll-1454 and elsewhere in Special Collections

....

Brown, Andrew

Andrew Brown (1763–1834) succeeded Hugh Blair as Professor of Rhetoric and Belles Lettres at the University of Edinburgh, and was an important historian of North America.

Born at Biggar, Peeblesshire, Brown was educated at Glasgow University. He entered the Church and was ordained minister of the Scottish Church in Halifax, Nova Scotia, in 1787, on the recommendation of his mentor William Robertson. Brown returned to Scotland in 1795 and held charges in Lochmaben and at New Greyfriars and Old St Giles' in Edinburgh. In 1801 he became Regius Professor of Rhetoric and Belles Lettres at the University of Edinburgh, a post first offered to Sir Walter Scott (who turned it down). His appointment proved

'Of the Languages of American Indians', MS by Andrew Brown

largely unsuccessful, however, for his interests lay in North American history rather than in literature, and he was an uninspiring lecturer.

Brown devoted much of his life to an unfinished and unpublished *History of North America*. He nonetheless achieved recognition as a historian during his lifetime due to his published work on the history of Nova Scotia, particularly on the expulsion of the French-speaking Acadian population. He was described by Benjamin Rush as 'a man of genius, learning, observation'.

The papers consist of notes and papers on the history of North America during the War of Independence and including material on Native Americans, Nova Scotia and colonial history. *Coll-9*

....

Brown, George Mackay

George Mackay Brown (1921–1996), was a key figure in 20th-century Scottish literature, achieving equal prominence as poet, novelist and short-story writer. His work was rooted in the history, mythology, landscape and speech of his native Orkney.

He was born in Stromness, Orkney, where he spent most of his life. During the war, the poet and lecturer Francis Scarfe was billeted with Brown's family during his own military service. Scarfe encouraged the young George to read D H Lawrence and Dylan Thomas and to develop his own poetry. In 1950, Brown met Edwin Muir, the great Scottish poet and a fellow Orcadian, who encouraged him to attend college at Newbattle Abbey. He subsequently attended the University of Edinburgh as a mature student in the late 1950s.

Brown believed that his place as a writer was at the heart of the community into which he was born. Although his work is confined in place it has a broad range, from poems, plays, children's books and essays, to novels and short stories. His poetry appeared in volumes such as *Loaves and Fishes* (1959), *The Year of the Whale* (1965), and *The Wreck of the Archangel* (1989). His novels include *Greenvoe* (1972), *Magnus* (1973) and *Beside the Ocean of Time* (1994). Among his best-known short story collections are *A Calendar of Love* (1967) and *A Time to Keep* (1969). Brown's essays are also highly regarded and are collected in *An Orkney Tapestry* (1969), *Letters from Hamnavoe* (1975), *Under Brinkie's Brae* (1979) and *Portrait of Orkney* (1981). A selection of poems entitled *Following a Lark* (1996) and an autobiography *For the Islands I Sing* (1997) were published posthumously. Brown was awarded an OBE in 1974 and became a Fellow of the Royal Society of Literature in 1977.

This substantial collection contains manuscript drafts, typescripts and proofs of poems, plays, stories and novels. These are often in Brown's original folders or envelopes. There are folders containing reviews, articles, essays, short stories and broadcasts; drafts of uncollected poems; scripts; newspaper cuttings; and small notebooks containing a weekly record of letters written and drafts of poems. There is also important correspondence, including letters to his one-time fiancée Stella Cartwright.

Coll-50

Brown, Gerard Baldwin

As Professor of Fine Art at the University of Edinburgh, Gerard Baldwin Brown (1849–1932) played a major role in the development of fine art as a new academic discipline, and also promoted the cause of university education for women.

Born in London, Brown was elected a Fellow of Brasenose College, Oxford in 1874 but, in 1877, decided that he wished to train

Ruthwell Cross, Dumfriesshire; photographs by Gerard Baldwin Brown

as an artist and subsequently studied painting at the National Art Training School in South Kensington. In 1880 he was appointed to the new Watson Gordon Chair of Fine Art at the University of Edinburgh, the first Fine Art chair in the UK. He occupied the post for half a century, retiring only in 1930. His many publications include *From Schola to Cathedral: A Study of Early Christian Architecture* (1886), *The Fine Arts* (1891), *William Hogarth* (1905), *The Glasgow School of Painters* (1908), *The Arts and Crafts of our Teutonic Forefathers* (1910), and *The Art of the Cave Dweller* (1928). Brown's 1905 work *The Care of Ancient Monuments* inspired the Secretary of State for Scotland to set up a royal commission to compile an inventory of ancient Scottish monuments in 1908. Brown himself was appointed as a member of the commission.

The collection consists largely of notes and notebooks relating to Brown's courses, and a great deal of correspondence. There are assorted notes, photographs and sketches of Anglo-Saxon antiquities; notes for lectures and lecture courses; field notebooks and manuscripts for publication. In addition, there are card-mounted photographs of archaeological and historical sites and landmarks across the British Isles. These show churches, stone crosses, decorated stonework and metal jewellery.

Brown also bequeathed some 1,000 printed volumes to the Library, all 19th- and 20th-century books on fine art and archaeology, which are in various locations.
Coll-314

Bruce, William Speirs

See main entry under Rare Books.
Coll-72

....

Bulfield, Grahame

Grahame Bulfield was born in Leeds in 1941 and attended school in Cheshire, where he developed an interest in agriculture and farming. Bulfield completed his BSc in Agriculture with Honours in Animal Production at the University of Leeds, and gained a diploma and a PhD at the Institute of Animal Genetics in Edinburgh. After a period as Lecturer and Medical Convenor of Medical Genetics at the University of Leicester – where he made the significant discovery of a mutation on the mouse X chromosome, which is still used to understand muscular dystrophy in humans – Bulfield returned to Edinburgh in 1981 as Head of the Genetics Group at the Poultry Research Centre.

In 1986, Bulfield was appointed Head of the Gene Expression group in the newly formed Edinburgh Research Station of the Institute of Animal Physiology and Genetics Research (IAPGR), becoming Head of Station in 1988. When the Station became independent from its sister institute in Cambridge, and was renamed the Roslin Institute, Bulfield became director and chief executive. Bulfield steered Roslin through a time of scientific innovation, the growth of various spin-out biotechnology companies, government scrutiny of research establishments, as well as unprecedented public and media attention, particularly surrounding the Institute's work on cloned and transgenic animals, including Dolly the sheep (1996).

Bulfield retired as Roslin's director in 2002, and moved over to the University of Edinburgh to become Vice-Principal and Head of the College of Science and Engineering. He is currently Emeritus Professor of Genetics at the University of Edinburgh. He was awarded a CBE for services to Animal Genetics in 2001.

The collection, which spans the 1970s to the 2000s, consists of reports, diaries, correspondence and papers concerning various ethical and political matters arising out of work conducted at the Roslin Institute, as well as publicity surrounding Dolly the sheep. *Coll-1644*

Butcher, Samuel Henry

Samuel Henry Butcher (1850–1910) was an eminent classical scholar and politician.

Born in Dublin, he was the son of Samuel Butcher, Bishop of Meath. He was educated at Marlborough College and Trinity

College, Cambridge, where he graduated in Classics in 1873. He was a Fellow of University College, Oxford from 1876 until 1882, when he was appointed Professor of Greek at the University of Edinburgh. Between 1889 and 1896 he was a member of the Scottish Universities Commission, which was tasked with drawing up new statutes and reforming the Scottish university system. In 1903 he was a founder member of the English Classical Association. He lectured at Harvard University in 1904 and was an honorary foreign member of the American Academy of Arts and Sciences, 1905. Butcher had extensive political interests, and after resigning his Edinburgh chair in 1903, served as Unionist MP for Cambridge University from 1906 until his death.

The collection consists largely of notes of lectures on Greek and Roman literature and history, but there is also some correspondence and a commonplace book. *Various locations in Special Collections*

Cameron, Colin

Colin Cameron (1933–) played a significant role as a lawyer and politician as British Nyasaland became independent Malawi.

Born in Lanark, Cameron was educated at Uddingston Grammar School and Glasgow University where he read Law. In 1957, he moved to the Federation of Rhodesia and Nyasaland (now Malawi) to work as a solicitor. During a state of emergency in 1959,

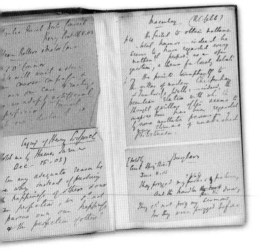

Pages from Samuel Henry Butcher's commonplace book

Cameron gave legal help to Africans who had been arrested and detained. He joined the African National Congress and became a vocal opponent of apartheid. In 1959, he also became a member of the Church of Central Africa Presbyterian. At the request of Hastings K. Banda, he stood in the 1961 General Election against the United Federal Party. Cameron was elected to the Council along with the first Africans elected to government, and in September 1961 became Minister of Works and Transport. In August 1964, Cameron resigned from the Cabinet when Banda amended the Constitution to allow detention without trial in the newly independent Malawi. On resuming private legal practice he represented the former Minister of Education, Henry Chipembere, in a constitutional case which challenged Banda in the High Court. This resulted in Cameron's expulsion from Malawi. During the next 30 years, Cameron established his own legal practice in Irvine, Scotland, and although unable to return to Malawi, he continued to support refugees from the country. After the first multi-party elections in Malawi in May 1994, Cameron and his wife were invited back and he was offered the position of Honorary Consul for the Republic of Malawi in Scotland.

The collection includes:
- ministerial and constituency material
- material for speeches
- material on Cameron's invitations, tours and visits
- business and personal correspondence.

Coll-70

Campbell, Archibald Hunter

See main entry under Rare Books.

Coll-221

Campbell, Colin

Colin Campbell of Achnaba (1644–1726) was a church minister and noted mathematician who won the admiration of Isaac Newton.

Born in Perthshire, Campbell was educated at St Salvator's College, St Andrews, graduating in 1661. In 1666 or 1667 he was admitted as minister of the parish church of Ardchattan and Muckairn

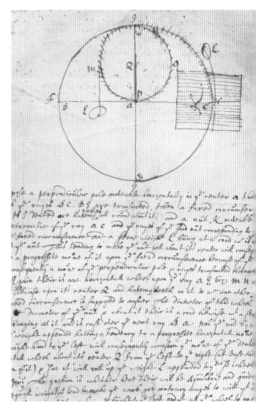

Drawing of 'Perpetual Motion Machine' by Colin Campbell

in Lorne. On 12 January 1676 he was suspended from the ministry on a charge of pre-nuptial intercourse but was restored on 25 June 1676. In addition to carrying out his professional duties, Campbell had a deep interest in mathematics and astronomy. Newton wrote to James Gregory, Professor of Mathematics at Edinburgh, that Campbell 'would make children of us all'.

The manuscript collection relating to Campbell and his family contains:

- letters from mathematicians to Colin Campbell and mathematical papers
- correspondence from 1664 onwards
- miscellaneous manuscripts including medical papers
- sermon notes and scripture expositions from 1703 onwards
- Gaelic songs and verse
- notebooks, accounts and letters of Patrick Campbell of Achnaba
- a body of accounts, the earliest being 1553.

The 65 printed books are mainly theological works, but also include some science, such as a copy of Sacro Bosco's *Sphaera* printed at Antwerp in 1573. The books have shelfmarks JA 4033–4079 and JY 1213–1225 and a separate author catalogue on slips is available. *Coll-38*

Carlyle, Thomas, and Jane Welsh Carlyle

The philosopher, historian, satirist and essayist Thomas Carlyle (1795–1881) is one of the great social commentators of the 19th century.

Carlyle was born in Ecclefechan, Dumfriesshire. He was educated at the village school and then at Annan Academy. In 1809 he began studies at the University of Edinburgh. Originally intended for the ministry, Carlyle

Thomas Carlyle and Jane Welsh Carlyle, photographs by Richard Tait

showed a keenness for mathematics, besides studying French, German, Latin and Greek. After leaving university, he became a mathematics teacher in Annan and then in Edinburgh. In 1824 he achieved prominence with his translation of Goethe's *Wilhelm Meister*. Other major publications followed in rapid succession, including *Signs of the Times* (1829), *Sartor Resartus* (1835), *The French Revolution* (1837), *On Heroes and Hero Worship* (1841), *Past and Present* (1843), *Oliver Cromwell's Letters and Speeches* (1845), *Latter-Day Pamphlets* (1850), and the six-volume *History of Friedrich II of Prussia* (1858–1865). Carlyle was a founder of the London Library and in later life served as Rector of the University of Edinburgh (1865–1868). Jane Welsh Carlyle (1801–1866), whom he married in 1826, is regarded as one of the great letter-writers of the 19th century.

The Carlyle material is scattered and consists primarily of correspondence, some 190 letters, mainly by Thomas. Other material includes class tickets, galley proofs, holograph drafts, autographed notes, photographs and an etched portrait.
Various locations in Special Collections

....

Carmichael–Watson

The papers of Alexander Carmichael (1832–1912) and Professor W J (William John Ross) Watson (1865–1948) constitute our most important collection relating to Gaelic and Celtic culture.

Alexander Carmichael was born in Taylochan, Lismore. After attending school, Carmichael entered the Civil Service as an exciseman. There he joined the team of pioneering folklorists collecting for *Popular Tales of the West Highlands* (1860–1862) under the direction of John Francis Campbell (1821–1885). He came to believe that it was his duty not only to record the present, but also to retrieve and reconstruct a glorious Gaelic past. In 1864 he was assigned to the Uists. His new post, initially based in Lochmaddy, allowed him to undertake arduous journeys through some of the richest areas for folklore in western Europe, scribbling down in a series of field notebooks an extraordinary range of material ranging from long Fenian tales and ballads, through historical narratives, songs, hymns and charms, to anecdotes, observations, proverbs, riddles and unusual words.

In 1882 he moved to Edinburgh, where he was to spend the rest of his life. Here he was at the heart of Edinburgh's Gaelic intellectual community, and a crucial player in Scotland's Celtic Renaissance, contributing, for instance, to the seminal journal *Evergreen* edited by Patrick Geddes (1854–1932). In 1900 he published his greatest and most enduring work, the two volumes of *Carmina Gadelica*. This substantial collection of sacred pieces, hymns and charms was intended to illustrate the refined mystical spirituality of the Scottish Gaels. With the help of his daughter Ella and the publisher Walter Biggar Blaikie (1847–1928), Carmichael was able to fashion a landmark in Scottish publishing, whose illustrations (by his wife) and hand-made paper suggest early Christian manuscripts.

Despite the enthusiastic response of most reviewers to *Carmina Gadelica*, and the award of an honorary LLD by the University

Alexander Carmichael beside a large ice boulder in Scalpay, drawn by his wife Mary Frances Macbean

of Edinburgh in 1906, scholarly doubts soon surfaced concerning Carmichael's editing techniques. Nevertheless, the publication and his manuscript collection remain an indispensable treasure trove, the fruits of a lifetime spent gathering, preserving, communicating and interpreting Gaelic culture, tradition and lore for future generations.

The collection was received under the wills of Carmichael's son-in-law William John Watson (1865–1948), Professor of Celtic in the University of Edinburgh, and William's own son James Carmichael Watson (1910–1942), his successor as Professor of Celtic.

The manuscripts include:

- invocations
- addresses to the saints
- seasonal hymns, including Christmas carols
- blessings for everyday tasks
- incantations used in healing
- prayers to the sun and moon
- rhymes about animals and birds
- blessings on cattle and other livestock
- praise songs, love songs, milking songs, fairy songs, waulking songs
- auguries
- information on custom and beliefs generally.

There are also notebooks, newspaper cuttings and lists of place names.

The 1,400 printed books are all listed in the pre-1985 typescript catalogue and there are online records for some of them.

Coll-97

HMS Challenger Papers

The Challenger Expedition of 1872–1876 was the first great voyage of oceanographical exploration.

In 41 months from December 1872 to May 1876, the wooden steam corvette HMS *Challenger* visited all the oceans of the world except the Arctic. The vessel and crew were provided by the Admiralty, and the naval command was given to Captain George Strong Nares. The scientific staff were supervised by Charles Wyville Thomson (knighted in 1876), a Scottish naturalist and student of marine invertebrates. The expedition was charged with determining deep-sea physical conditions including depth, temperature and ocean currents. Charting, surveying and biological investigations were also carried out. In its programme of research, the expedition covered 68,890 nautical miles, gathering observations from 362 stations and making 492 deep soundings and 133 dredgings. Thomson had been appointed Professor of Natural History at the University of Edinburgh in 1870, and much of the preparation for this voyage took place in Edinburgh. At the end of the expedition the Challenger Office was set up in the city. The *Report on the Scientific Results of the Voyage of H.M.S. Challenger* was issued in 50 volumes between 1850 and 1895. When Thomson died in 1882, John Murray succeeded him as Director of the Challenger Office and editor of the *Report*. Much of the information gathered by the Challenger Expedition is still used today.

The Challenger Papers contain:
- sheets of plates illustrating various marine life forms, and original drawings of marine life forms
- engravings, lithographs and photographs of marine life forms
- drawings, photographs and engravings of Challenger equipment and staff
- statistical material, graphs, charts and maps.

There is also miscellaneous textual material and engraved proof illustrations. The printed report volumes are all in the rare book collections. *Coll-46*

HMS Challenger *moored at St Paul's Rocks,* 28 August 1873

Chalmers, David Patrick

David Patrick Chalmers (1835–1899) was a leading political and legal figure in colonial Africa.

Educated at the Edinburgh Institution and at the University of Edinburgh, Chalmers was called to the Scottish Bar in 1860. He was appointed Magistrate of Gambia in 1867, with full powers of a judge. In 1869, he became the Magistrate of the Gold Coast (modern-day Ghana) with similar powers. In 1872, Chalmers was appointed Queen's Advocate of Sierra Leone. He served on the Gold Coast during the Ashanti (Asante) invasion. In 1876, he became first Chief Justice of the Gold Coast, and in 1878 Chief Justice of British Guiana (Guyana). Chalmers was appointed as the Royal Commissioner to enquire into the 1898 revolt in Sierra Leone which had arisen from the imposition of a hut tax and because ruling chiefs had not been consulted before protectorate status was proclaimed in 1896. Chalmers also served in Jamaica on a Judicial Commission of Enquiry in 1893, and as a special judge in a prosecution for fraud in Newfoundland in 1897. He was knighted in 1876.

The collection consists of:

- manuscripts, typescripts, newspaper cuttings and printed ordinances relating to the Gambia, 1867–1869; the Gold Coast, 1869–1878; and Sierra Leone, 1898–1899
- material relating to British Guiana, 1879–1894; Jamaica, 1895–1896; and Newfoundland, 1897
- pamphlets and articles relating to the Sierra Leone Hut Tax Enquiry in 1898
- correspondence and diaries covering the period 1859–1878
- a diary kept by W H Campbell on an expedition from Georgetown to Upata, British Guiana, in 1857.

Coll-239

'Outline Map Shewing the British Possessions on the Gambia', 1865
David Patrick Chalmers Papers

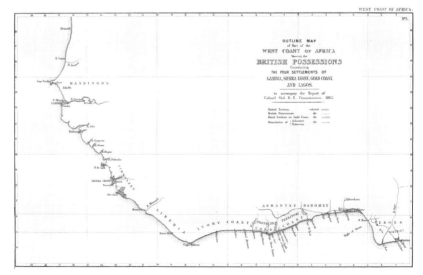

Clark, Arthur Melville

Arthur Melville Clark (1895–1990) was a distinguished scholar of English literature.

Born in Edinburgh, Clark was educated at Daniel Stewart's College and the University of Edinburgh, where he graduated MA with first-class honours in 1919. From 1924 to 1928 he was an Assistant in English Literature at the University of Edinburgh, then Lecturer from 1928 to 1946, as well as Director of Studies from 1931 to 1947. In 1946, he was appointed Reader in English Literature, remaining in post until his retirement in 1960. His publication record spans six decades and includes *The Realistic Revolt in Modern Poetry* (1922), *A Bibliography of Thomas Heywood* (1924), *Thomas Heywood, Playwright and Miscellanist* (1931), *Autobiography, its Genesis and Phases* (1935), *Spoken English* (1946), *Studies in Literary Modes* (1946), *Two Pageants by Thomas Heywood* (1953), *Sonnets from the French, and Other Verses* (1966), *Sir Walter Scott: The Formative Years* (1969), and *Murder under Trust, or, The Topical Macbeth* (1982). Clark also edited the *Edinburgh University Calendar*, 1933–1945. In addition to a DPhil from Oxford University (1929), Clark was awarded the Edinburgh University DLitt in 1947. He was made a Knight of Polonia Restituta for his work on international relations during the Second World War and was also a Knight of the Military and Hospitaller Order of St Lazarus of Jerusalem.

The papers contain:
- lecture notes, articles and other material on Shakespeare, Scott, and poetry generally
- material on heraldry and genealogy, and on the Order of St Lazarus
- speeches and reviews
- correspondence, personal material and some photographs
- books and a notebook containing poems with some inserted letters.

Coll-65

Clermiston Estate papers

The Edinburgh suburb of Clermiston, which lies to the west of Corstorphine Hill and Edinburgh Zoo, was originally the Clermiston Estate.

The Clermiston Mains area began to be developed for housing in 1957 and street names there were borrowed from *Kidnapped* by Robert Louis Stevenson.

The collection consists of some 70 legal documents including:
- instruments of sasine
- heritable bonds
- bonds of corroboration
- documents of discharge and renunciation
- searches of incumbrances
- a plan of Cramond Muir Road
- a sketch of parts of Cramond Moor
- a description of Clermiston House
- measurement of turnips sold on the estate
- pages from accounts books.

The archive includes papers particular to, and signed by, Sir Alexander Dick (1703–1785), a notable medical man of the time.

Three of the legal documents relate to dealings of Walter Scott (1729–1799), father of Sir Walter Scott, who in 1774 raised a

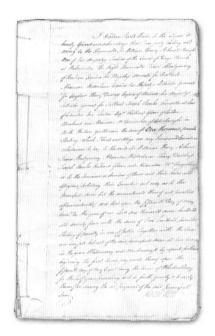

Clermiston Estate document in the hand of Walter Scott senior

loan of one thousand pounds on security of part of the Clermiston Estate.

Coll-720

. . . .

Collinson, Francis Montgomery

Musicologist and composer Francis Montgomery Collinson (1895–1985) made a major contribution to the collection and study of Gaelic and Scots song.

After serving in the Army Service Corps during the First World War, Collinson studied music at the University of Edinburgh, where he was awarded the degree of MusB in 1923. While at Edinburgh, Collinson played in the Reid Concert Orchestra and was conductor of the student Yahoo Orchestra. After working as a conductor in London, Collison took charge of the BBC's *Country Magazine*

programme in 1941, in which capacity he collected folksongs from all parts of Britain and later published arrangements of many of his finds.

In 1951, he was invited back to Edinburgh to become the first musical research fellow at the newly founded School of Scottish Studies, where he concentrated on collecting, studying and transcribing traditional song in both Scots and Gaelic. His research is collected in *The Traditional and National Music of Scotland* (1966), a landmark publication. Later works include *The Bagpipe* (1975), and the three-volume *Hebridean Folksongs* (1969, 1977, 1981) under the editorship of John Lorne Campbell.

The Collinson Papers consist of songs, correspondence and notebooks, in three boxes, as well as a small collection of printed broadside ballads.

Coll-90

. . . .

Coltness Papers

The Coltness Papers are an invaluable resource for many aspects of 17th- and 18th-century Scotland.

Coltness (part of modern Wishaw), was the seat of the aristocratic and influential Steuart family who played a major role in the legal and political life of Scotland. The collection contains papers from the following representatives of the family:

1. Sir James Steuart (1608–1681), twice Lord Provost of Edinburgh

The collection contains both printed and manuscript materials, particularly by Sir James Steuart Denham (1713–1780). There is part of the manuscript of his *Inquiry*, notes on Mary Queen of Scots, notes on the coinage of Bengal, translations and letters.

There are also:

- papers by both male and female members of the family, including recipes, estate papers and accounts
- genealogical and heraldic material
- military papers and letters to General Sir James Steuart Denham from William Pitt, Prime Minister
- verses, historical and religious writings, and a wide range of correspondence
- commonplace books of Elizabeth Steuart and others.

Coll-17

2. Sir James Steuart (1635–1713), who, after a period of political exile under the Stuarts, was appointed Lord Advocate in 1692 and wrote much of the official report on the Glencoe Massacre

3. Sir James Steuart (1681–1727), who served as Solicitor-General of Scotland

4. Sir James Steuart Denham (1713–1780), a prominent Jacobite who went into exile after Culloden and published the first systematic treatise on economics to appear in English, the groundbreaking and influential *Inquiry into the Principles of Political Oeconomy* (1767)

5. Sir James Steuart Denham (1744–1839) who rose to the rank of general in the British Army and served as MP for the county of Lanark.

Corson, James

See main entry under Rare Books.
Coll-1022

Cruickshank, Helen Burness

An important poet in her own right, Helen Burness Cruickshank (1886–1975) also played a major role as a mentor to other writers of the Scottish Literary Renaissance movement.

Cruickshank was born near Hillside, Montrose, in Angus. She was educated at the local Hillside Public School and at Montrose Academy. In 1903, she began a career in the Civil Service, initially working for the Post Office in London. There she became involved with the suffragette movement and in particular with the Woman Clerks' Association which campaigned for better pay for women. In 1912, Cruickshank returned to Edinburgh to work in the newly established National Health Insurance Scheme. She became friends with Christopher Murray Grieve (1892–1978), otherwise known as Hugh MacDiarmid, and William Soutar (1898–1943), among many other writers and artists, whose work she tirelessly supported and encouraged. In 1926 she was a founder member of Scottish PEN, part of an international writers' organisation which fosters cross-cultural exchange and champions freedom of expression. Ten years later, she was also part of the founding committee of the Saltire Society, a body set up to promote understanding of the culture and heritage of Scotland. Cruickshank's poems, in Scots and English, are rich in the sights and sounds of 20th-century Scotland and show a sharp political perception of the position both of women and of Scotland in general. She published three volumes of verse: *Up the Noran Water*

(1934), *Sea Buckthorn* (1954) and *The Ponnage Pool* (1968); and a *Collected Poems* in 1971. At a graduation ceremonial on 2 July 1970, Cruickshank was awarded the honorary degree of MA from the University of Edinburgh for her services to literature.

Cruickshank's papers and correspondence include:

- manuscripts of poems, plays, short stories, lectures, talks and articles
- letters from writers such as Hugh MacDiarmid (and his wife Valda Grieve) and Lewis Grassic Gibbon
- autobiographical notes
- pencil sketches, photographs and press cuttings
- contributions to Scottish PEN
- correspondence connected with her career in the Civil Service covering the years 1913–1945.

Coll-81

Cullen, William

William Cullen (1710–1790) was one of the leading medical figures of Enlightenment Scotland, focusing on the role of the nervous system in disease. It was he who introduced the term 'neurosis' into medicine. After an initial period of study at Glasgow University, Cullen

William Cullen
William Gowan
© The University of Edinburgh

went to London in 1729 to enlist as a surgeon on a merchant ship sailing to the West Indies. On his return to London, he continued his studies and worked for an apothecary. In the early 1730s, Cullen returned to Scotland to provide for his family after the death of his father and eldest brother. After two years as a practitioner at Auchinlee near his native Hamilton, he studied at the Edinburgh Medical School under Alexander Monro *primus* (1697–1767) from 1734 to 1736. He then worked as a surgeon in Hamilton, graduating MD at Glasgow University in 1740. In 1744 he moved to Glasgow with the aim of founding a medical school there. While in the city he lectured on medicine and other subjects to students who included Joseph Black (1728–1799). In 1751, Cullen was appointed Professor of Medicine at Glasgow University, then in 1755 he was elected joint (subsequently sole) Professor of Chemistry at the University of Edinburgh. In 1757 he began to give clinical lectures at Edinburgh Royal Infirmary with great success, and in 1766 he was elected Professor of the Theory (or Institutes) of Physic. From 1768 he and his rival, Dr John Gregory (1724–1773), lectured on the theory and the practice of physic in alternate years, but on the death of Gregory in 1773 Cullen succeeded him and gave both courses.

In the 1740s, Cullen made important discoveries regarding the evolution of heat in chemical combination and the cooling of solutions. These were described in his first publication, *Essay on the Cold Produced by Evaporating Fluids* (1756). His other major works include *Synopsis nosologiae methodicae* (on the classification of diseases) (1769) and his magnum opus *First Lines of the Practice of Physic* (1777 1784). He also took an active part in preparing a new edition of the *Edinburgh Pharmacopoeia* (1774).

The collection includes correspondence, lecture notes, abstracts and commentaries. *Various locations in Special Collections.*

Cunningham, Daniel John

Daniel John Cunningham (1850–1909) is best known for his *Text-Book of Anatomy* and *Manual of Practical Anatomy*, which long maintained their position as standard works in the field.

Born in Crieff, Perthshire, Cunningham graduated MB from the University of Edinburgh in 1874. He returned to the University as Demonstrator in Anatomy from 1876 until 1882, when he was appointed Professor of Anatomy at the Royal College of Surgeons of Ireland, in Dublin. The following year he was elected to the Chair of Anatomy at Trinity College Dublin. He remained there until appointed

Photograph by Daniel John Cunningham from South African War Royal Commission album

to the Edinburgh chair in 1903. Although essentially remembered for his textbooks, Cunningham carried out original research in human and comparative anatomy as well as in the wider field of anthropology, including studies of gigantism, right-handedness and left-brainedness. He undertook a number of important public duties including service in 1900 with the Royal Commission on the Care of the Sick and the Wounded during the South African War. He was elected FRS in 1891.

The papers include a substantial sequence of notebooks and working papers containing detailed notes of experiments and dissections, together with drawings and drafts for lectures. There are autograph letters from eminent anatomists and medical men, including ten letters from Joseph Lister. An item of particular interest is an album of 96 photographs from Cunningham's service on the South African War Royal Commission. The subjects include army camps and infirmaries, railroads and the indigenous population. Many of the documents bear annotations by Cunningham's son, John (see below).

Coll-11

Cunningham, John

John Cunningham (1881–1968) was both a pioneering bacteriologist and an early advocate of occupational therapy.

The son of anatomist Daniel John Cunningham (see page 79), John Cunningham was educated at Loretto School, Epsom College and the University of Edinburgh, before completing his medical training at Trinity College Dublin. He entered the Indian Medical Service in 1905, was appointed Assistant Director of the Bombay Bacteriological Laboratory in 1910, and Assistant Director of the Central Research Institute of India in 1912.

After serving on the Indian North-West Frontier during the First World War,

John Cunningham in Brewery Garden, Kasauli, 1916

he became Director of the King Institute, Madras, 1919–1926, where he initiated mass production of smallpox vaccine and constructed experimental filter stations. In 1926, he was appointed Director of the Pasteur Institute, Kasauli, where he was involved in the preparation of an anti-rabies vaccine and conducted groundbreaking research into bacillary dysentery. He was also Organising Secretary of the Seventh Congress of the Far Eastern Association of Tropical Medicine held at Calcutta in 1927. Returning to Scotland in 1929, Cunningham became the first medical superintendent of the Astley Ainslie Institution, Edinburgh, where he set up the first school of occupational therapy in Scotland.

The papers include full documentation (case histories, experimental notes and data) of Cunningham's medical research in India, and in particular of his work on the bacteriology and immunology of relapsing fever, and the treatment of rabies. An important feature of the collection is the many photographs taken in India. The subjects are both professional and personal, and include the institutes and laboratories where he worked, their personnel, equipment and facilities, his own family and their quarters, the scenery and people of India, and his military service. Almost all of these bear dates and descriptions in Cunningham's hand. The papers also include Cunningham's reports, press cuttings and other material relating to the 1927 Calcutta Congress.

Coll-30

Dalyell, John Graham

After making his mark as an antiquary devoted to early Scottish history and literature, John Graham Dalyell (1775–1851) turned to natural history and made a series of major contributions to marine biology.

The second son of Sir Robert Dalyell of the Binns, he was educated at the Universities of St Andrews and Edinburgh and became a member of the Faculty of Advocates in 1797. In the same year, Dalyell was elected to the Society of Antiquaries of Scotland and became its first Vice-President. His publications include *Fragments of Scottish History* (1798), the two volumes of *Scotish* [sic] *Poems of the 16th Century* (1801), *Observations on Some Interesting Phenomena in Animal Physiology, Exhibited by Several Specia of Planariae* (1814), the engraved *Rare and Remarkable Animals of Scotland* (1847) and, his magnum opus, *The Powers of the Creator Displayed in the Creation* (1851–1853). Dalyell was a member of the Highland and Agricultural Society of

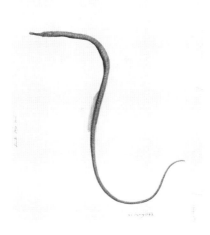

Sea snake, drawing by John Graham Dalyell, 1843

Scotland, was one of the original promoters of a Zoological Gardens for Edinburgh, and served as President of the Society of Arts for Scotland in 1839–1840. Dalyell was knighted on 22 August 1836 for his services to science and literature. The papers consist of some 158 volumes of notebooks of manuscript notes and printed matter. The subjects of the notebooks are wide and varied: antiquities, superstitions, human society, tours, musical practice, natural history, rare and remarkable animals, properties of animals, the will and power of the creator, experiments, observations and extracts from records. There are also four packets of Dalyell's original drawings for *Rare and Remarkable Animals* and *The Powers of the Creator*.
Coll-244

Medals to mark the graduation of
Pavel Mikhailovich Dashkov

Dashkov Medals

In 1777 Princess Ekaterina Romanovna Vorontsova Dashkova arrived in Scotland with her son Paul (Pavel Mikhailovich Dashkov) who enrolled at the University of Edinburgh. In 1779 the Princess, still resident in Edinburgh, gave a collection of Russian commemorative medals to mark the occasion of her son's graduation as Master of Arts. The 94 medals, all made of copper, were first entrusted to the care of Professor John Robison (see page 170), Professor of Natural Philosophy in the University and a Fellow of the Royal Society of Edinburgh. In the early 1770s, Robison had briefly held the Chair of Mathematics in the Imperial Naval Cadet Corps at Kronstadt, St Petersburg, where he had been awarded the rank of colonel.

The medals were handed back to the University after Robison's death in 1805.

Some of the medals show rulers of Russia, military figures, statesmen, and events of the reign of Peter the Great. Others mark events such as coronations, accessions, marriages and deaths of Russian rulers. Imperial institutions are commemorated, as are cities and buildings of the Russian Empire. All are located within the University Archives small objects collection. There is a detailed inventory of the medals.
Coll-21

Davies, Reginald

Reginald Davies (1887–1971) was a leading figure in the colonial administration of Africa.

He was educated at Hymers College, Hull, and St Catharine's College, Cambridge, where he was awarded the degree of BA (Hons Maths) in 1909. He entered the

Sudan Political Service in 1911, and held a succession of posts. He retired from the Service in 1935 and moved to Egypt. There he became Deputy Director-General of Alexandria Municipality between 1935 and 1939, before working for the British Embassy in Cairo and then the British Council, where he worked until his final retirement in 1953. His publications include *The Camel's Back: Service in the Rural Sudan* (1957). He was awarded the Order of the Nile, 3rd Class, in 1932, and in 1950 he was awarded the Order of St Michael and St George.

The papers consist of correspondence concerning the Sudan from 1901 to 1961, and also include diaries (1920–1934), photograph albums, loose photographs and slides, verses, addresses, articles and biographical information. Among the correspondence are letters from explorer and travel-writer Freya Stark (1893–1993). *Coll-191*

....

De la Mare, Walter

The poet, short-story writer and novelist Walter de la Mare (1873–1956) is perhaps best remembered for his many poems and anthologies for children.

Born in Charleton, Kent, de la Mare was educated at St Paul's Cathedral Choristers' School in London. From 1890 until 1908, he worked for the statistics department of the Anglo-American Oil Company in London. However, after his *Songs of Childhood* were published in 1902, he devoted more and more time to writing, and the award of a Civil List

pension in 1908 permitted him to commit to it full time. He produced a steady stream of works for adults and children throughout the rest of his life. His works include the novels *Return* (1910) and *Memoirs of a Midget* (1921), the verse collections *Poems* (1906), *The Listeners (1912), Peacock Pie (1913)*, and *Inward Companion* (1950), and the anthologies *Come Hither* (1923), *Behold, This Dreamer!* (1939) and *O Lovely England* (1953). He was made Companion of Honour in 1948, and received the Order of Merit in 1953.

The collection includes letters and other papers. There are author's proofs of *Desert Islands and Robinson Crusoe* (published 1930) as well as ten folders of letters in both manuscript and typescript form. There are also letters to educationalist William Fraser Mitchell, to writer Jessie Georgina Sime, 1940–1952, and to Dr Frank Carr Nicholson, Librarian of the University of Edinburgh, 1940–1956.

Various locations in Special Collections.

....

Donaldson, Gordon

Gordon Donaldson (1913–1993) was one of the 20th century's leading Scottish historians.

Born in Leith, Donaldson was educated at the Royal High School and the University of Edinburgh where he obtained a first-class honours degree in history. His postgraduate study was conducted at the Institute of Historical Research, University of London. After graduating with a PhD in 1938, Donaldson was appointed as an assistant in the Scottish Record Office where he became skilled as a reader of difficult early-medieval and late-medieval manuscripts. Throughout

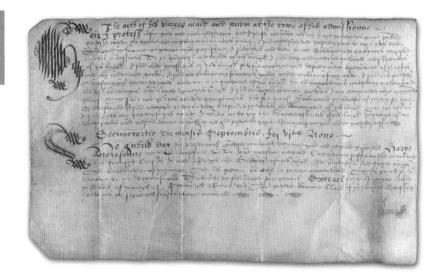

MS from Gordon Donaldson's palaeography collection

his life he maintained an interest in the material there, making an enormous contribution to the editing of historical records. In 1947 he became a Lecturer in Scottish History at the University of Edinburgh. In 1955 he was appointed Reader, and in 1963 was awarded the Chair of Professor of Scottish History and Palaeography. His output of edited texts, books, articles and reviews was immense and included *The Making of the Scottish Prayer Book of 1637* (1954), *Scotland: James V to James VII* (1965), *Scotland: Church and Nation through Sixteen Centuries* (1960), *Isles of Home: Sixty Years of Shetland* (1984), *Scottish Church History* (1985) and *The Faith of the Scots* (1990). Of particular significance is Donaldson's work on the Reformation period and on the national church as originally established by John Knox. Between 1972 and 1977 he was editor of the *Scottish Historical Review*. In 1979, Donaldson was appointed Historiographer to the Queen in Scotland, and in 1988 was awarded the CBE.

The papers consist of:
- letters, including correspondence with institutions and publishers
- materials and notes on churches, crofters, emigration, genealogy and the Northern Isles
- lectures and notes
- personal and family papers
- photographs and press cuttings
- manuscript material, typescript material and proofs.

These all cover the period 1935–1993.

Further material acquired later includes some 60 manuscripts and fragments dated from 1549 to 1740. This is Donaldson's private collection of formal legal and historical Scottish documents which he used to illustrate his Scottish documents and palaeography courses in the 1970s. A further collection of colour and black

and white slides shows houses, castles and Scottish domestic architecture generally, plus views of other places, including the Faroe Islands, Scandinavia, England, France, the Mediterranean, the USA and Canada.
Coll-78

Duncan, Andrew (the elder)

See main entry under Rare Books.
Coll-199

Duncan, Andrew (the younger)

Andrew Duncan the younger (1773–1832) was a pioneer in the fields of forensic medicine and public health.

The son of Andrew Duncan the elder, Professor of the Institutes of Medicine at the University of Edinburgh (see above), he was born in Edinburgh and was the only one of his father's 12 children to follow him into the medical profession. Having studied medicine at the University of Edinburgh, he was apprenticed to the Edinburgh surgeons Alexander and George Wood. He graduated with the degree of MA in 1793 and MD in 1794. He then studied in London and at a number of European medical schools including Göttingen, Vienna, Pisa and Naples. On his return to Edinburgh in 1796 he became a Fellow of the Royal College of Physicians and a Physician to the Royal Public Dispensary. He subsequently became Physician to the Fever Hospital at Queensberry House. Duncan's travels

abroad had shown him the necessity of closer cooperation between the medical profession and the state. In 1807 a Chair of Medical Jurisprudence and Medical Police was set up at the University of Edinburgh (amidst much opposition from the Faculty of Medicine) with Duncan as its first Professor. In addition, from 1809 to 1822, he performed the duties of Secretary of the Senatus and Librarian to the University. In 1819 he resigned as Professor of Medical Jurisprudence on being appointed to assist his father in the Chair of the Institutes of Medicine. In 1821, Duncan was elected Professor of Materia Medica at the University of Edinburgh. His best-known publication is the *Edinburgh New Dispensary* (1803), which was translated into French and German and widely republished in the USA. From 1816 until his death, Duncan was an active member of the Commission for the re-building of the University (the Adam-Playfair buildings of the Old College).

The papers include letters and other material mostly about his travels and studies abroad. There are also notes of lectures on materia medica delivered between 1831 and 1832.
Coll-7

Edinburgh Association for the University Education of Women (EAUEW)

The Edinburgh Association for the University Education of Women (EAUEW) played a crucial role both in lobbying the University of Edinburgh to admit female students and in providing further education for women.

Mary Crudelius, founding member of the
Edinburgh Ladies' Educational Association

The EAUEW has its roots in the second
half of the 19th century. The first association
of its kind in Scotland, it was part of a vigorous
nationwide campaign demanding the provision
of higher education for women. Prior to
this period, women had rarely attended
University of Edinburgh lectures, although
Dr James Miranda Barry had graduated
MD from Edinburgh in 1812, served in the
British Army as a medical officer, and only
at her death was revealed as a woman. With
the arrival of Sophia Jex-Blake in Edinburgh
in the 1860s, the campaign for the medical
education of women in particular became
intense. On 15 October 1868, the forerunner
of the EAUEW was founded – the Edinburgh
Ladies' Educational Association (ELEA) – and
the following year Jex-Blake won the right
for women to attend medical classes in the
separate Extra-Mural School. The guiding
force behind the setting up of the ELEA,
however, was Mary Crudelius. Crudelius
and others were able to use their influence
to win the support of a number of Edinburgh
academics, in particular David Masson,
Professor of Rhetoric and English Literature.

By 1873, women were enrolled in
Association classes as diverse as mathematics,
moral philosophy, chemistry, physiology,
botany and Bible criticism. In 1874 a University
Certificate in Arts was introduced, and by 1877
the Rules and Calendar of the Association were
being printed in the University Calendar. With
a change in name (to EAUEW) the Association
continued to attract students to its classes,
while rigorously campaigning for universities
to admit women. Their campaign culminated
in the Universities (Scotland) Act 1889 which
led to the drawing up of Regulations for the
Graduation of Women and for their instruction
in the Universities. In 1893 eight women,
who had all been EAUEW students, graduated
from the University of Edinburgh. Right from
the start, classes were mixed except in the
Faculty of Medicine. With its main objective
now achieved, the EAUEW turned to the
provision of facilities and amenities for women
at the University. By 1897, a library and
accommodation for women were available at
Masson Hall in George Square. By 1914 more
than a thousand women had graduated from
the University. The EAUEW was wound up in
the 1970s.

The collection contains:

- reports and calendars of the
  Association between 1868 and
  1888 as well as class register books,
  1867–1892

- minutes spanning 1868 to 1970
- certificates in arts and register of names, addresses and subjects passed
- printed pamphlets on the history of the Association
- photographs of the first women graduates
- the correspondence of Mary Crudelius (with portraits).

There are also EAUEW membership lists, 1950 and 1968, and material relating to the winding up of the Association, 1970–1974.
Coll-42

Edinburgh Geological Society

The Edinburgh Geological Society was formed in 1834 in order to stimulate public interest in geology and promote the advancement of geological knowledge.

It was formed by 11 students of a class in mineralogy and geology conducted by Alexander Rose at (the now defunct) Queen's College, Edinburgh. They met on Thursday 4 December 1834 in Robertson's Tavern, Milne's Close, and voted to establish a society for 'Discussion and Mutual Instruction', which would initially meet in Rose's house at 2 Drummond Street. Its first President was John Castle, and its first Secretary was James Brodie. Its first scientific meeting was held on 8 December 1834, the subject for discussion being whether or not Arthur's Seat was of volcanic origin. In 1863, the Society elected Sir Roderick Impey Murchison as its first Patron (1863–1871), followed by Sir Charles Lyell (1871–1875). The Society continues to thrive today.

The collection contains:

- minute books of general and council meetings from 1834 to 1982
- treasurer's accounts
- laws, lists and rolls of members
- membership applications
- billets of meetings, 1879–1990
- correspondence
- papers read, 1863–1864.

Letter from Hugh Miller to Alexander Rose, founding member of Edinburgh Geological Society

Printed items include a history of the Edinburgh Geological Society, proceedings of the Society, copies of the *Edinburgh Geologist*, leaflets and geological excursion guides.
Coll-43

Edinburgh University Archives

The University of Edinburgh was formally established by Royal Charter in 1582. It was originally called the Tounis College, as it was set up by the Town Council of Edinburgh using part of a legacy left by Robert Reid, Bishop of Orkney. The opening of the University took place in 1583. In 1617 when King James VI and I visited the College its name was officially changed to King James' College, although the older title continued to be more widely used.

Teaching began in 1583 under Robert Rollock, with a four-year course to gain a Masters of Arts degree. When Rollock was appointed as the first Principal of the University in 1586, there were four Philosophy regents and one regent of Humanity, while Rollock himself henceforth specialised in Divinity. Until the beginning of the 18th century the University remained essentially an Arts College, with a Divinity School attached. In the course of the 17th century the Chairs of Divinity, Oriental Languages, Ecclesiastical History and Mathematics were founded. By the end of the 17th century there was also regular teaching in Medicine, and sporadic teaching in Law.

In the 18th century, the University was at the centre of the European Enlightenment. A Faculty of Law was established in 1707.

The first medical chair had been established in 1685 and was closely followed in the first half of the 18th century by six more, leading to the formal creation of a Faculty of Medicine in 1726. The Chair of Rhetoric (English Literature) was founded in 1760. Further posts emerged from the mergers with New College, the Royal (Dick) Veterinary School, Moray House Institute of Education, the Roslin Institute and Edinburgh College of Art.

The University was governed by the Town Council until the Universities (Scotland) Act of 1858, when it received self-governing status. A University Court and General Council were introduced, which decided on matters and management pertaining to the whole University. The Senatus Academicus was already in place before 1858 and this continued to manage academic matters but was now answerable to the Court and Council.

Alongside the archives of the University itself sit those of the Students' Association and of clubs, societies and other organisations closely related to the University.

Major records series and types include:
- minutes of University Court, Senatus and committees
- minutes of Faculties
- matriculation and graduation records
- student class lists
- University Calendars and publications
- records of departments, centres, institutes, etc.
- examination papers
- records of clubs and societies
- photographs of staff, students and spaces.

There are also objects – not all formally part of the University Archives – which tell the story of the University. Notable items include Sophia Jex-Blake's address and casket. In 1869 Jex-Blake (1840–1912) determined to study medicine at the University of Edinburgh though its doors were still closed to women. After a bitter struggle, which divided the faculty and ended with Jex-Blake suing the University unsuccessfully in the Court of Session, she moved to Berne to qualify. In 1889, however, largely as a result of her struggles, degrees for women were sanctioned by Act of Parliament. This address was presented by students to congratulate her on the establishment of the independent Edinburgh School of Medicine for Women, which opened in 1886. The casket was made for the presentation and the silver decoration includes the initials SJB in monogram.
Dc.3.103 and Medals.125

Another remarkable object is Edinburgh Professor of Medicine James Young Simpson's chloroform bottle. Simpson first anaesthetised a patient in January 1847, using ether, but subsequently experimented on himself and his assistants in search of a more satisfactory anaesthetic. A trial of chloroform was made on 4 November 1847 when the experimentalists 'proved its efficacy by simultaneously falling insensible below the table'. As well as the bottle, the collection holds a photograph of the first child born to a mother under the influence of chloroform. According to a letter written by Simpson's daughter the baby was actually christened Anaesthesia. Her full name was Agnes Anaesthesia Carstares.
Special Collections Dc.2.85

James Young Simpson's chloroform bottle, 1840s

Edinburgh College of Art Archives

See also Rare Books.

Edinburgh College of Art is one of the most influential art schools in the UK. It has its roots in the Trustees Academy set up by the Trustees of the Board of Manufacturers in 1760, the earliest art college in Britain. This was part of a forward-looking scheme to foster aesthetic design quality and promote innovation. Practical instruction in art and design was made available from about 1820 in partnership with the Royal Scottish Academy and later with the short-lived School of Applied Art set up by Edinburgh architect Sir Robert Rowand Anderson. In 1908 all teaching activities were brought together in one central institution, the newly built Edinburgh College of Art, henceforth the principal provider of a wide range of teaching and skills in the practical arts. The College became an integral part of the University of Edinburgh in 2011.

The majority of the collection covers the period 1906–2011. It contains administrative and teaching records which provide an overview of practices, trends and technology in the art scene. Student records and social activity are well represented. The collection has a few volumes of minutes and student records for the predecessor bodies of the Trustees Academy and School of Applied Art. A particular strength of the collection is the photographs and design work for the annual Revel Party. The correspondence of Sir Robin Philipson in his role as Head of Drawing and Painting provides an insight into the impact the college had in the 1960s and 1970s.

There is a substantial photographic element to the collection, together with numerous press cuttings.

Moray House College of Education Archives

See also Rare Books.

Moray House, a 17th-century town house on Edinburgh's Royal Mile, has been home to a pioneering centre for teacher training since 1848. In 1987, it incorporated the Dunfermline College of Physical Education, founded by the Carnegie Trust in 1905. Moray House College merged with the University of Edinburgh in 1998.

The archives of Moray House and Dunfermline College of Physical Education are an important record of teacher training, education policy and physical education from the mid-19th century to the present. The collection also includes records of the Moray House College's Demonstration School and Nursery, and the Newington Hostel for female students.

The Colleges and Schools covered include:
- Edinburgh Church of Scotland Training College and Normal School, 1845–1907
- Edinburgh United Free Church Training College, 1843–1907
- Edinburgh Normal and Model Free Church School (and its successors), 1867–1968
- Edinburgh Provincial Training College, 1907–1959
- Moray House College of Education, 1959–1986

• Moray House Institute of Education, 1986–1998.

It also includes the records of the following institutions, which were associated to or merged with Moray House Institute of Education and its predecessors:
  • Callendar Park College, 1964–1986
  • Dunfermline College of Physical Education, 1905–1986
  • Edinburgh College of Domestic Science, 1918–1970
  • St George's Training College, 1886–1939.

The collection includes personal papers alongside records of hostel provision, clubs and societies, reflecting the lives of students and staff. The collection also includes the archives of the Dunfermline College of Physical Education Old Students Association.

Royal (Dick) Veterinary College Archives

See also Rare Books.

The Royal (Dick) Veterinary College was originally founded by William Dick in 1823 as the Highland Society's Veterinary School. It was the first veterinary college in Scotland and only the second in the UK. Dick was a pioneer in veterinary practice and developed high standards for veterinary practice and education. He was appointed Veterinary Surgeon in Scotland to Queen Victoria in 1844. Among his students were the founders of veterinary schools in Glasgow, Liverpool, Ireland, Canada, the USA and Australia. The College's international reputation grew in the 20th century with eminent veterinarian Orlando Charnock Bradley as Principal and

the building of new facilities at Summerhall. From 1943 to 1948 the 'Dick Vet' hosted a veterinary school set up by some 50 Polish students and staff exiled from their homeland. The College was reconstituted as an integral part of the University of Edinburgh in 1951 and became a full faculty in 1964.

This collection includes the administrative records of the teaching and practice at the college and a large photographic archive depicting animals, people and events of the college. Artefacts used for practical classes and demonstration are included. An overview of student life and extramural activities is provided by the parts of the collection that cover societies and clubs. These include the Officer Training Corps and Dramatic Society. There are also research papers, published works and some personal papers by staff such as Charnock Bradley (Principal, 1911–1937).

EUA

Ewart, James Cossar

Zoologist James Cossar Ewart (1851–1933) was a pioneer in the improvement of domestic animals by selective breeding.

Born in Penicuik, Midlothian, Ewart studied medicine at the University of Edinburgh from 1871 to 1874. After graduating, he initially stayed on at the University as an anatomy demonstrator under William Turner, then took up the position of Curator of the Zoological Museum at University College, London, where he played a key role in establishing the first course of practical zoology. In 1882, he was appointed Regius Professor of Natural History at the University of Edinburgh in 1882, a position he held for 45 years. Ewart is best known for his cross-breeding work with zebras and horses, which disproved the long-held theory of telegony (the belief that a female's first mate can determine the characteristics of later offspring from different sires) and which he described in his 1899 book *The Penycuik Experiments*. Ewart was instrumental in the creation of a Lectureship in Genetics at the University of Edinburgh in 1911 (the first in the UK). It was largely due to Ewart's presence that Edinburgh was chosen as the location for what became the Institute of Animal Genetics, a decision which had a significant impact on Edinburgh's development as a major centre for biological research and teaching.

The collection spans the period 1866–1935, and includes:

- lecture notes
- correspondence with colleagues and scientists around the world
- personal notebooks, books of press cuttings, certificates, diplomas and letters of appointment
- a collection of medals and badges from school and university
- photographs, including pictures of Ewart with his zebra hybrids.

Coll-14

Ferguson, Adam

The philosopher and historian Adam Ferguson (1723–1816) is one of the key figures of the Scottish Enlightenment and has been called the father of modern sociology

Born at Logierait, Perthshire, Ferguson studied at St Andrews University, taking his MA in July 1742. He went on to study divinity, first at St Andrews and then at the University of Edinburgh. In 1745, Ferguson was appointed as Deputy-Chaplain (subsequently Chaplain) to the (42nd) Black Watch but left military service in the same year to embark on a literary career. For a brief period in 1757–1758, Ferguson succeeded David Hume as librarian at the Advocates' Library, Edinburgh. In 1759 he was appointed as Professor of Natural Philosophy at the University of Edinburgh, and in 1764 to the Chair of Pneumatics and Moral Philosophy. In 1773 he became tutor to Charles, the 3rd Earl of Chesterfield, accompanying him on a tour of Europe where he met Voltaire. In 1778, Ferguson was appointed as Secretary to the Commissioners to the American Colonies, accompanying them to Philadelphia for the negotiation of a settlement; we have a letter from George

James Cossar Ewart with 'Romulus', a horse/zebra cross

Washington refusing him passage. Ferguson retired from the Chair of Moral Philosophy in 1785, but so that he might still draw a salary was appointed to the Chair of Mathematics.

Ferguson's masterpiece is *An Essay on the History of Civil Society* (1767) which influenced Schiller and Hegel, and, later, Karl Marx. Other works include *Institutes of Moral Philosophy* (1769), *History of the Progress and Termination of the Roman Republic* (1783) and *Principles of Moral and Political Science* (1792).

The Ferguson papers include:
- correspondence with Sir John Macpherson, 1773–1808
- correspondence with Alexander Carlyle, 1775–1802
- letters about religious intolerance among the Greeks and Romans
- family correspondence
- a collection of essays
- lectures on pneumatics and moral philosophy, 1776–1785
- *Proceedings of the British Commissioners at Philadelphia*, 1778–1779.

We also hold his roll-top writing desk.
Various locations in Special Collections.

Ferguson, James

James Ferguson (1710–1776) was a self-educated astronomer, inventor and instrument maker.

Born to a humble background near Rothiemay in Banffshire, Ferguson acquired an interest in mechanics as a small child. Tending sheep at the age of ten, he was able to study the stars at night and make models of spinning-wheels and mills during the day. As a young man he first earned a living by cleaning clocks and repairing domestic machinery. In his spare time he constructed a wooden clock and watch with wooden wheels and whalebone springs. This mechanical talent would later assist in his construction of astronomical models. Possessed of considerable artistic talent too, he supported his family and funded his research by painting miniature portraits, first in Edinburgh in 1734, then in Inverness from 1736. While in Inverness, Ferguson published his *Astronomical Rotula for Showing the Motions of the Planets, Places of the Sun and Moon*, and in 1742 he constructed an orrery. In 1743, he moved to London where he would live for the rest of his life, again initially combining portraiture with astronomical research. He presented a number of papers to the Royal Society, including 'On the Phenomena

Adam Ferguson (1790)
Henry Raeburn
©The University of Edinburgh

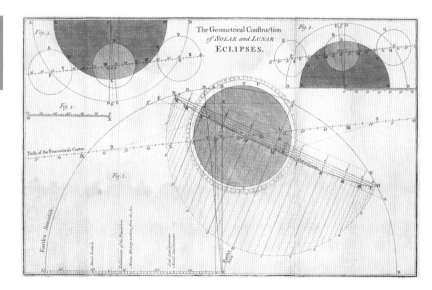

of Venus, Represented in an Orrery' in March 1746. In 1748, Ferguson began a successful career as a highly popular lecturer in astronomy and experimental science. In 1752–1753 he lectured on the reform of the calendar and the lunar eclipse of 1753. By 1760 he was able to give up portrait-painting and commit himself fully to science. In 1763 he presented to the Royal Society a projection of the partial solar eclipse of 1 April 1764 showing its times and phases at Greenwich. In his later years he developed an interest in the science of electricity and incorporated it into his lectures.

His principal publications include: *Astronomy Explained upon Sir Isaac Newton's Principles* (1756), *Lectures on Select Subjects in Mechanics, Hydrostatics, Pneumatics, and Optics* (1760), *An Introduction to Electricity* (1770), *Select Mechanical Exercises* (1773), and *The Art of Drawing in Perspective Made Easy to Those Who Have No Previous Knowledge of the Mathematics* (1775).

'The Geometrical Construction of Solar and Lunar Eclipses', astronomical table by James Ferguson

The collection of printed and manuscript items includes astronomical tables, the design of an astronomical clock, tracts relative to several branches of science, a commonplace book and a memorandum book.
Various locations in Special Collections.

. . . .

Flint, Robert

Robert Flint (1838–1910) was a philosopher and theologian whose works argue for the reasonableness of belief in God in the light of 19th-century scientific advances.

Born at Applegarth near Dumfries, Flint was educated at the University of Glasgow. He was licensed to preach in 1858 and held successive charges at the East Church of Aberdeen, 1859–1862, and at Kilconquhar, Fife, 1862–1864. In 1864 he was appointed to the Chair of Moral Philosophy and Political Economy in the University of St Andrews, where his *Philosophy of History in France and Germany* (1874) cemented his scholarly reputation. In 1876, he took up the Chair of Divinity in the University of Edinburgh. His books and pamphlets exercised a worldwide influence. They included *Socialism* (1894) and the trilogy represented by *Theism*, *Anti-Theistic Theories* (delivered as Baird Lectures in 1876 and 1877) and *Agnosticism* (1903). He received honorary degrees from the Universities of Aberdeen, Edinburgh and Glasgow, and from Princeton and Yale.

The collection includes:
- notes of lectures, 1843–1851
- essays, lectures, sermons, admonitions and speeches
- letters, including correspondence with publishers, and accounts
- photographs and newspaper cuttings.

Robert Flint (1903)
George Reid
© The University of Edinburgh

There are also papers connected with his University of Edinburgh courses, student names and essay marks, and galley proofs of *The Life of Professor Flint* by Donald Macmillan. *Coll-57*

Firth of Forth Defences

This important collection on the military defence of the Scottish coast, focusing, in particular, on the Firth of Forth, was built up by Captain Bruce Alexander Stenhouse (1911–1991).

Born in Sheerness, Kent, Stenhouse attended Edinburgh Academy from 1920 to 1930, then the University of Edinburgh where he graduated MA in 1936. He joined the Royal Artillery, achieving the rank of captain, initially commanding an anti-aircraft battery in the Firth of Forth, and later seeing other active service in North Africa and Italy. After the War he returned to his old school, the Edinburgh Academy, where he was appointed first as Secretary of the Academical Club (1946–1965) and later as Registrar (1950–1976).

Stenhouse had a strong interest in military history, especially maritime and naval, and began compiling a history of coastal defence in Scotland. He collected Public Record Office references from the Admiralty, the Committee for Imperial Defence, and the War Office, and interviewed ex-Forth Coast Gunners and other former military personnel.

Stenhouse's research was presented to the University by his widow in 1996.
The collection includes:

- Public Record Office references, 1879–1956
- correspondence with Major D Rollo (retired), HQ Royal Artillery, Woolwich, 1979–1987, relating to research on coastal defence, and further miscellaneous correspondence 1976–1990
- material relating to batteries and forts, including Forth Artillery Defences 1880–1980
- papers relating to the defence of islands
- newspaper cuttings
- material on attacks and disasters
- photographic materials (aerial photographs, camp and group photographs, photographs of ships, armoured trains, forts and batteries).

Coll-61

Forbes, Eric

Eric Gray Forbes (1933–1984) played a major international role in the establishment of history of science as an academic discipline.

Forbes was educated at Madras College, St Andrews, and at the University of St Andrews where he graduated in astronomy and mathematics in 1954. While studying for a PhD in solar astronomy at St Andrews, he spent much time working in observatories in Florence and Göttingen, acquiring an excellent knowledge of both Italian and German, which proved important for his later career. At Göttingen, he also helped discover archives left by the 18th-century astronomer Tobias Mayer, stimulating his interest in the history of astronomy.

In 1961, Forbes was appointed Lecturer in Physics at St Mary's College, Twickenham, and from 1963 to 1965, was a Senior Lecturer in Mathematics at the same institution. At the same time he studied for an MSc in history and philosophy of science at University College London, conducting research in 19th-century astronomy and navigation at the Royal Greenwich Observatory. Upon being awarded his MSc in 1965, he took up a post as Lecturer in the History of Science at the University of Edinburgh. Continued research on Tobias Mayer led to a PhD from University College London and a number of publications in the 1970s. A book to mark the tercentenary of the Royal Observatory in 1975 triggered an interest in John Flamsteed, the first Astronomer Royal. Forbes embarked on a project to publish Flamsteed's collected correspondence (subsequently completed by his widow Maria Forbes).

In 1978 Forbes was awarded a personal chair in History of Science at the University of Edinburgh and shortly afterwards was appointed Director of the History of Medicine and Science Unit. From the 1960s onwards, he played an active role in both national and international bodies concerned with the history of science. In 1977, he organised a congress in Edinburgh for the International Union of the History and Philosophy of Science. He subsequently served as the Union's secretary-general and vice-president.

He was also elected to the Royal Society of Edinburgh and the International Academy of the History of Science.

The papers consist of material under the following headings: astronomers, conferences, faculty and departmental papers, journals, lectures and lecture notes, Medical Archive Centre, observatories, publications and publishing, research projects and funding, reviews, societies and institutions.

Coll-132

Forth Bridge Archive

The Forth Rail Bridge, opened in 1890, is an iconic symbol of Scotland and indeed of Britain at the height of Victorian industrial confidence. Designed by Sir John Fowler and Sir Benjamin Baker, it was the longest single cantilever bridge in the world.

This collection includes important original photographs showing the development of the bridge, visitors' books recording important visits to the construction site, and associated plans, sketches and cuttings. This is a major research resource for the history of engineering and bridge technology.

Coll-1151

Forth Rail Bridge under construction

Geddes, Patrick

Patrick Geddes (1854–1932) was a pioneer of modern town planning, civic sociology and environmentalism. Geddes wrote and campaigned on topics ranging from the architecture of Edinburgh's Old Town to the teaching of evolutionary theory through his radical summer schools. His wide and varied output had a huge influence on many fields, and is reflected in the rich collections at the University of Edinburgh.

Born in Ballater, Aberdeenshire, Geddes was educated at Perth Academy, then studied natural sciences under Thomas Huxley at the Royal School of Mines, London. Huxley sent Geddes for further scientific training to the Sorbonne, Paris, where he first developed an interest in social evolution. He worked as a demonstrator in the Department of Physiology at University College London, then as a Lecturer in Zoology at the University of Edinburgh from 1880 to 1888. In 1887, while working at the University of Edinburgh, Geddes opened the first of a series of student residences at Riddle's Court. Furthering his expertise in town planning, Geddes worked to improve the slums of Edinburgh – and, later, the planning of other cities, such as Tel Aviv and Bombay – by focusing on the relationship between inhabitants and their surrounding environment. Geddes went on to hold the Chair of Botany at University College Dundee (1888–1919), and the Chair of Sociology at the University of Bombay (1919–1924). He was knighted

'The Valley Section' devised by Patrick Geddes for 1910 Cities and Town Planning Exhibition

in 1932, but died later that year in Montpellier, France.

The archives were formerly held at the Outlook Tower on Castlehill, Edinburgh, which Geddes had founded as a civic museum and educational centre, and which later became a base for studies relating to Geddes and his ideas. They include Geddes' own papers, papers of the Association for Planning and Regional Reconstruction (APRR), and much other material relating to planning, city exhibitions and the environment from the 19th to the late 20th century. There are also photographs taken for the Survey of Edinburgh from 1895, which provide an important documentary resource for the history of the city.

A published catalogue describes the collection as it was while still at the Outlook Tower (*Catalogue of the Archives of the Patrick Geddes Centre for Planning Studies*, 1998). The first volume is available in digital format online. There are now online catalogue descriptions for the contents of the second volume, which focuses on the Edinburgh Survey photographs.

Coll-1167

Geikie, Archibald

Archibald Geikie (1835–1924) was one of the founders of modern geology.

He was educated at the Royal High School in Edinburgh and at the University of Edinburgh. In 1854, Geikie joined the staff of the British Geological Survey which was then under the directorship of Sir Roderick Impey Murchison. Largely through the influence of Murchison, he was admitted as a Fellow of the Royal Society, London, at the age of 29, and in 1867 he was appointed as the first director of the Geological Survey of Scotland. In 1871 he became the first Murchison Professor of Geology and Mineralogy at the University of Edinburgh. Geikie was the foremost advocate of the fluvial theories of erosion which illustrated the physical interaction of flowing water and the natural channels of rivers and streams, and the processes behind the denudation of land surfaces. His works include *The Scenery of Scotland* (1865), *Life of Sir Roderick I. Murchison* (1875), *Text-Book of Geology* (1882), *The Founders of Geology* (1897), and *The Ancient Volcanoes of Great Britain* (1897). His autobiography, *A Long Life's Work*, was published in 1924. Geikie was President of the Geological Society of London, 1891–1892 and 1906–1908, and President of the Royal Society 1908–1913. He was knighted in 1891. Geikie was succeeded in the University of Edinburgh's Chair of Geology and Mineralogy by his younger brother James Geikie (see page 207).

The papers include:

- lectures and lecture notes
- correspondence with Murchison and with other figures (alphabetically arranged)
- notes on raised beaches, on Arran and Skye, on the Sorby Research Fund, and on the Geological Survey
- sketches and a photograph album of the Geikie family.

A substantial number of Archibald Geikie's books were in the Geology Library, and some of these are now scattered throughout Special Collections.

Coll-74

Watercolour of Dunvegan Head by Archibald Geikie

Geikie, James

See main entry under Rare Books.
Coll-99

. . . .

Greenwood, Alan

Alan William Greenwood (1897–1981) was a pioneering poultry geneticist, known for his work on the secondary sexual characteristics of the domestic fowl.

Born in Melbourne, Australia, Greenwood read chemistry and biology at Melbourne University before gaining a scholarship to study in the UK in 1923. His original intention was to work on poultry genetics under Reginald Punnett at the University of Cambridge, but James Cossar Ewart, Professor of Natural History at the University of Edinburgh, persuaded him to study under F A E Crew at the newly founded Animal Breeding Research Department (later the Institute of Animal Genetics) in Edinburgh. Crew's influence would direct

the whole course of Greenwood's future research on the reproductive physiology of the fowl, particularly the secondary sexual characters and endocrine activity. Greenwood was placed in charge of the Institute during the Second World War before becoming director of the new Poultry Research Centre (PRC) in 1947, a position he held until his retirement in 1962. The PRC's remit was wide, encompassing such areas as egg production, heredity, sexual characteristics and environmental factors in development and productivity. The PRC also housed a group of workers supported by the British Empire Cancer Campaign, and Greenwood remained honorary director of this unit until his retirement.

The collection includes: biographical information, notebooks, visitors' books, scrapbooks, articles, lectures and papers, newspaper cuttings, correspondence and an extensive collection of photographs, mainly of the PRC and conferences and events around the world. There is a separate collection of Greenwood's lectures and articles.

Coll-1057

Gregory, David

David Gregory (1659– or 1661–1708), was the first university professor to teach astronomy in the light of Newton's theory of gravitation.

Having studied at Aberdeen Grammar School and Marischal College, Aberdeen, Gregory took the Mathematics Chair at the University of Edinburgh in 1683, by unseating the incumbent in a series of public debates. It helped that the chair had been occupied briefly some years before by his uncle, James Gregory (1638–1675). David was awarded a hasty MA although he had never studied in Edinburgh. His lecture notes show that he covered a broad range of subjects: not just mathematics but also optics, mechanics, hydrostatics and even anatomy.

In 1689 a violent dispute between the University and its paymasters, the Town Council, led to Gregory being libelled before the new Presbyterian Committee of Visitation. He was said to be a violent, drunken atheist, who kept women in his chambers and once visited a prisoner in the Canongate tollbooth; worse, he was a superficial teacher and a crypto-Cartesian. He was saved from dismissal by influential friends, but moved to Oxford in 1691 to take up the Savilian Chair of Astronomy. There he came to know personally figures such as Isaac Newton, Edmond Halley and John Flamsteed, the first Astronomer Royal. He also travelled to the continent, to exchange views with prominent colleagues like Jan Hudde and Christiaan Huygens.

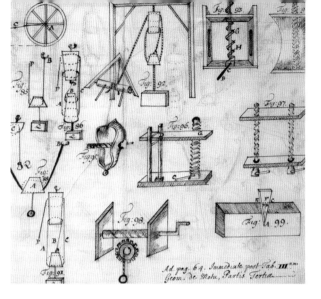

His first significant publication was
Exercitatio geometrica de dimensione figurarum
(1684). He then published his Edinburgh
lectures on optics as *Catoptricae et dioptricae
sphaericae elementa* (1695) which was rapidly
established as an influential textbook.
Subsequently his *Astronomiae physicae et
geometricae elementa* (1702) was the first
textbook to apply Newtonian gravitational
principles to astronomy. Newton himself
assisted with the work, which one publisher
immodestly declared would 'last as long
as the sun and the moon'. His final major
publication was an edition of Euclid, which
appeared in 1703. His special interests
included the catenary curve, eclipses, the
contemporary 'parallax problem', and the
Cassinian orbital model for heavenly bodies.

Late in his life, in 1707, the Act of
Union between Scotland and England called
Gregory away from his work on an edition of
Apollonius (eventually finished by Halley), to
work instead on rationalising the Scottish Mint
(just as Newton was doing with the London
Mint), and on calculating the enormously

complex 'Equivalent', a payment to Scotland
to offset new customs and excise duties.

The papers are substantial and
complex. They include mathematical and
personal papers, lecture notes and letters
from Alexander Pitcairne (1652–1713).
Related material includes manuscripts and
correspondence of his uncle Professor James
Gregory the Elder.
Coll-33

Guthrie, Douglas

Douglas Guthrie (1885–1967) was an eminent
doctor and a pioneering historian of medicine.

Born in Dysart, Fife, Guthrie graduated
in medicine from the University of Edinburgh
in 1907. After further studies at Jena and
Paris on a travelling scholarship, he spent
six years in general practice in Lanark.
During the First World War he served in
the Royal Army Medical Corps and then as
Commandant of a Royal Air Force officers'
hospital. In 1919 he became ear and throat
surgeon to the Royal Hospital for Sick

Children in Edinburgh, and surgeon to the Ear and Throat Infirmary. From 1920 he was Lecturer on Diseases of Ear, Nose and Throat at the School of Medicine of the Royal Colleges of Physicians and Surgeons, Edinburgh. On his retirement from practice in 1945, Guthrie was appointed Lecturer on History of Medicine at the University of Edinburgh in succession to Dr John Comrie, holding the post until 1956. Guthrie is perhaps best remembered for his *History of Medicine* (1945), which was widely republished and translated and remains popular to this day. Other publications include *Lord Lister: His Life and Doctrine* (1949), *The Royal Edinburgh Hospital for Sick Children, 1860–1960* (1960), *Janus in the Doorway* (1964), and *Dr John Leyden, 1775–1811* (1964). In 1948, Guthrie founded the Scottish Society of History of Medicine. He was elected a Fellow of the Royal College of Surgeons of Edinburgh in 1913, and Fellow of the Royal College of Physicians of Edinburgh in 1961.

The papers include lecture notes on clinical surgery, newspaper cuttings and offprints, correspondence, notebooks and a scrapbook relating to the publication and reviews of *A History of Medicine*.

In addition to his papers, Guthrie left the Library some 100 volumes from his library on the history of medicine.
Coll-52

Halliwell-Phillipps, J O
See main entry under Rare Books.
Coll-103

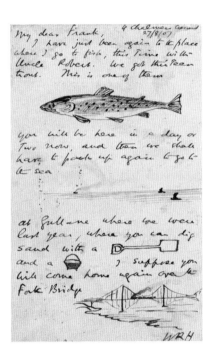

Postcard from William Ross Hardie to his son Frank, 27 August 1907

Hardie, William Ross

William Ross Hardie (1862–1916) was an innovative Classical scholar and teacher.

Born and educated in Edinburgh, Hardie graduated MA from the University in 1880. He pursued further studies at Balliol College, Oxford, where he won a number of scholarships and prizes. Elected to a fellowship at Balliol in 1884, he remained there as a tutor until 1895, when he was appointed Professor of Humanity (Classics) at the University of Edinburgh. A conscientious and inspirational teacher, he introduced to Edinburgh a system of individual teaching along Oxford lines. His publications include *Lectures on Classical*

Subjects (1903), *Latin Prose Composition* (1908),
and *Silvulae academicae* (1911), a series of
experiments in Latin and Greek poetry. His
Res metrica, an analysis of Latin verse rhythms,
was posthumously published in 1920.

The papers include lectures, notes and
biographical material, along with annotated
editions of classical texts and of publications
by Hardie and his contemporaries.
Coll-92

Heatley, David Playfair

David Playfair Heatley

David Playfair Heatley (1867–1944) was
a leading historian of British politics and
international relations.

Born in Northumbria, Heatley was
educated at Edinburgh's Royal High School
and studied at the University of Edinburgh
from 1884 until 1890 without graduating.
He embarked on research into Northumbria
at the time of St Aidan, then was appointed
Assistant in History at the University of
Edinburgh in 1892. In 1900, he became
Lecturer in Modern History and Political
Science, and, from 1920 to 1935, Reader
in Political Science. His publications include
Studies in British History and Politics (1913),
Diplomacy and the Study of International Relations
(1919) and *Viscount Grey of Fallodon* (1934).

The papers include:
- manuscripts of unpublished works
  on British politics, relations between
  Great Britain and the United States,
  the politics of Richard Hooker,
  and the humanist politics of
  Shakespeare and Bacon
- materials towards a memoir

- Heatley's notes of lectures attended
  as a student.

Various locations in Special Collections.

Henderson, Hamish

Hamish Henderson (1919–2002) was the
father of Scotland's post-war folk revival,
as well as a major poet, songwriter and
political activist.

Born in Blairgowrie, Perthshire,
Henderson won a scholarship to Dulwich
College and went on to read modern
languages at Downing College, Cambridge.
During the Second World War, he served as an
intelligence officer in North Africa and Italy,
an experience that would inspire his award-
winning poetry collection *Elegies for the Dead
in Cyrenaica* (1948) and songs such as 'The 51st
(Highland) Division's Farewell to Sicily'.

Immediately after the war, Henderson
took various teaching engagements, including
one at a German high school teachers' summer

school in Bad Godesberg, and another working with German prisoners of war in Comrie, Perthshire. Between 1948 and 1949 he was also a district secretary for the Workers' Educational Association. At the same time he began writing and publishing literary and political criticism, poetry and songs (in both Scots and English).

In 1951 Henderson was appointed a lecturer and research fellow at the University of Edinburgh's School of Scottish Studies. His work there as a folk-song collector provided the catalyst for the Scottish folk revival. His many writings, for both academic and non-academic audiences, displayed a keen and deep appreciation of internationalism, foreign literature and people's culture.

Throughout Henderson's life, he corresponded with many of the finest minds of the day. As a political activist, he played a major role in the Campaign for Nuclear Disarmament and the anti-apartheid struggle, and wrote extensively on land rights.

Among Henderson's best known songs are 'The Freedom Come-All-Ye', 'The Men of Knoydart' and 'Rivonia', now all part of the folk tradition themselves. Major publications include *Ballads of World War II* (1947), *Prison Letters of Antonio Gramsci* (1974), *Alias MacAlias: Writings on Songs, Folk and Literature* (1992), and *The Armstrong Nose: Selected Letters of Hamish Henderson* (1996).

The papers include manuscripts of poems and songs (some unpublished), notebooks, letters, journals, off-prints, photographs, memorabilia, and School of Scottish Studies material. There are also articles, scripts and essays sent by others to Henderson.

Henderson's correspondents include many of the 20th century's leading folk singers, musicians, collectors and scholars, together with a wide range of political, literary and cultural figures.

Coll-1438

Hodgson, W B

See main entry under Rare Books.

Hope, Thomas Charles

Thomas Charles Hope (1766–1844) was a leading chemist who discovered the element strontium and was a prominent figure in the Edinburgh social scene.

The son of John Hope (1725–1786), Professor of Botany at the University of Edinburgh, he was educated at the Royal High School and then the University of Edinburgh, where he graduated in 1787. In the same year, he was elected Lecturer in Chemistry and Materia Medica at Glasgow University, becoming Professor in 1791. In 1793, he gave a paper to the Royal Society of Edinburgh on strontianite, the first known compound of strontium (named after the village of Strontian, Argyll, where Hope came across the mineral). Joseph Black, Professor of Chemistry at Edinburgh, was so impressed by the discovery that he manoeuvred to have Hope appointed as his assistant. When Black died, Hope succeeded him in the chair, remaining in post for nearly half a century. In 1805, he devised an experiment (now known as the Hope Experiment) which established that water attained its maximum

density several degrees above the freezing point. Other important scientific papers concerned the chemical composition and colouring of the leaves and flowers of plants. Hope was a proponent of the pioneering chemistry of Lavoisier, and an early advocate of the geological theories of James Hutton. However, he ceased to spend much time on research once he realised that he could make substantial sums from his dramatic chemistry lectures. Among his pupils was a young Charles Darwin, for whom Hope's lectures were a highlight of the Edinburgh curriculum.

The papers include Hope's manuscripts and notes for his lectures on chemistry. There are also notes taken as a student by Hope on lectures by Professors Joseph Black, William Cullen, Alexander Monro *secundus*, John Robison and John Walker. More recently acquired is a small collection shedding light on the social side of his career, including lists of detailed monthly expenses, names of gentlemen recommended to him, and suppers given. (Hope was apparently capable of eating eight plates of turtle at one sitting.)

Coll-12

Coll-1371

List of suppers given by Thomas Charles Hope

Horn, David Bayne

David Bayne Horn (1901–1969) published many important works on British and European history and was a major historian of the University of Edinburgh.

Horn was educated at the Edinburgh Institution and at the University of Edinburgh, graduating MA in history (first class) in 1922. The following year, he joined the staff of the history department of the University as an assistant. In 1927 he was promoted to Lecturer in History, and in 1929 was awarded the degree of DLitt at the University for his thesis on 'Sir Charles Hanbury Williams and European Diplomacy'. In 1954, he was appointed to the newly created Chair of Modern History. Horn's main interest lay in the field of 18th-century diplomatic history and 18th-century British foreign policy in particular. His publications include *A History of Europe, 1871–1920* (1927), *British Diplomatic Representatives, 1689–1789* (1932), *Scottish Diplomatists, 1689–1789* (1944),

British Public Opinion and the First Partition
of Poland (1945), British Diplomatic Service,
1689–1789 (1961), Frederick the Great and the
Rise of Prussia (1964), and Great Britain and
Europe in the Eighteenth Century (1967). At the
time of his death in 1969, Horn was writing
a full-length history of the University, having
previously published A Short History of the
University of Edinburgh, 1556–1889 (1967).

The most significant material in the collection
relates to the proposed 'long history' of the
University. There are also:

- background materials (drafts, notes,
  bibliographies, offprints, etc.) relating
  to Horn's publications on 18th-century
  British diplomatic history
- lecture notes, correspondence,
  award medals and loose papers
- notes, maps, technical data, clippings,
  photos and offprints relating to
  Scottish mountains and climbing.

Coll-26

Department of Animal Genetics, c.1930

Institute of Animal Genetics

The Institute of Animal Genetics had its
origins in the early 20th century, when the
Development Commissioners formulated
a scheme to encourage research into genetics
and its application to animal breeding and
livestock improvement. Partly due to the
presence of individuals such as the zoologist
James Cossar Ewart (1851–1933) and
geneticist Arthur Dukinfield Darbishire
(1879–1915) at the University of Edinburgh,
it was decided to locate the Animal Breeding
Research Station there in 1920, under the
direction of Francis Albert Eley Crew
(1886–1973). By 1930, the Station
became known as the Institute of Animal
Genetics, occupying a new building on the
University's King's Buildings site. Under
Crew's leadership, research in the fields
of reproductive physiology and classical
genetics was encouraged to develop
alongside practical animal breeding
experiments. The Institute also housed
the Imperial (later the Commonwealth)
Bureau of Animal Genetics, which was
established to disseminate information
through reviews and bibliographies.

In 1945 the Agricultural Research
Council (ARC) formed the National Animal
Breeding and Genetics Research Organisation
(later ABRO), and it was decided that the
genetics laboratory would be located within
the Institute. Crew had left by this time
and directorship of the Institute passed to
C H Waddington (1905–1975). Under this
arrangement, the Institute passed out of
existence in its previous format, although
the name was retained to denote the building
and became a byname for the various bodies

it contained. The Institute was formally disbanded in 1990. The Genetics Building was renamed the Crew Building and is currently home to the University's School of GeoSciences.

These records span the 1920s to the 1990s and contain committee minutes, reports, visitors' books, notebooks, historical information, artefacts, photographs and the departmental files of C H Waddington. *EUA IN1/ACU/A1*

....

Jameson, Robert

Robert Jameson (1774–1854) was a pioneering mineralogist and collector of natural history specimens.

Born and educated in Leith, Jameson was apprenticed to a local surgeon, initially with the aim of going to sea. He also attended classes at the University of Edinburgh, studying medicine, botany, chemistry and natural history. By 1793, and influenced by the Professor of Natural History, John Walker (1731–1803), he abandoned medicine and focused instead on the natural sciences, particularly geology and mineralogy. In 1793, he went to London, meeting naturalists and visiting museums to take notes. In 1794 he visited his father's native Shetland Islands, exploring their geology, mineralogy, zoology and botany. This led to the publication of *An Outline of the Mineralogy of the Shetland Islands and of the Island of Arran* (1798). Jameson rejected the vulcanist interpretation of the formation of Earth proposed by Edinburgh geologist James Hutton (1726–1797). Hutton argued that the features of the Earth's crust were caused by natural processes over geologic time: the principle of uniformitarianism. Instead, Jameson supported the ideas of Abraham Gottlob Werner (1750–1817) who believed that rocks were formed when immense quantities of minerals precipitated out of the waters of the biblical flood. Jameson's *Mineralogy of the Scottish Isles* (1800) was a fuller description of his views and the three-volume *System*

Letter from Robert Jameson on a live ocelot kept at the University Museum, 1823 *of Mineralogy* which followed is probably his most important work. Jameson founded the Wernerian Natural History Society in 1808, but was later won over to the views of Hutton.

In 1803, Jameson was appointed Regius Professor of Natural History and Keeper of the University Museum. Over his 50-year tenure, he built up a huge collection of mineralogical and geological specimens for the museum, including fossils, birds and insects. Shortly after his death, the University Museum was transferred to the Crown and became part of the Royal Scottish Museum (now the National Museum of Scotland) in Edinburgh's Chambers Street.

The collection includes correspondence covering a great variety of subjects. The letters are mostly in English, but include some in German and French, and discuss matters ranging from accounts and bills, the health of Abraham Gottlob Werner, Jameson's own health, specimens and catalogue of minerals, contributions to journals, and various introductions. There are also 13 volumes of notebooks from 1790 to 1850, containing diaries of tours, mineralogical notes of works, and summaries of correspondence.

Coll-44

Coll-1373

Johnson-Marshall, Percy

Percy Edwin Alan Johnson-Marshall (1915–1993) was one of the generation of town-planners who, in the wake of the Second World War, dedicated their lives to the creation of a new world of social equity through the radical transformation of the human environment.

Born in India, he was brought by his parents to England in the 1920s. After gaining a Diploma in Architecture from the University of Liverpool in 1936, Johnson-Marshall entered public service as an assistant architect, initially with Middlesex County Council. He was Senior Assistant Architect at Coventry when the city was devastated by bombing in 1940. After military service in India and Burma he became Senior Planner at the London County Council, overseeing several comprehensive development areas, including Lansbury Estate. In 1959 he moved to the University of Edinburgh as Lecturer in Planning at the newly created Department of Architecture. In 1964, he became Professor of his own Department of Urban Design and Regional Planning. While in Edinburgh he founded the planning consultancy Percy Johnson-Marshall & Associates, which master-planned the University of Edinburgh's Comprehensive Development Area in the 1960s. The practice was also extensively involved in urban planning and redevelopment projects in the UK and internationally. Johnson-Marshall retired from his chair in 1985, becoming the director of the Patrick Geddes Centre for Planning Studies until 1988.

The collection includes papers, plans, books, journals and photographs collected or created by Johnson-Marshall throughout the course of his career. These reflect both his architectural and academic careers; his involvement in professional organisations, educational bodies and world development issues; and his general interest in architecture and planning.

In total there are some 178 metres of material, making this one of our largest single collections.

PJM

. . . .

Keith, Arthur Berriedale

See main entry under Rare Books.

Coll-34

. . . .

Kennedy-Fraser, Marjory

A major figure in the Celtic Revival, Marjory Kennedy-Fraser (1857–1930) was a collector and arranger of Gaelic songs, and an accomplished singer in her own right.

Born in Perth, she was the daughter of singer David Kennedy, who from 1866 onwards toured extensively with his family across the world, taking traditional Scots songs to emigrants and their descendants. Kennedy-Fraser then trained as a piano accompanist in London and a vocalist in Milan and Paris. After her father's death in 1886 and her marriage the following year, she made a living as a music teacher in Edinburgh. Here she became interested in Gaelic songs and, with encouragement from Professor John Stuart Blackie, studied the Gaelic language and musical tradition. In 1905, she visited the island of Eriskay to collect songs from its declining population, returning there in 1907 and recording material on wax cylinders. In 1907–1908, she researched and recorded further songs on the Isle of Barra. She subsequently arranged the materials gathered

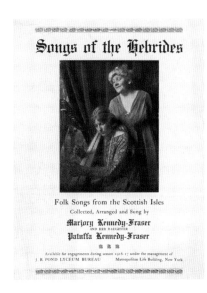

Poster for recitals by Marjory and Patuffa Kennedy-Fraser, 1916–1917

for voice and piano (sometimes for harp or clàrsach for her daughter Patuffa), had the words translated into English by the Reverend Kenneth MacLeod, and published them as the three volumes of *Songs of the Hebrides* (1909, 1917, 1921). Acclaimed as a key work of the Celtic Revival, this sealed Kennedy-Fraser's reputation, leading to lecture tours, performances and recitals throughout the world. In 1928 the University awarded her the honorary degree of Doctor of Music, and in 1930 she presented to the University Library her archive of song, including 280 original wax cylinders of recordings which were re-recorded on tape for the Sound Archive of the School of Scottish Studies.

The collection includes a manuscript volume of Gaelic songs, manuscripts and proofs of *Songs of the Hebrides,* papers relating to Granville Bantock's opera *The Seal Woman* (for which Kennedy-Fraser wrote the libretto), proofs of her autobiography *A Life of Song*, along with newspaper cuttings and other memorabilia. There are also letters, including family correspondence.

The book collection includes about 100 modern books on Scottish topics, especially Highland music and dance, history and literature. They were presented in the 1950s by Kennedy-Fraser's children, Patuffa Kennedy-Fraser Hood and David Kennedy-Fraser.

Additional items from Mrs Patuffa Kennedy-Fraser Hood were acquired in 2012–2013.

Coll-1036

Letter from Rudyard Kipling declining an invitation to stand as Rector of the University of Edinburgh, 1935

Kipling, Rudyard

Joseph Rudyard Kipling (1865–1936) is one of the best-known authors of the late 19th and early 20th centuries, whose writings on empire and politics remain controversial.

Born in Bombay, India, on 30 December 1865, he was the son of the architectural sculptor and designer John Lockwood Kipling and a cousin of Stanley Baldwin. He was educated at United Services College, Westward Ho!, North Devon, an experience fictionalised in his *Stalky & Co.* (1899). In 1882, he joined the staff of the *Civil and Military Gazette* in Lahore, and stayed in India as an increasingly successful journalist until 1889. He then settled in London though travelled widely in China, Japan, America, Africa and Australia. From 1902 he lived in Burwash in Sussex. Early writing included *Plain Tales from the Hills* (1888), *Soldiers Three*

(1888) and *Wee Willie Winkie* (1889). Further volumes of narrative and verse, such as *The Light That Failed* (1890), *Barrack-Room Ballads* (1892), and, in particular, *The Jungle Book* (1894) and *The Second Jungle Book* (1895) brought him to the height of his fame. Subsequent major publications included *Kim* (1901), the *Just So Stories for Little Children* (1902), *Puck of Pook's Hill* (1906) and *A School History of England* (1911). In 1907 Kipling was awarded the Nobel Prize in Literature.

The manuscript material is composed of sheets of verse from *A Diversity of Creatures* (1917) and *The Eyes of Asia* (1918). There is also a letter from Kipling to students James Couper H Brash and Agnes Christian Gillan declining an invitation to be nominated as a candidate in the University of Edinburgh rectorial election, 1935.

Coll-393

....

Koestler, Arthur

Arthur Koestler (1905–1983) was a prolific author on politics, science and philosophy who continues to attract controversy and interest from many different angles.

Born in Budapest, Hungary, Koestler attended the Technical University of Vienna until 1926, when the failure of his father's business left him unable to pay the fees. He spent the next five years as a foreign correspondent, reporting on the Middle East, Paris and Berlin before joining the Graf Zeppelin Arctic Expedition in 1931. He subsequently travelled in Russia and what was then Soviet Central Asia before being sent to Spain by the *News Chronicle* to cover the Civil War in 1936–1937. As a result of this he was imprisoned and sentenced to death by General Franco's forces, and was spared only following extensive lobbying by his wife Dorothy Ascher in Britain. After his release he saw Second World War service in the French Foreign Legion and the British Pioneer Corps, and after the war became a full-time writer, having achieved international success with the anti-totalitarian novel *Darkness at Noon* in 1941. He spent the rest of his life in Britain where he campaigned for many political causes (including the abolition of capital punishment and the legalisation of euthanasia) and wrote novels, memoirs and biographies. He was elected a Fellow of the Royal Society of Literature in 1960,

was awarded the Sonning Prize in 1968 for his outstanding contribution to European culture, and was made a CBE in 1972.

Koestler set up a trust fund to establish, after his death, a chair of parapsychology at a British university. Edinburgh won this honour, and with it Koestler's own archive of most of his surviving manuscripts, correspondence and annotated books from his library.

The book collection includes more than 1,000 items. Apart from copies of his own works, with translations into numerous languages, it contains other works on a wide range of topics, often presented by the author. One especial rarity is a copy of Koestler's first book, *Von weissen Nachten und roten Tagen,* about his travels in the Soviet Union (Kharkov, printed in about 1934). The original collection has been augmented by gifts from the London Library, bequests from Koestler's literary executor Harold Harris, and purchases from the sculptor Daphne Hardy Henrion (Koestler's former

Arthur Koestler as a student in Vienna

partner who smuggled the manuscript of *Darkness at Noon* into Britain from Nazi-occupied France).

All the books appear in the Library's online catalogue. Shelflists (SC 3875–4988; SCF 151; JA 3904–3908; SD 4026–4034) and provenance files are available via staff.

The archive consists of Koestler's manuscripts and papers from 1940 to March 1983. These include:

- literary manuscripts including interviews, broadcasts and speeches
- material on specific subjects such as extrasensory perception and euthanasia
- correspondence with a wide range of figures (including members of Koestler's family)
- personal material including diaries, address books and medical files
- business and financial papers
- literary manuscripts by other authors
- non-print material such as photographs, medals, tapes and records
- files gifted by publishers Hutchinson comprising papers and correspondence on particular books.

Most of Koestler's earlier papers were lost when France fell in 1940 and he left for England. Later papers bequeathed in 1993 include personal files which are restricted until 2045.

The Koestler Archive in Edinburgh University Library: A Checklist, by Susan Smyth, was published by the Library in 1987 and remains the main finding aid until an online listing is complete.

Coll-146

Laing, David

Our most important manuscript collection was assembled by the great antiquarian David Laing (1793–1878).

The son of an Edinburgh bookseller, Laing became the leading Scottish expert on early books and manuscripts. In many ways he could be described as a 'consulting bibliographer' – a man who tried to help anyone with a question about books. He travelled across Europe to buy precious volumes, but also rescued countless important papers from offices and family homes. When he died, his library of printed books was sold and is scattered throughout the world. His collections of art works and objects are now held in the National Galleries of Scotland and the National Museums of Scotland. However, his manuscript collection was gifted to Edinburgh University Library.

Laing was a friend of the University over many years. His first publication was a reprint of the catalogue of the library of William Drummond of Hawthornden, given to the University in 1626, and it may be that Drummond's example inspired Laing to make his later, even greater gift. Before 1878, Edinburgh University Library had only a handful of manuscripts; since then, building on the Laing bequest, it has become an internationally important centre for special collections.

The Laing Collection is one of the great Victorian collections but differs from most of the 'gentleman's collections' of the era with its focus on particular themes. It includes beautiful items of iconic importance, such as Michael Van Meer's wonderfully illustrated Album Amicorum, but also many boxes of

Psalter of Thomas Wode, Vicar of St Andrews,
16th century

- manuscripts on science, alchemy
  and medicine
- finely painted manuscripts on
  European heraldry and travel
- early writing by women, such as the
  17th-century poet Elizabeth Melville
- Laing's personal papers, journals
  and 9,000 letters, including
  correspondence with great writers
  such as Thomas Carlyle, Sir Walter
  Scott and William Wordsworth
- crucial Scottish governmental and
  legal documents.

densely packed, closely written manuscripts,
the raw primary source material on which
historians rely.

Some of the known highlights include:

- 103 Western medieval manuscript
  books, very finely illuminated or
  textually important, and a substantial
  number of fragments, some of the
  highest historical significance
- early Islamic manuscripts, including
  fragments from a 9th-century Koran
- letters by Kings and Queens of
  Scotland and England
- poems in the hand of Robert Burns
  (see page 23)
- more than 3,000 charters, many with
  original wax seals
- manuscripts on the arts and performance,
  including dance and theatre
- early manuscripts in Gaelic and
  Middle Scots
- early manuscript music books

Access to the collection is currently through
a variety of handlists and printed finding aids,
but work is in progress to develop a project
that will create a modern online catalogue.

David Laing's outstanding library was
sold by Sotheby, Wilkinson & Hodge in
almost 12,000 lots over 31 days in 1879
and 1880, and realised £16,137. However,
many of the annotated books were treated
as manuscripts and so were included in the
bequest of material to the Library in 1878.
An example is the fine copy of the 1566
Acts of the Scottish Parliament with the

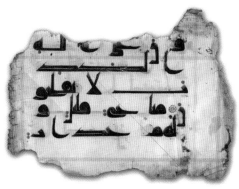

Early Koran fragment

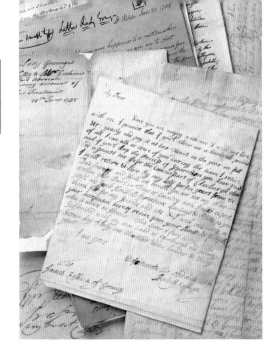

Letters by Lady Grange from St Kilda where she had been incarcerated by her husband

magnificent woodcut royal arms (La.III.655). The bulk of the printed material is in Laing division III; a few items are catalogued online but most can only be found by examining the printed handlists.

Coll-1

Lang, Andrew

Andrew Lang (1844–1912) was a leading poet, anthropologist and historian, who remains widely read as a collector of folk and fairy tales.

Born in Selkirk, Lang was educated at Edinburgh Academy, St Andrews University and Balliol College, Oxford, where he graduated in Classics in 1868. In the same year, he was elected as a Fellow of Merton College but resigned his fellowship when

he married in 1875. Thereafter Lang made his living as a professional writer, working for a wide range of periodicals, and initially making a name for himself as a poet with *Ballads and Lyrics of Old France* (1872), *XXXII Ballades in Blue China* (1881) and *Grass of Parnassus* (1888). His major work, however, lay in the fields of anthropology and folklore, including *Customs and Myth* (1884), *Myth, Ritual and Religion* (1887), *The Making of Religion* (1898), *Magic and Religion* (1901), *Social Origins* (1903) and *The Secret of the Totem* (1905).

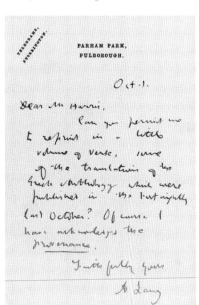

Letter from Andrew Lang to Frank Harris, c.1888

Lang's extraordinarily fertile intellect found expression in a wide range of disciplines. In particular, he made major contributions to classical studies in *Homer and the Epic* (1893), *Homer and his Age* (1906) and *The World of Homer* (1910), and to Scottish historiography with the controversially pro-Stuart *The Mystery of Mary Stuart* (1901), *John Knox and the Reformation* (1905) and the *History of Scotland from the Roman Occupation to the Suppression of the Last Jacobite Rising* (1900–1907). As a children's writer, he remains popular as the author of the 'coloured' compilations of folk tales, beginning with *The Blue Fairy Book* (1889) and continuing through to *The Lilac Fairy Book* in 1910. Lang was a founding member of the Folklore Society in 1878.

The collection is composed of 35 letters to various individuals including W E Henley and Frank Harris.

Coll-732

Robert Laws

Laws, Robert

Robert Laws (1851–1934) was a dedicated missionary whose papers are a key component of our African collections.

Born in Aberdeen, Laws studied divinity at the United Presbyterian Theological Hall, Edinburgh, 1872–1875, but also pursued medical studies at the University of Aberdeen, 1871–1873; Anderson's College, Glasgow, 1873–1874; and the University of Glasgow, 1873–1874. Between 1873 and 1875, Laws was a missionary in the City of Glasgow Fever and Smallpox Hospitals. In 1875 he was ordained by the United Presbyterian Presbytery of Aberdeen, and

the same year was appointed as medical missionary of the Free Church of Scotland Mission, Livingstonia, Lake Nyasa (modern-day Malawi). Laws was in full control of the mission station between 1877 and 1927. For a time he was also Principal of Overtoun College, Livingstonia, and in 1894 acted as deputy at the Hope Waddell Training Institution in Calabar (now in Nigeria). During his career as a missionary, Laws developed a Christian community of some 60,000 and founded more than 700 schools. He translated the New Testament into Nyanja, published an English-Nyanja dictionary, compiled Gunda-English and English-Gunda vocabularies, and published works in the Tonga language. For three years he was a senior unofficial member of the Nyasaland Legislative Council.

The papers consist of notebooks and papers mainly relating to the work of the Livingstonia Mission in Nyasaland (now Malawi), including notebooks on African languages. There is correspondence and other papers and also printed items including translations from the Bible and grammars of African languages.

Coll-75

Leighton, Kenneth

Kenneth Leighton (1929–1988) was a popular and versatile composer who became Reid Professor of Music at the University of Edinburgh.

Born in Wakefield, Yorkshire, Leighton studied at Queen's College, Oxford, graduating BA in Classics in 1950 and Bachelor of Music in 1951. His first works were performed in Oxford, London and Liverpool with support from Gerald Finzi and Ralph Vaughan Williams. In 1951 he was awarded a Mendelssohn Scholarship, enabling him to study with Goffredo Petrassi in Rome. On his return from Italy, Leighton taught at the Royal Marine School of Music in Deal, before taking up a Gregory Fellowship in Music at the University of Leeds in 1953. In 1956, he was appointed Lecturer (subsequently Reader) in Music at the University of Edinburgh. In 1968, he moved to Oxford University as Fellow in Music of Worcester College, but returned to Edinburgh in 1970 as Reid Professor of Music, holding the post until his death in 1988.

His widely ranging compositions include church and choral music, pieces for piano, organ, cello, oboe and other instruments, chamber music, concertos, symphonies and an opera. Influenced by modern Italian music, Leighton worked on fugue and counterpoint and was hailed as the 'musician's composer'. He received many prizes and honours, including the Royal Philharmonic Society Prize and the Cobbett Medal for distinguished services to chamber music.

The collection is not catalogued, but amounts to 15 boxes of archival material.

Coll-1144

Leslie, John

John Leslie (1630–1681) was a major political and military figure in 17th-century Scotland, who fought for the restoration of monarchy and episcopacy.

Leslie succeeded to the earldom of Rothes at the age of 11. He was one of the first noblemen to attend Charles II on his arrival in Britain from Breda in 1650 and at his coronation as King of Scotland he carried the Sword of State. He commanded a regiment of the Scottish army that descended into England but was taken prisoner at the Battle of Worcester in 1651, and committed to the Tower of London. In 1652 he was freed but his liberty extended only to within ten miles of the City of London. Under heavy security, however, he was permitted to visit Scotland on business in 1652, 1653 and 1654. He was authorised to stay for a longer period in 1656–1657, but Cromwell had him committed to Edinburgh Castle to prevent a duel with Viscount Morpeth over the attention that Leslie was supposedly paying

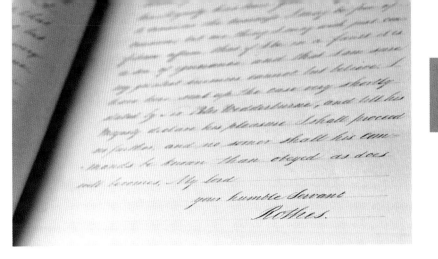

Letter from John Leslie to the Duke of Lauderdale, 4 January 1665

his wife. Leslie was finally released in 1658, and, on the return of Charles in 1660, Leslie was again among the first to wait on him. He was appointed President of the Council in Scotland, and in 1661 Lord of Session, and Commissioner of the Exchequer. In 1662 he went to London to press for the establishment of episcopacy, and in 1663 he was appointed Lord High Treasurer and a Privy Councillor in England. In 1664 he became Keeper of the Privy Seal. Although marital scandal caused him to lose many of his official functions he was created Duke of Rothes in 1680.

The papers, in eight volumes, are composed primarily of letters to the Duke of Lauderdale, 1660–1671.

Coll-477

. . . .

Liddell, Eric Henry

Edinburgh graduate Eric Henry Liddell (1902–1945) was an Olympic Gold-winning athlete and Christian missionary.

Liddell was born in 1902 in China, the son of Scottish missionaries. He was educated in Blackheath and Eltham, London, then studied at the University of Edinburgh where he was a rugby blue and gained his BSc in 1924. He was outstanding as a runner and was selected for the British team in the Paris Olympics of 1924. He refused to run in the heats for the 100 metres as they were held on a Sunday and instead entered the 400 metres, which he won in a world record time. In the film *Chariots of Fire* (1981), the part of Liddell was played by another Edinburgh graduate, Ian Charleson. (A third Edinburgh graduate, Sally Magnusson, wrote the biographical account *The Flying Scotsman* (1981) which was inspired by the film.) At his graduation in July 1924 the Principal of the University capped him with a crown of wild olive and the now-famous words: 'Mr Liddell, you have shown that none can pass you but your examiners.'

Liddell went on to study at the Scottish Congregational College and in 1925 went to China as a missionary with the London Missionary Society. He began by teaching science at the Anglo-Chinese College in

Tientsin then moved to rural Siochang where he worked despite the difficult conditions caused by poverty and war. He married Florence Mackenzie in March 1934 in Tientsin but he last saw his wife and children in 1940 when, for safety, they went to Canada to live with family. Liddell was interned by the Japanese in 1943 in Weihsien prison camp, Weifang, where he died of a brain tumour in 1945. His death was widely mourned not least in the camp itself where he had become a teacher, friend and guide to scores of imprisoned children.

In May 1992 Mrs Patricia Russell presented to the University the three medals won by her father in 1924: the gold for the 400 metres, the bronze for the 200 metres and his participant's medal. The Library also holds annual sports programmes of Edinburgh University Athletic Club, 1923–1925, showing Liddell's times in the races entered, and an annotated Scottish Inter-Universities programme, 1923. There is also correspondence in New College Library. *Coll-218*

Eric Liddell's Olympic Gold Medal

Lindsay, Maurice

Maurice Lindsay (1918–2009) was a tireless champion of Scotland's literary and artistic renaissance in the 20th century. As a prolific poet, broadcaster, anthologist, editor and all-round man of letters, he was at the heart of Scottish cultural life for more than 60 years.

Lindsay was educated at Glasgow Academy, 1926–1936, then attended the Scottish National Academy of Music in Glasgow, 1936–1939. During the Second World War, he volunteered to fight with the 9th Cameronians, but an injury during military training led to a secondment to the War Office. While still in uniform, Lindsay began a period of precocious and prolific activity as a poet, publishing three volumes by the age of 25. He became a passionate advocate of the Scottish Literary Renaissance, which he introduced to a wider audience through his editorship of the annual *Poetry Scotland* (1942–1946) and the seminal anthology *Modern Scottish Poetry* (1946). After the war, he turned to journalism, becoming drama critic for the *Scottish Daily Mail*, music critic for the *Bulletin* and a feature writer for *Scottish Field*. This would lead to a new career as one of Scotland's foremost broadcasters.

In 1946 Lindsay became a freelance broadcaster with the BBC in his native Glasgow, contributing to many arts programmes. He rose to prominence as co-editor and presenter of the radio series *Scottish Life and Letters* and of *Counterpoint*, the first arts programme on Scottish television. He was also one of BBC Scotland's first

roving reporters, appearing almost daily and becoming an early Scottish television celebrity. He left the BBC in 1961 to become programme controller, features executive and senior interviewer for Border Television in Carlisle. He returned to Scotland in 1967 to take up the post of Director of the Scottish Civic Trust.

A prolific, versatile and undervalued poet, Lindsay published more than 20 books of verse including *Hurlygush* (1948), *Snow Warning* (1962) and *This Business of Living* (1969). He also wrote on an enormous range of Scottish subjects, including music, art, architecture, landscape and tourism. He co-edited the journals *Scottish Poetry* (1966–1976) and *Scottish Review* (1975–1985). His lifelong advocacy of Scottish writing culminated in his co-editorship (with Lesley Duncan) of *The Edinburgh Book of Twentieth-Century Scottish Poetry* (2005).

The papers contain:
- poetry notebooks
- drafts, manuscripts and typescripts of a wide range of publications, including poetry, fiction and drama
- radio and television scripts
- incoming correspondence and some carbon replies
- manuscripts by Hugh MacDiarmid, Sydney Goodsir Smith and other Scottish authors.

Coll-56

Lister, Joseph

Joseph Lister (1827–1912) is the great pioneer of antiseptic surgery.

Born in Upton, Essex, he qualified as a doctor at London's University College Hospital, graduating BA and MB in 1852. He became a Fellow of the Royal College of Surgeons, London in the same year. In 1853 Lister came to Edinburgh to develop his surgical experience, and was subsequently elected to vacancies that arose at the Royal Infirmary and at the Royal College of Surgeons in the city. He was elected a Fellow of the Royal College of Surgeons, Edinburgh, in 1855. In 1860 he was appointed Professor of Surgery at Glasgow University and, at the same time, a surgeon at the city's Royal Infirmary. He eventually returned to the University of Edinburgh in 1869 as Regius Professor of Clinical Surgery, then in 1877 took up the post of Professor of Surgery at King's College, London. Lister took Louis Pasteur's research on air-borne organisms a stage further. He realised that such organisms could cause post-operative wound infections like tetanus, blood-poisoning and gangrene. He countered this by using carbolic acid soaked in lint or calico around the wound and replaced slow-to-absorb silk stitching with cat-gut stitching, which absorbed the carbolic acid better. He also experimented with gauze swabs and a disinfectant spray for operating theatres. Lister was appointed Serjeant-Surgeon to Queen Victoria in 1878, and was created a baron in 1897.

The collection includes some 73 letters plus miscellaneous material (including testimonials, certificates and the commission of Queen Victoria appointing him to the Edinburgh Chair of Clinical Surgery).

Various locations in Special Collections

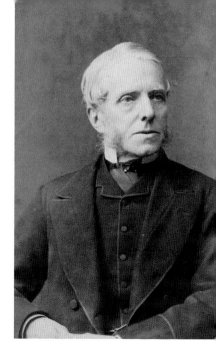

Henry Duncan Littlejohn, photograph by John Moffat

....

Littlejohn, Henry Duncan and Littlejohn, Henry Harvey

Sir Henry Duncan Littlejohn (1826–1914) is one of the fathers of modern forensic medicine. His work was continued by his son Henry Harvey Littlejohn (1862–1927).

Born in Edinburgh, Sir Henry Duncan Littlejohn was educated at Perth Academy and the Royal High School, Edinburgh. He graduated MD from the University of Edinburgh in 1847, and undertook postgraduate training at Edinburgh Royal Infirmary (1847–1848) and in Europe (visiting Vienna, Paris and Berlin). After a year in general practice in Selkirk, he returned to Edinburgh where he became a Fellow of the Royal College of Surgeons in 1854. In the same year, he was elected by

Edinburgh Town Council to the position of police surgeon. Littlejohn became a brilliant jurist, appearing in more than a hundred criminal cases involving deaths caused by everything from strangling to poisoning. He famously presented evidence in the 1893 Ardlamont murder trial, in which Alfred John Monson was tried for the attempted murder of Lieut. W C Hambrough. In 1856, he also began lecturing in medical jurisprudence at the Extra-Mural School of Medicine in Surgeons' Hall. In 1862 he was appointed as Edinburgh's Medical Officer of Health, a post which he held until 1908. He greatly advanced the cause of public health in Scotland, particularly through his *Report on the Sanitary Condition of the City of Edinburgh* (1865). Littlejohn was knighted in 1895. Two years later, at the age of 71, he was elected to the

Chair of Forensic Medicine and Public Health at the University of Edinburgh, retiring in 1906. A popular lecturer, his students included Joseph Bell, thought to be the model for Conan Doyle's Sherlock Holmes.

Littlejohn materials in the University Archives include notes of his lectures on medical jurisprudence, public health and forensic medicine. There are also notebooks on such topics as infanticide and poisoning.

In 1906 Littlejohn was succeeded as Professor of Forensic Medicine by his son, Henry Harvey Littlejohn (1862–1927), also appointed Chief Police Surgeon for Edinburgh in 1906. From his time the collections include post-mortem casebooks, post-mortem photograph albums, and other notebooks. *Various locations in Special Collections.*

....

Lodge, Richard

Sir Richard Lodge (1855–1936) helped turn the subject of modern history into a thriving academic discipline.

Born in Penkhull, Staffordshire, Lodge graduated from Balliol College, Oxford, with a first-class degree in history in 1877. The following year, he was elected a Fellow of Brasenose College, in which capacity he researched and published *The Student's Modern Europe* (1885), the first of the textbooks which would make his name. In 1894, he was appointed to Glasgow University's newly created Chair of Modern History. Finding, however, that the city's climate did not agree with him, he applied for and obtained the equivalent Chair at Edinburgh (itself only established in 1894). Lodge played a major

role in making the study of modern British and European history a credible and respected academic subject. Through his influence, Edinburgh became a centre for historical study, and Lodge himself was recognised as a leading authority on 17th-century English history and 18th-century European diplomacy. His publications include *Richelieu* (1896), *The Close of the Middle Ages* (1901), *English Political History, 1660–1702* (1909), *The History of England: From the Restoration to the Death of William III, 1660–1702* (1910), *A History of Modern Europe from the Capture of Constantinople, 1453, to the Treaty of Berlin, 1878* (1914), and *Great Britain and Prussia in the Eighteenth Century* (1923).

The papers comprise correspondence along with offprints of articles by Lodge on historical subjects, as well as articles given to him by others, 1889–1933.

Related material includes notes of lectures on British history, 1907 and 1922–1923, and correspondence with Professor David B Horn about historical research and publications. *Coll-252*

....

Lorimer, James

Jurist and political philosopher James Lorimer (1818–1890) was a powerful voice for educational and political reform in 19th-century Scotland.

Born in Perth, Lorimer studied at the Universities of Edinburgh, Geneva, Berlin, Bonn, and was admitted as a member of the Faculty of Advocates in 1845. Although he had some practice at the bar, and acted as sheriff-

substitute of Midlothian, he essentially devoted his energies to writing, making his name with two works on constitutional reform, *Political Progress Not Necessarily Democratic* (1857) and *Constitutionalism of the Future* (1865). He also lobbied for university reform, arguing in his *The Universities of Scotland, Past, Present, and Possible* (1854) that existing universities were mere extensions of high school rather than genuine centres for teaching and original research. His views exerted a major influence on the Universities (Scotland) Act 1858, which encouraged a broad liberal approach to legal education. The Chair of Public Law and the Law of Nature and of Nations at the University was revived in 1862, and Lorimer was appropriately appointed to it.

His teaching focused on public and private international law and is encapsulated in his *The Institutes of Law* (1872) and *The Institutes of the Law of Nations* (1883–1884). In his work he discussed neutrality, nationality and proportional disarmament. Lorimer even put forward a scheme for the organisation of an international government of Europe with Geneva as its centre. He was an advocate of further political reforms such as proportional representation and the enfranchisement of women, although his views on the naturally progressive or degenerative character of different societies were often explicitly racist.

He was survived by his wife and three sons, one of whom was the artist John Henry Lorimer, and the architect Sir Robert Stodart Lorimer (1864–1929) (see below).

The Lorimer papers consist of:
- manuscripts materials for *The Institutes of Law*
- manuscript materials and proofs for *The Institutes of the Law of Nations*
- lectures and University papers
- a biography of Lorimer, compiled by his son from a family history written by Lorimer himself
- articles, offprints and correspondence
- pamphlets on the Eastern Question
- printed papers and cuttings.

Coll-230

Lorimer, Robert

Robert Stodart Lorimer (1864–1929) was a prolific architect and furniture designer who brought the highest standards of craftsmanship to both public and private commissions.

The son of Professor James Lorimer (see above), he was educated at Edinburgh Academy and the University of Edinburgh. In 1885 he began his career in architecture working first with Sir Robert Rowand

Hallyburton House, Coupar Angus, designed by Robert Lorimer

Anderson in Edinburgh, then with George Frederick Bodley in London. In 1891, he returned to Edinburgh to form his own practice. Deeply influenced by William Morris and the Arts and Crafts Movement, he became known both for new work in Scottish vernacular styles and for the sensitive restoration of historic houses and castles. Lorimer also built significant public works including the Thistle Chapel in the High Kirk of St Giles, Edinburgh (1909) and the Scottish National War Memorial within Edinburgh Castle (1927). Among his final commissions was the restoration of Paisley Abbey (1923).

The papers include office letters relating to projects throughout the UK, along with plans of buildings and further building details.

Coll-27

Lothian Health Services Archive

Overview

Lothian Health Services Archive (LHSA) is one of the leading National Health Service (NHS) archives. The holdings comprise the historically important records of NHS Lothian (NHSL) hospitals and other health-related organisations, and have been managed by the University since 1980. Of particular significance are the 11 individual collections, covering the period 1983–2010, which chart the unprecedented rise of HIV/AIDS in Edinburgh and Lothian. These were inscribed to the UNESCO UK Memory of the World Register in May 2011.

The LHSA collection spans the period 1594 to date and amounts to 3,000 linear metres. The largest collections are the 69 created by NHSL and its predecessor bodies. There are a further 200 smaller collections of non-NHS institutional records and personal papers relating to the local history of healthcare and the history of Scottish medicine.

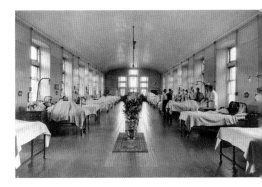

Royal Infirmary of Edinburgh ward, 1937
© Lothian Health Services Archive

Title deed to the first Infirmary site
in Edinburgh, 1594
© Lothian Health Services Archive

LHSA's other main collections include 20th-century folder-based case notes which, with approximately one million items, are likely to form the largest accumulation of such historically significant material in the UK. Objects, audiovisual material (including oral history recordings), architectural plans, artwork and approximately 40,000 still images (1850 to the present) provide a view of health history beyond the written record.

For more information, see:
www.lhsa.lib.ed.ac.uk.

NHS Hospitals and Administrative Bodies (LHBs)

The largest collections held are those produced by the hospitals within the Edinburgh and Lothian region and, since the creation of the NHS in 1948, the historical records of the NHS Boards

Staff member, Edinburgh and South East Scotland Blood Transfusion Service, c.1945
© Lothian Health Services Archive

of Management and related units of administration. They comprise records which have long-term legal, administrative, epidemiological and historical value; they have reference codes with the prefix LHB. Although they range in size and scope, the majority of these collections contain richly informative documents such as minutes, annual reports and accounting information; clinical records such as registers of patients and post-mortem registers; and staff records such as training registers and wages books. Larger collections may be supplemented by architectural drawings and plans, photographs, correspondence and staff publications.

Perhaps the most notable collection is that of the Royal Infirmary of Edinburgh (RIE), the first, and once the largest, voluntary hospital in the UK. It opened its doors to the sick poor in 1729. The archival material covering about 1,500 metres is rich in clinical and administrative records and includes LHSA's oldest item: a 1594 title deed to the building occupied by the hospital during its first 14 years of operation. Now housed in its fourth building, it remains the largest general hospital within the NHSL region, with transfers of records continuing up to the present day. The early financial records reveal the facts and figures associated with raising funds to establish a hospital, and the people involved. The annual reports, for example, list each individual, church and company to contribute money to the running of this 'ever open door' up until the formation of the NHS. This continuous run of nearly 300 years' worth of records makes this collection a unique link with the past.

The most heavily used records are those of the Royal Edinburgh Hospital (REH), which celebrated its bicentenary in 2013. The REH was founded in response to the death of the Scots poet Robert Fergusson in the city's Bedlam, at the age of 24. His medical attendant, Dr Andrew Duncan, was so moved by the poet's plight that he resolved to found a hospital in Edinburgh where the mentally ill could be cared for humanely. In 1792, Duncan launched an appeal for funds, and

Royal Charter,
Royal Infirmary of
Edinburgh, 1736
© Lothian Health
Services Archive

125

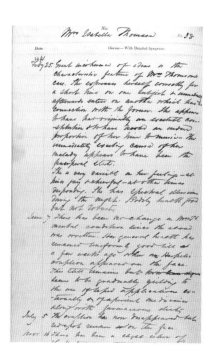

Case history of Royal Edinburgh Hospital
psychiatric patient, 1841
© Lothian Health Services Archive

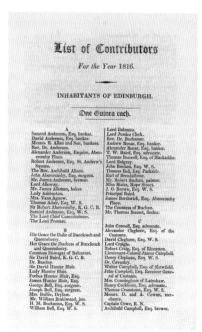

Financial donors listed in an early Royal Infirmary
of Edinburgh Annual Report, 1816
© Lothian Health Services Archive

in 1806 Parliament granted a sum of £2,000 out of the funds of the estates forfeited in the aftermath of the Jacobite Rising of 1745. A villa in Morningside was purchased with four acres of grounds, a Royal Charter was granted and, in 1809, the foundation stone was laid. The first patient was admitted in July 1813. The collection, dating from 1792 to the present day, spans some 200 linear metres of objects, photographs, architectural plans and administrative, operational and clinical records. Its patient casebooks (1840–1932) have proved invaluable for history of medicine research into topics such as post-traumatic stress disorder and general paralysis of the

insane, and are consulted frequently for family history research. They have also been used to discover more about 'outsider' art and patient writings, both of which form an important part of the collection.

A final example from the rich LHB collections is the material relating to the Western General Hospital (WGH), which started life as one of Edinburgh's poorhouses and, along with several others, became a hospital after the 1929 Local Government (Scotland) Act. The WGH collection amounts to three linear metres dating from 1930 to 2010, and mainly comprises patient registers, plans and administrative files. The site has been home to many significant institutions whose legacy is preserved in the Archive, such as the Children's Home serving the poorhouse. This was built in 1911, and later became the Paderewski Hospital during the Second World War. In 2010, as the Paderewski was demolished during redevelopment works, a time capsule dating from 1911 to 1913 was found containing Edinburgh City Council minutes, a photo, newspapers and a map of the city. The time capsule was transferred to LHSA and copies were made for a new time capsule placed in the replacement Royal Victoria Building on the same site.

In addition to its expansive LHB collections, LHSA holds 200 smaller collections of non-NHS institutional records and personal papers concerning the local history of healthcare and the history of Scottish medicine. These collections increase the breadth of LHSA's holdings, and have reference codes with the prefix GD. From a single nurse training badge to editions of First World War magazines, from historic cinefilm to patient artwork, these collections are as varied as they are intriguing. They offer a more rounded, and often more personal, take on the history of healthcare. They include papers collected by prominent medical individuals such as Elsie Stephenson, the first Director of what became known as the Nursing Studies Unit (1956) and later of the Department of Nursing at the University of Edinburgh (1965), and organisations such as the Scottish National Blood Transfusion Service and the South Eastern Association of the Medical Women's Federation.

A notable GD is a bound volume of Dr John Gregory's clinical cases at the RIE, 1771–1772. Gregory had studied medicine at the University of Edinburgh, as well as at Leiden and Aberdeen, before gaining his position at the RIE. He was appointed First Physician to His Majesty in Scotland in 1766 and in the same year Professor of Medicine at the University of Edinburgh. Although not the earliest patient records held at LHSA, they represent the most detailed clinical notes from the 18th century in the Archive and form a good link

Royal Infirmary of Edinburgh nurse training record, 1881
© Lothian Health Services Archive

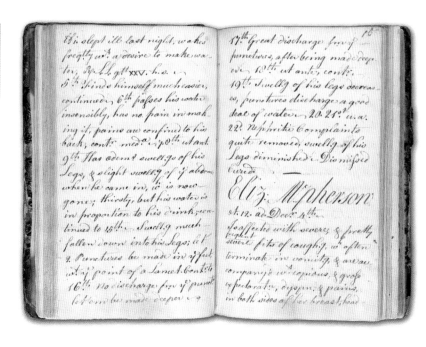

Case histories by John Gregory, 1771
© Lothian Health Services Archive

records of Jessie MacLaren MacGregor,
1863–1906, a pioneering Edinburgh
doctor at a time when prejudices against

with collections within Edinburgh
University Archives.

A number of oral history recordings
make up a small but important part of
the GD collections. One of the gems is an
interview with Mr Lockie, a 99-year-old
recorded in 1965, who describes his time
as a patient at the RIE as a child. GD1/60
contains a collection of oral history
recordings made by clinical psychologist
Jill Birrell in the early 1990s. The interviewees
were staff and former staff of the REH
and were collected in preparation for a
written history of the hospital.

The lives of notable Edinburgh medical,
and medical-related, women are also
contained within the GDs. These include

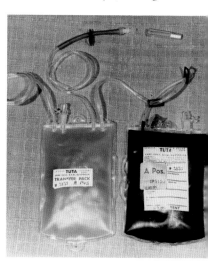

'Tuta' packs used in the separation of plasma from
blood, Edinburgh and South East Scotland Blood
Transfusion Service, 1971
© Lothian Health Services Archive

female medical education abounded. The daughter of a Newington builder, she studied art before registering as a medical student at Sophia Jex-Blake's Edinburgh School of Medicine for Women in 1888. After intensive and distinguished prize-winning studies there, she gained the Triple Qualification of the Scottish Royal Colleges of Physicians in 1892. Thereafter she was able to take advantage of new University regulations (Ordinance No.18 of 1892) which permitted women to graduate in medicine. She eventually graduated MB, CM in 1896 and, although not among the earliest women medical graduates, she was the first to gain a MD in 1899 with her thesis 'On the comparative anatomy of the eighth nerve'. She held posts in Edinburgh's Sick Children's and Bruntsfield Hospitals and went into private practice with Elsie Inglis, subsequently the leading light of the First World War's Scottish Women's Hospitals movement.

The papers of Helen Millar Lowe, one of Scotland's first three female chartered accountants, form GD34. Millar Lowe had a lifelong interest in the medical profession, mounting a successful campaign in 1957 to ensure that the Bruntsfield Hospital and the Elsie Inglis Memorial Maternity Hospital employed only qualified female medical staff. She was treasurer of both hospitals when they were transferred to the NHS in 1948. Millar Lowe's campaign papers, legal documents and publications complement Bruntsfield Hospital and Elsie Inglis Memorial Maternity Hospital LHB collections.

Edinburgh and Lothian HIV/AIDS Collections

The Edinburgh and Lothian HIV/AIDS Collections contain material that is both unique and of world importance in contextualising the city's pioneering initiatives in HIV prevention. It is unlikely that any equivalent collection exists elsewhere.

These 11 collections are composed principally of management, administrative and policy papers, publicity and educational materials, and reference literature. The three largest collections are the Lothian Regional Aids Team Papers and Lothian Health Board AIDS Papers (files of Lothian NHS departments in response to the outbreak of the disease), and the Take Care campaign (papers of a regional HIV prevention

Take Care campaign safe sex postcard, c.1990
© Lothian Health Services Archive

Take Care campaign safe sex postcards, c.1990
© Lothian Health Services Archive

campaign). Smaller collections include papers of Save the Children Scotland and of the Waverley Care Trust. The latter includes material relating to World AIDS Day, 1993–1998.

The collections reflect the evolution of prevention strategies as understanding of the virus developed. They chart internal NHS policy discussions and evidence subsequent initiatives enacted across the Lothians and beyond. Reference literature includes regional, national and international publications, policy documents and promotional materials, connecting local public health with the global.

Case Note Collections

Holding approximately one million individual patient records, LHSA possesses one of the largest historically significant, loose-leaf medical case note collections

in the UK. These case notes are unbound documents and images that have been kept together, tracing the treatment histories of individual patients. Their use superseded the creation of bound, indexed volumes. Case note folders hold typed or handwritten summaries of cases, presenting their information in a rich variety of forms, from photographs and X-rays to medical charts, laboratory reports, surgical sketches and medical and personal correspondence. They not only build a picture of medical careers and the progression of clinical practice, but also fill in social contexts behind often groundbreaking treatments.

Although the majority of LHSA case note collections originate from the RIE, the Archive holds documents of this kind from a variety of institutions. Case notes present a wealth of sociological and scientific

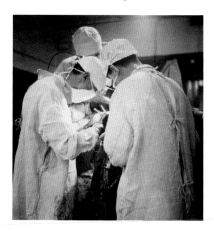

Norman Dott and his team in theatre, 1937
© Lothian Health Services Archive

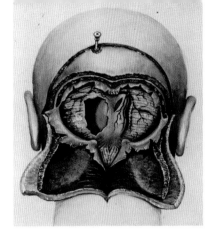

Medical illustration from Norman Dott
case note, 1926
© Lothian Health Services Archive

Special Collections also holds a significant collection of personal papers, photographs and documents relating to Dott's career at the University of Edinburgh Medical School, where he was made Professor of Surgical Neurology in 1947 (Coll-32).

Lyell, Charles

Charles Lyell (1797–1875) was the leading geologist of his day, whose groundbreaking work was a major formative influence on Charles Darwin.

Born in Kirriemuir, Forfarshire, Lyell graduated MA from Oxford University in 1821, and entered practice as a barrister. He combined his legal work with the scientific observation of geological phenomena, presenting his first paper in 1822, and being elected joint secretary of the Geological Society the following year. By 1827, he had abandoned law to devote himself full time to geological research. He embarked on a tour of France and Italy (1828–1829), studying,

information to medical humanities, clinical and genealogical researchers. LHSA has undertaken conservation work and cataloguing projects funded by the Wellcome Trust to open up this research-rich resource.

The case notes of Norman Dott – a University of Edinburgh graduate, renowned neurosurgeon and pioneer in surgical practice – serve as an exemplar. His case notes are augmented by teaching photographs, sketches and glass plate negatives, which are held in separate collections by LHSA.

Geological section of the coast of Forfarshire by Charles Lyell

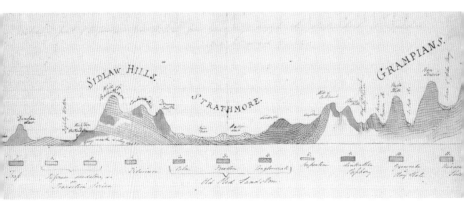

in particular, the volcanic formations at Vesuvius and Etna, which culminated in the publication of his *Principles of Geology* (1830–1833). In 1831 he was appointed Professor of Geology at the newly founded King's College London and in the following years conducted further research tours of Germany, Switzerland, Italy and Scandinavia. In the 1840s he travelled extensively in the United States and wrote two popular works which combined travel-writing with geology: *Travels in North America* (1845) and *A Second Visit to the United States* (1849). Lyell contributed significantly to Darwin's thinking on evolution and helped to arrange the simultaneous publication of papers on natural selection by Darwin and Arthur Russel Wallace in 1858. Lyell tackled Darwin's evolutionary theories in his own final work *Geological Evidences of the Antiquity of Man* (1863), which broadly accepted Darwin's thesis while still insisting that there was a radical discontinuity between humankind and the rest of the animal kingdom.

Lyell's significance as a geologist lies in popularising James Hutton's concept of uniformitarianism, which argued that the earth has been gradually shaped by processes still in operation today. This ran counter to the prevailing theory which assumed that mountain-building and other geological phenomena could have occurred only as a result of major cataclysmic events in the past. The vast time scales required by uniformitarianism helped Darwin to develop his theories.

This substantial collection includes correspondence with many major scientific figures, manuscripts of lectures and papers, and notes relating to matters from the New Zealand earthquake of 1855 to sea serpents. *Coll-203*

MacAlpine, Alexander Gillon

Alexander Gillon MacAlpine (1869–1957) was a missionary and linguist who conducted important research into the languages of Malawi.

Born in Linlithgow, MacAlpine was educated at the University of Edinburgh and Glasgow Free Church College. Upon his ordination in 1893, he travelled as a missionary to Bandawe, Nyasaland (modern-day Malawi). With the exception of a brief period as Minister of Monquhitter and New Byth, Aberdeenshire (1914–1921), he spent the rest of his career in Nyasaland, mainly in Bandawe but moving later to Chintechi and Livingstonia. A skilled linguist, he prepared a dictionary of the Chitonga language, and translated the New Testament into Chitonga. In retirement, he returned to Scotland.

The papers were presented in 1964 and 1993, by MacAlpine's son, the Reverend Alexander Gillon MacAlpine junior. A further small tranche of material was acquired in 2010.

The papers consist of:
- biographical notes on African and missionary colleagues dating from 1893
- diaries from 1897 onwards
- wayside and travel notes
- notes on folklore

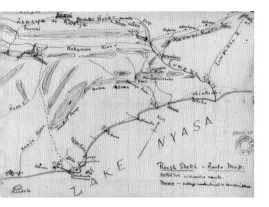

- correspondence with church
  colleagues in Scotland
- a collection of photographs
  of local people, the mission at
  Bandawe, missionary home life
  and geographical landmarks
- sketch maps of the Malawi highlands
  and the shore of Lake Nyasa
- a film strip documenting
  missionary work
- extracts from newspapers.

There are printed items, including liturgical
texts in Chitonga and Tonga, grammatical
studies of these two languages, and works on
the development of the Church in Nyasaland.
Coll-48

MacCaig, Norman

Norman MacCaig (1910–1996) was one
of Scotland's best-loved and most influential
poets. Marked by a striking gift for metaphor,
his poetry moves between his native Edinburgh
and his 'spiritual home' of Assynt in the
north-west of Scotland.

MacCaig was educated at Edinburgh's
Royal High School and the University of
Edinburgh, graduating MA in
Classics in 1932. After training
at Moray House College, he
embarked on a career as a
schoolmaster, working first as a
Latin teacher, then at a number
of Edinburgh primary schools. His pacifism
led him to register as a conscientious
objector during the Second World War,
but he was able to resume his career
after the Armistice. After retiring from
schoolteaching, he served as the University
of Edinburgh's first Writer in Residence
(1967–1969) and went on to become Reader
in Poetry at Stirling University (1972–1977).
His best-known volumes include *Riding
Lights* (1955), *Surroundings* (1966), *A Man
in my Position* (1969), *The White Bird* (1973),
The World's Room (1974), *Tree of Strings*
(1977), *A World of Difference* (1983) and
Voice-Over (1989). MacCaig was awarded
the OBE in 1979.

The collection includes manuscripts or
typescripts for more than 1,000 poems written
between 1947 and 1992, together with working
materials for all of MacCaig's collections of
verse from *Riding Lights* (1955) onwards.

The papers also include drafts of
(or notes for) broadcasts, talks, lectures
and reviews, along with diaries, personal
materials and some correspondence
(including poetical Christmas cards from
Seamus Heaney).

The printed collections include 139 books from MacCaig's personal library (all catalogued online at shelfmarks SD 9008–9155). Other copies of first editions of his own works are to be found in the manuscript collection. These include inscribed copies of works by fellow poets including Hugh MacDiarmid, Edwin Morgan, Seamus Heaney and Sydney Goodsir Smith. Of particular interest is a copy of MacDiarmid's *A Drunk Man Looks at the Thistle,* which is heavily annotated by MacCaig.

Coll-69

. . . .

MacCormick, Neil

Professor Sir Donald Neil MacCormick (1941–2009) was a renowned legal philosopher, an internationally acknowledged authority on the legal theory of the European Union and a prominent figure in both Scottish and European politics.

MacCormick was educated at the High School of Glasgow and Glasgow University, where he graduated MA in Philosophy and English in 1963. He went on to study jurisprudence at Balliol College, Oxford, graduating in 1965. He then spent two years lecturing in jurisprudence at University College, before returning to Balliol in 1968 as a Fellow and Tutor in the same discipline. In 1972, at the remarkably young age of 31, MacCormick was appointed to the Regius Chair of Public Law and the Law of Nature at the University of Edinburgh. He held this post until his retirement in 2007 while also pursuing an active political career. MacCormick held office as Member of the European Parliament for the Scottish National Party from 1999 to 2004, where he dealt with many constitutional and legal affairs. His mandate coincided with the re-establishment in 1999 of the Scottish Parliament and much of his work concerned the proper representation of regions and sub-state nations in Europe, with special regard to the principle of subsidiarity. In 2007 he was appointed as special adviser to the First Minister on European and External Affairs.

The papers represent MacCormick's time in office as MEP, 1999–2004, and consist of documents relating to topics such as legislative work, policy shaping, rights implementation, constitutive work, communications, the Convention on the Future of Europe, parliamentary questions and answers, and parliamentary immunity.

Coll-1049

. . . .

MacDiarmid, Hugh

Hugh MacDiarmid, the pseudonym of Christopher Murray Grieve (1892–1978), was the pre-eminent Scottish literary figure of the 20th century. As a poet, critic, essayist and political activist, he dominated the nation's cultural scene for more than five decades.

Born in Langholm, Dumfriesshire, and educated at Langholm Academy, MacDiarmid worked as a journalist before joining the Royal Medical Corps at the outbreak of the First World War. He served in Salonica, Greece and France before being invalided home to Scotland in 1918. He resumed his journalistic career in Montrose while publishing the works *Sangschaw* (1925), *Penny Wheep* (1926) and *A Drunk Man Looks at the Thistle* (1926), which placed him at the forefront of the Scottish Literary Renaissance – a movement which sought to revitalise Scottish writing by fusing the heritage of the medieval makars with an international, modernist outlook. Soon recognised as the major Scots-language poet since Burns, MacDiarmid inspired other poets such as William Soutar to take up Scots as a literary medium. Further major publications in Scots followed, such as *To Circumjack Cencrastus* (1930) and the first and second *Hymns to Lenin* (1931, 1935). From *Stony Limits* (1934) onwards, however, MacDiarmid increasingly turned to English, rejecting the lyricism of his early volumes in a favour of an austere, philosophical diction. In his post-war poetry he increasingly shunned the personal and subjective in favour of open-ended epics such as *In Memoriam James Joyce* (1955) and *The Kind of Poetry I Want* (1961) which celebrated political and scientific materialism. MacDiarmid continued to inspire younger Scottish poets and in the 1950s and 1960s was at the heart of the group, including Sydney Goodsir Smith, Norman MacCaig and George Mackay Brown, which met in Edinburgh's legendary literary pub, Milne's Bar.

MacDiarmid combined literary and political activism. He was a founding member of the Scottish National Party in 1928 but left in 1933 due to his Marxist-Leninist views. He joined the Communist Party the following year only to be expelled in 1938 for his nationalist sympathies. He subsequently stood as a parliamentary candidate for both the SNP (1945) and British Communist Party (1964). As a follower of the Scottish revolutionary socialist John Maclean, he saw no contradiction between international socialism and the nationalist vision of a Scottish workers' republic, but this ensured a fraught relationship with organised political parties.

The substantial manuscript collection includes typescripts and manuscripts of MacDiarmid's poems and correspondence with many leading writers. There are also many literary manuscripts sent to MacDiarmid by fellow writers.

We also hold the bulk of MacDiarmid's personal library. Most of this was acquired in 1979. Some further material was given to the Library by his son, Michael Grieve, in 1990. This is primarily a literary collection, but it also reflects MacDiarmid's interest in Scottish and international politics. It includes a large number of verse pamphlets and separate issues or short runs of periodicals. The collection comprises some 5,000 printed items, not all catalogued.

Coll-18

Mackenzie, James

James Mackenzie (1853–1925) was a physician and medical researcher who made an outstanding contribution to the study of heart disease.

Born near Scone, Perthshire, Mackenzie studied at Perth Academy and the University of Edinburgh, where he obtained the degrees of Bachelor of Medicine and Master in Surgery in 1878. After graduation he worked for colliery practices in County Durham and then as house

'Student Days at Edinburgh' (James Mackenzie seated far left)

The papers consist of:

- correspondence, largely dating from 1900 to 1925
- manuscripts of and notes towards publications
- offprints of articles for medical journals and other printed materials (including reviews of his work)
- press cuttings
- personal materials including photographs of people and places, and Mackenzie's birth certificate.

Coll-84

physician and assistant to professors of clinical medicine at the Royal Infirmary in Edinburgh. In 1879 Mackenzie joined a general practice in Burnley, Lancashire, where he also served as physician to the Victoria Hospital. Here he began a series of painstaking clinical studies which were slowly to win him a global reputation. In 1907, he left Burnley to take up practice in London. He became a consulting physician at the London Hospital in 1913 and during the First World War acted as consultant to the Military Heart Hospital. In 1918, Mackenzie returned to Scotland to set up the Institute for Clinical Research at St Andrews. His major publications include *The Study of the Pulse* (1902), *Diseases of the Heart* (1908), *Symptoms and their Interpretation* (1909), *Principles of Diagnosis and Treatment* (1916), *The Future of Medicine* (1919) and *Heart Disease and Pregnancy* (1921). He was knighted in 1915.

Mackenzie, Kenneth

Kenneth Mackenzie (1920–1971) was a Scottish missionary in Central Africa who later became a prominent anti-apartheid campaigner.

Born in Strathpeffer, Ross-shire, Mackenzie was educated at Dingwall Academy and Aberdeen University where he graduated MA in 1940. Mackenzie then underwent theological training at the Free Church College, Edinburgh, 1940–1942, and New College, 1942–1944. He was licensed by the Presbytery of Edinburgh in 1944, and ordained as a missionary the following year. He first served in Mlanje and Zomba in Nyasaland (modern-day Malawi), 1946–1948, learning the essentials of the languages spoken there. He then moved to Northern Rhodesia (modern-day Zambia), working in Lubwa, 1948–1950, and Chitambo, 1952–1954, where he again made an in-depth study of the languages and cultures of the region. Mackenzie regarded his true mission as making the people of Scotland, and especially the Church of Scotland, aware of the Central African situation at a time of great political change for the continent. He also played a prominent part in the transfer of mission schools to Government control, and in the discussions leading to Church union in the region. During this period he persuaded the Northern Rhodesian Christian Council of the need for urgent action on the proposals for a Central African Federation and of the need for firmer safeguards for African interests. Through this work, he became the confidant of African leaders as their nations moved towards independence. Mackenzie returned to Scotland in 1956 for family reasons. He was seconded to the staff of St Colm's College, Edinburgh, in 1957, and later served as Minister of Restalrig Parish Church, 1968–1971. In these years, Mackenzie became one of the founders and leading spirits of the Anti-Apartheid Movement in Scotland.

The collection includes papers relating to:
- Central Africa, 1958–1964; and Rhodesia, 1965–1970
- South Africa, particularly in connection with the Anti-Apartheid Movement, including the Springbok tour controversy
- race relations and immigration.

There are also newspaper cuttings and pamphlets, along with printed grammars, vocabularies and dictionaries of African languages.

Coll-64

Mackie, Charles

Charles Mackie (1688–1770) was the University of Edinburgh's first Professor of History.

Born in Limekilns, Fife, Mackie studied at the University of Edinburgh, graduating in 1705. He continued his education in the Netherlands, at Groeningen, 1707–1708, and at Leiden in 1715. On his return to Edinburgh he joined the Rankenian Club, one of the earliest literary societies of 18th-century Scotland, which numbered such major Enlightenment figures as David Hume and Colin Maclaurin among its members. In 1719 Mackie was appointed to the new Chair of Universal History at the University of Edinburgh, the first history chair in Scotland. As his title indicates, Mackie's remit was extensive, encompassing Western history, Scottish history, and Greek, Roman and British antiquities. Mackie's conception of the historian's duties was exceptionally broad, and his courses covered many topics later taught by professors of constitutional history, Roman law, and rhetoric and belles lettres. He was a popular lecturer, despite teaching in Latin at a time when many lecturers were turning to English. His pupils included such future luminaries as William Robertson.

The archive is composed of:
- the manuscript of an alphabetical biographical dictionary
- notes of lectures by William Law, Professor of Moral Philosophy, taken down by Mackie as a student
- Mackie's catalogue of his own library
- commonplace books containing notes and extracts on Roman, Scottish and universal history

Index Funereus 29 Annorum.
from 11ᵗʰ June 1727, to 11ᵗʰ June ~~1755~~ 1756
(By Charles Mackie, Professor of Civil History in the University of Edinburgh)
General Register.

Abercromby (Capt: Alexʳ) of Glasrough, Janry 1729.

Agnew (Thoˢ) Bʳ: to Lady Wallace, sudden. Febry, 1736.

- an 'index funereus' of peoples deceased, 1727–1756
- chronological notes on the birth and death of Mackie's children
- accounts and miscellaneous papers.

Coll-423

Charles Mackie's index of people deceased, 1727–1756

MacKinnon, Donald

Donald MacKinnon (1839–1914) was the University of Edinburgh's first Professor of Celtic.

Born and schooled on Colonsay in the Hebrides, MacKinnon attended the Church of Scotland Training College, Edinburgh, before working as a schoolteacher in Lochinver, Sutherland, 1860–1863, where he made a close study of the dialects and literature of the North Highlands. MacKinnon then returned to Edinburgh where he obtained the degree of MA from the University of Edinburgh in 1870. In the following decade he published a series of scholarly articles in the groundbreaking journal *An Gaidheal*. In 1882, he became the first appointee to the newly created Chair of Celtic at the University of Edinburgh, a post he held until 1914. His experience and intimate knowledge of the North Highlands served him

well as a member of the Royal Commission of Inquiry into the Condition of Crofters and Cottars in the Highlands and Islands chaired by Lord Napier in 1883. MacKinnon's contribution to the Commission's Report was impressive enough to speed up subsequent legislation for the improvement of conditions for Scotland's crofters. Among his publications were the *Reading Book for the Use of Students of the Gaelic Class at Edinburgh University* (1883) and *On the Dialects of Scottish Gaelic*. As a scholar, MacKinnon is best remembered

The Crofter

A MONTHLY RECORD FOR THE PEOPLE.
"KNOWLEDGE IS POWER."

No. 4. JUNE, 1885. PRICE ONE PENNY.

JOHN STUART BLACKIE,
EMERITUS PROFESSOR OF GREEK, EDINBURGH.
From a Photograph by Thomas Annan, Edinburgh.

The Crofter, No. 4, June 1885
MacKinnon Collection

for editing, translating and annotating the 15th-century Glenmasan Manuscript, a codex that contains a version of the Deirdre story.

The papers are substantial, and include:
- a 15th-century manuscript on medieval physiography
- a 16th-century summary or abstract of the Treatise of Maighstir Ricairdi compiled from Hippocrates and others
- manuscripts of 18th-century tales and verse
- lecture notes on Gaelic grammar and Gaelic literature
- notebooks containing transcripts of Gaelic poetry
- notes on the history of Scotland
- draft versions of MacKinnon's published works
- newspaper cuttings.

There are also some 1,700 books and 300 pamphlets from MacKinnon's library on Celtic studies and Scottish theology mainly published in the 19th or early 20th centuries. The bulk of the collection was bequeathed to the Library by Dr Roger McNeill, Medical Officer of Health for Argyllshire, in 1924. All the books are fully catalogued online, with shelfmarks starting 'MacKinnon Coll.'.
Coll-98

Macleod, Norman

Dr Norman Macleod was a Lecturer in Chemical Engineering at the University of Edinburgh from 1957 to 1990 and was a keen amateur naval historian. The material consists of papers and correspondence, including:

- the manuscript of an unpublished book on the Admiralty together with related correspondence
- material on shipwrights in Naval dockyards
- material on Holbrook Naval School and Greenwich Hospital
- manuscripts of lectures on the historical development of the Admiralty
- articles and notes on Royal dockyards
- reports on Royal dockyards in Singapore, Palestine and Malta.

Coll-426

Macmurray, John

John Macmurray (1891–1976) was a leading moral philosopher, a critic of Cartesian thought, whose works ranged broadly across religion, political science and education.

John Macmurray

Born in Maxwellton, Kirkcudbrightshire, Macmurray was educated in Aberdeen and at Glasgow University from which he graduated in Classics in 1913. He won a scholarship to Balliol College, Oxford, but his studies were interrupted by the First World War. He served in the Royal Medical Corps from 1914 to 1916, then enlisted as Lieutenant in the Cameron Highlanders from 1916. Wounded in the Battle of Arras, he was awarded the Military Cross in 1918. After the war, Macmurray held teaching posts in philosophy at Manchester University (1919–1921), the University of Witwatersrand, Johannesburg (1921–1922) and Balliol College (1922–1928). In 1928, he was appointed Grote Professor of the Philosophy of Mind and Logic at the University of London. In the 1930s, he began a second career as a popular BBC radio commentator on cultural, political and moral questions. In 1944, he returned to Scotland as Professor of Moral Philosophy at the University of Edinburgh, remaining in post until 1958. Macmurray's most significant works are *The Self as Agent* (1957) and *Persons in Relation* (1961), originally delivered as Gifford lectures in Glasgow, 1953–1954. Other important publications include *Freedom in the Modern World* (1932) and *The Search for Reality in Religion* (1965). He was also credited with influencing the thought of Tony Blair.

The papers contain manuscripts of and notes towards lectures, talks, radio broadcasts and publications, together with some offprints. A substantial additional gift of papers was received in 2013 including poetry, diaries and extensive correspondence.

Coll-35

Maconochie, Allan

Allan Maconochie, Lord Meadowbank (1748–1816), was one of the leading figures in Scots Law during the Enlightenment period.

Born in West Lothian, Maconochie was privately educated by Alexander Adam (1741–1809), later Rector of Edinburgh's Royal High School. Maconochie then studied at the University of Edinburgh, studying moral philosophy under Adam Fergusson and rhetoric and belles lettres (English literature) under Hugh Blair. He also read Roman law under Professor Robert Dick. While a student, he co-founded the Speculative Society, an institution which 'trained' young men in 'public speaking, talent, and liberal thought'. In 1770 he was admitted as an advocate and the following year entered Lincoln's Inn in London but was not ultimately called to the English Bar. In 1779 Maconochie was appointed Professor

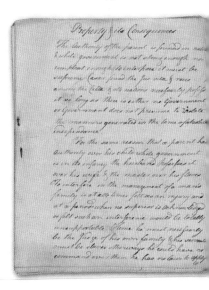

'Property and its Consequences', MS by Allan Maconochie

of Public Law and the Law of Nature and Nations at the University of Edinburgh. His teaching, which traced the rise of political institutions, is encapsulated in his *Essay on the Origin and Progress of the European Legislatures* (1784). Maconochie combined academic work with an active career at the Bar. In 1779 he was elected treasurer of the Faculty of Advocates and in 1788 he became Sheriff-Depute of Renfrewshire. When he was finally promoted to the Bench as Lord Meadowbank in 1796, he resigned his Edinburgh chair. As a judge Maconochie took a keen interest in proposals to reform the Court of Session, publishing *Considerations on the Introduction of Jury Trial in Civil Causes into Scotland* (1814).

The collection consists of manuscripts of lectures and notes dating from the 1780s and covering subjects as diverse as education, monarchy, international and constitutional law, currency, trade, medicine, agriculture and the development of language.
Coll-1137

Earle Monteith Macphail, photograph by Nicholas and Co., Chennai, India

Macphail, Earle Monteith

Earle Monteith Macphail (1861–1937) was a prominent missionary, educationist and politician in colonial India.

Born in Aberdeen, Macphail was educated at Edinburgh Academy and then at the University of Edinburgh where he graduated MA in 1883. He was one of the founders of the Edinburgh University Students' Representative Council, 1883–1884, and was President of the Council in 1885. Macphail went on to read divinity at New College, Edinburgh, and pursued further studies abroad at Jena, Tübingen and Berlin Universities. In 1890 he was ordained as a missionary of the United Free Church of Scotland and travelled to India to take up an appointment as Professor of History and Economics at Madras Christian College (in modern-day Chennai). He would eventually become Principal of the College in 1921. From 1899 onwards, he was also a Fellow of Madras University, represented the university on a number of bodies, and eventually served as its Vice-Chancellor from 1923 to 1925. Macphail was also active in politics as a member of the Indian Council of State in 1924 and Representative of the European Constituency of Madras in the Legislative Assembly of India between 1925 and 1927. In 1919, Macphail was awarded the CBE, and in 1924 was made Companion of the Order of the Indian Empire.

The collection consists of:
- notes of lectures attended at the University of Edinburgh
- notes of lectures given in India
- material relating to the University of Edinburgh's tercentenary celebrations
- materials relating to the Students' Representative Council, the University Union and various student societies
- papers relating to Madras Christian College
- personal papers including correspondence, school papers and photographs.

Coll-91

Marwick, William Hutton

William Hutton Marwick (1863–1940) was a literary scholar and a missionary in Nigeria, Jamaica and India.

Marwick studied at Arbroath High School, the University of Edinburgh and the United Presbyterian Training College in Edinburgh. He was an assistant at Lossiemouth Manse from 1887 to 1888, but had difficulty securing a permanent position and spent some time travelling to Orkney and pursuing literary interests. In particular he organised the Ruskin Reading Guild and edited its journal *Igdrasil* as well as another periodical *World Literature*. He was also the founder and the first secretary of the Carlyle Society. Marwick was ordained by the World Congregational Church in Dundee in 1890. In 1892 he was appointed a missionary at Calabar (in modern-day Nigeria) where he met Elizabeth Hutton, whom he married in 1893. Marwick returned to Scotland

for health reasons in 1894 but resumed his mission in 1898. Marwick taught himself Efik and in 1899 he prepared a bilingual (Efik and Akunakuna) service book. The Marwicks travelled to Scotland on leave in 1900 expecting to return to Calabar but Marwick was sent instead as a missionary to Jamaica. He was later a civil chaplain at Meerut, northern India.

The collection consists of correspondence, personal papers and diaries, including in particular:
- personal correspondence including letters from Marwick's family
- letters from Marwick to his wife Elizabeth Hutton
- correspondence relating to the Ruskin Reading Guild and to his editorship of journals
- correspondence relating to the Calabar Mission
- diaries of Marwick (1892, 1895) and of Elizabeth Hutton (1891–1894).

Coll-219

Matthew, Robert

Robert Hogg Matthew (1906–1975) was a leading 20th-century architect responsible for designing Scottish new towns, rebuilding war-damaged London and devising major modernist building projects in Edinburgh.

Born in Edinburgh, Matthew was educated at Melville College and then at the School of Architecture in Edinburgh College of Art. His professional career began in the office of Lorimer and Matthew, the architectural practice founded by Matthew's father John Fraser Matthew and

Sir Robert Lorimer (see page 122). From 1936 to 1946 he worked for the Department of Health for Scotland, and, during the Second World War, helped draw up the Clyde Valley regional plan, making the first sketches for the new towns of East Kilbride and Glenrothes. In 1946, Matthew was appointed architect to London County Council, where he worked on the city's post-war reconstruction and was involved in the building of the Royal Festival Hall on London's South Bank. In 1953 he was appointed to the joint post of Professor of Architecture at the University of Edinburgh and Head of the School of Architecture in the Edinburgh College of Art. At the same time, he set up a private architectural practice in Edinburgh which was responsible for designing Edinburgh Turnhouse Airport, the Royal Commonwealth Pool, Stirling University and Cockenzie Power Station. Matthew was also closely involved with the University of Edinburgh's development plan for George Square, and his practice designed the University's David Hume Tower, Adam Ferguson Building and William Robertson Building. In 1962 he was elected president of the Royal Institute of British Architects (RIBA) and did much to expand its activities and influence. From 1970 Matthew was consultant adviser on building conservation policy to the Secretary of State for Scotland. He was awarded the CBE in 1952, and was knighted in 1962.

The collections consist of papers relating to subjects including:
- Matthew's architectural practice
- Matthew's University of Edinburgh work
- architectural competitions
- international organisations including the Union Internationale des Architectes and the Commonwealth Association of Architects
- The Scottish Civic Trust
- amenity societies
- personal materials (including letters relating to his knighthood).

There are also many printed publications (some on ecology) and pamphlets.

Coll-89

Medieval Manuscripts

Some of the most beautiful books in Scotland are preserved in our collection of about 270 western medieval manuscripts. These are all books and documents written by hand, from the 11th to the 16th centuries. Many are finely illuminated and decorated.

The greatest treasure of the collection is the small, brightly coloured copy of the Psalms known as the Celtic Psalter (MS.56), which dates from the early 11th century and is possibly the oldest surviving Scottish book still in Scotland. There are also Books of Hours produced for royalty, copies of classical works by authors such as Virgil, medical treatises and examples of pre-Reformation Scottish music. There are manuscripts in English, French, Gaelic and Greek, as well as Latin.

The collection was formed by bringing together pre-Reformation manuscripts from across the Library. About half the manuscripts come from the David Laing collection. Many manuscripts display evidence about their different owners through the centuries, from monks to rich private collectors. We do not have the resources to acquire medieval manuscripts on a regular basis but have received some very fine examples as donations, such as the 14 manuscripts, mainly Books of Hours, received through the Cathcart White bequest in 1943.

Work is in progress to create a full online listing. Some 230 of the manuscripts are described in detail by Catherine Borland, *A Descriptive Catalogue of the Western Mediaeval Manuscripts in Edinburgh University Library* (Edinburgh, 1916). Other finding aids are available in the Centre. There are also five western medieval manuscripts in New College Library.

Coll-101

MS of Virgil by Florius Infortunatus, c.1460

Mitchell, William Fraser

William Fraser Mitchell (1900–1988), was an educationalist and poet with wide-ranging interests in religion, literature and history.

Born in Dundee, Mitchell was educated at Dundee High School and at the University of Edinburgh, where he graduated in English in 1922. He went on to Exeter College, Oxford to conduct postgraduate research on the rhetoric of English preaching in the 17th century. He was awarded the degree of BLitt, and later published his thesis as *English Pulpit Oratory from Andrewes to Tillotson* (1932). After Oxford, Mitchell studied education at Moray House and the University of Edinburgh, and served as personal assistant to Sir Godfrey Thomson, Bell Professor of Education at the University of Edinburgh. After a temporary post lecturing in English at Armstrong College, Newcastle, Mitchell was appointed Lecturer in Education at the University of Reading in 1928 where he remained until 1944. A secondment to Farnborough Grammar School as an English master was followed by his appointment as Professor of Education in the Selly Oak Colleges, Birmingham, where he instructed teachers of religious knowledge, missionaries, overseas student teachers and youth leaders. When his department closed in 1951, Mitchell took a post as Assistant Lecturer in English at Huddersfield Technical College, then in 1955 took part in the establishment of the Malayan Teachers' College in Wolverhampton. After a brief further spell at Huddersfield Technical

dia aiam meam ad confitendū no
mini tuo : me expectant iusti donec
retribuas michi . cum vsiculis ⁊ ora
nibus que dicebantur ad . Placebo .
Hic incipit commendacio aïarum .

Beati im
maculati i
uia : qui
ambulant
in lege dñi .
Beati qui
scrutantur
testimonia
eius : in toto corde exquirunt eum .
Non enim qui operantur iniquita
tem : in vijs eius ambulauerunt .
Tu mandasti : mandata tua custo
diri nimis . Utinam dirigantur

College and a lectureship at the University of Sheffield (1957–1958), he was appointed Assistant English Master at Colne Valley High School. When he retired in 1965, he returned to Dundee where he conducted research into the life of James Burnett, Lord Monboddo (1714–1799). Mitchell was also a talented poet, publishing collections including *Off Parade and Other Verses* (1919), *Cobweb and Mustardseed* (1928) and *A Slim Volume* (1960).

The collection includes:

- manuscripts of poems, plays, literary essays and an unfinished novel *Moth and Peaseblossom*
- papers and letters on educational research
- papers on contemporary poets and artists
- material on religion, tolerance and pulpit teaching

Postcards from William Fraser Mitchell's albums of Victorian and Edwardian ephemera

- papers and card indexes related to Mitchell's research on Monboddo
- albums of Victorian and Edwardian ephemera
- material on the history of Dundee.

There are also personal materials including Mitchell's academic hoods.

Coll-86

Moir, John William

John William Moir (1851–1940) was an evangelical African trader who opposed the slave market.

Born in Edinburgh, Moir studied at the University of Edinburgh and in Switzerland and Germany. In 1877, inspired by his evangelical Christian faith and the example of David Livingstone, he went with his brother Frederick Lewis Maitland Moir to the Zanzibar coast (modern-day Tanzania). They initially worked on William Mackinnon's unsuccessful scheme to build a road from Dar es Salaam to Lake Tanganyika, before founding the African Lakes Company Ltd, of which they were joint managers. Their company steamers plied Lake Nyasa and the Zambezi and Shire Rivers, trading with the local people and with Arab merchants, and supplying missionaries in the region. They thus built up a transport system that opened up large parts of Central-East Africa to commerce. The brothers sought to combat the slave trade and were both wounded during the violent conflicts that followed (known as the 'Arab War'). John Moir retired to Edinburgh in 1900. Moir was also an enthusiastic beekeeper and he built up a large and well-known collection of books on beekeeping.

The collection contains:

- John and Frederick Moir's journal, 1866
- John Moir's journal, 1877–1878
- family correspondence, 1883–1900
- photographs and news cuttings
- a report to the directors of the African Lakes Company, 1890
- a Bible presented to John Moir in 1859
- a catalogue of the Moir Beekeeping Library and a typescript on book-collecting.

Coll-240

....

Monro, Alexander (I–III)

The three Alexander Monros constituted a remarkable dynasty of anatomists whose lectures exerted a formative influence on generations of Edinburgh students.

Alexander Monro *primus* (1697–1767) was born in London. He was educated at the University of Edinburgh, after his family moved to the city, then returned to London to attend lectures on experimental philosophy and dissection. A visit to Paris followed before a study period at Leyden in the Netherlands in 1718 under Herman Boerhaave. In 1720 he became the first Professor of Anatomy at the University of Edinburgh, which has been seen as the birth of the medical school here. His course of lectures included the history of anatomy, osteology, the relation between animal and human anatomy, surgical operations and general physiology. In 1745 he tended to the wounded on the battlefield of Prestonpans. His published works include *The Anatomy of the Humane Bones* (1726) and *An Account of the Inoculation of Smallpox in Scotland* (1765). In 1758 he resigned his professorship in favour of his son (who had been joint professor since 1754) but continued to give clinical lectures.

Papers related to Alexander Monro *primus* include records of students, lecture notes, case histories and treatises.

Alexander Monro *secundus* (1733–1817) was born in Edinburgh and studied medicine at the University of Edinburgh. From 1753, he occasionally lectured in place of his father and in 1754 he became Joint Professor of Anatomy with him. In October 1755 he took the degree of Doctor of Medicine then went to London to attend William Hunter's lectures, before going abroad to pursue further medical studies at Paris, Leyden and

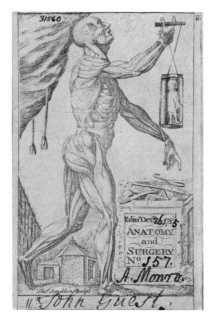

School and then studied at the University of Edinburgh, where he was awarded his MD in 1797. Between 1798 and 1808 he was Joint Professor of Anatomy at the University of Edinburgh with his father, although he pursued further studies in Paris in the earliest years of this co-occupancy. When his father finally retired in 1808, Monro *tertius* fully assumed the chair and delivered the whole lecture programme. His published works include *Observations on Crural Hernia* (1803), *Engravings of the Thoracic and Abdominal Viscera* (1814), *Anatomy of the Pelvis of the Male* (1827) and *Anatomy of the Urinary Bladder and Perinaeum in the Male* (1842).

Paper relating to Alexander Monro *tertius* include notes of his lectures taken down by students, a letter and a pen-and-ink sketch of Monro from 1834 or 1835.
Various locations in Special Collections.

Berlin. In 1758 he fully succeeded his father as Professor of Anatomy at the University of Edinburgh and the following year was elected Fellow of the Royal College of Physicians (serving as president of that body in 1779). An outstandingly influential anatomist, his works included *Observations on the Structure and Functions of the Nervous System* (1783), *The Structure and Physiology of Fishes Explained* (1785), *A Description of All the Bursae Mucosae of the Human Body* (1788) and *Three Treatises: On the Brain, the Eye, and the Ear* (1797).

Our papers relating to Alexander Monro *secundus* consist of lecture notes on anatomy taken down by his students (Coll-1029).

Alexander Monro *tertius* (1773–1859) was educated at the city's Royal High

Morrison, William Shepherd

William Shepherd Morrison (1893–1961) was a prominent British Conservative politician who served as Speaker of the House of Commons and Governor-General of Australia.

Born at Torinturk, Argyll, Morrison was educated at George Watson's College in Edinburgh, then went to the University of Edinburgh in 1912 to read Arts and Law. In many ways his career echoes that of John Buchan – from provincial Scottish upbringing to integration into the English and colonial elite. His studies were interrupted by the First World War, where he served in the Royal Field Artillery, winning the Military Cross in 1915 and rising to the rank of captain. Morrison resumed his studies after the war and served as both President of Edinburgh University Union and Senior President of the Students Representative Council. He graduated MA in 1920, and in 1923 he was called to the English Bar (Inner Temple) in London. Morrison then sought to enter politics, standing for election

Letter by William Shepherd Morrison from the Western Front, 11 June 1915

in the Western Isles as a Unionist in 1923 and 1924, and campaigning in Gaelic. He eventually became an MP in 1929, winning the constituency of Cirencester and Tewkesbury, in England, for the Conservatives. He held the seat until 1959 while occupying a succession of government positions. In 1935, he became Financial Secretary to the Treasury. In 1936 he was appointed Minister of Agriculture and Fisheries, and a member of the Privy Council. He was Chancellor of the Duchy of Lancaster and Minister of Food, 1939–1940; Postmaster-General, 1940–1942; and Minister of Town and Country Planning, 1943–1945. From 1951 to 1959 he was Speaker of the House of Commons, in which capacity he presided over the debate on the Suez crisis in 1956. When he retired from the House, he was created Viscount Dunrossil of Vallaquie (on the island of North Uist, Outer Hebrides). In the same year, he was appointed Governor-General of Australia but died in post in 1961. As an MP, he was known as 'Shakes' Morrison for his habit of quoting from his beloved Shakespeare.

The collection is composed of some 100 items of correspondence between Morrison and his brother Dr Donald John Morrison (whom Morrison addressed as 'Pwe'). Dating from 1915 to 1961, the letters cover a wide range of topics including both world wars, parliamentary politics, the abdication crisis of 1936, Winston Churchill, Gaelic phrases and Morrison's own poems.

Coll-1142

Muir, William

William Muir (1819–1905) was an administrator of colonial India with a deep interest in the history and literary heritage of the Islamic world.

Born in Glasgow, Muir studied briefly at Edinburgh and Glasgow universities before gaining a post with the East India Company. He entered the Bengal Civil Service in 1837, and after a series of postings in the revenue and judicial services, became Secretary to the Lieutenant-Governor of the North-Western Provinces in 1852. His service during the Indian Rebellion of 1857 (when he was responsible for intelligence) brought him to the attention of Governor-General Lord Canning, who appointed him his secretary in 1858. By 1865, he was Foreign Secretary to the Government of India, and by 1868 Lieutenant-Governor of the North-Western Provinces.

As an administrator, Muir introduced educational reforms, promoting, in particular, female and tertiary education. The Muir Central College opened in Allahabad in 1872, and became the province's first university. Muir's many scholarly publications on Islam, drawing on Arabic sources, were regarded as authoritative in his day. These included *The Life of Mahomet* (1858–1861), *Annals of the Early Caliphate* (1883) and *The Caliphate: Its Rise, Decline and Fall* (1891). Although written from a Protestant, evangelical standpoint, they nonetheless contain many original historical and linguistic insights.

Muir retired to Britain in 1876 but continued to take an active interest in Indian affairs as a member of the Council of India in

served with distinction during the Peninsular War. He retired from the army in 1815, and after several years devoted to travel and leisure, moved to London in 1824. Here he attended lectures at the Royal Institution which kindled an interest in geology. Fieldwork in England, Scotland (with Adam Sedgwick), France and Italy (with Charles Lyell) led to a series of papers which soon made him one of the most prominent members of the Geological Society. In 1831 he began a study of the Early Palaeozoic rocks in Wales that were to form the basis of his landmark work *The Silurian System*. Published in 1839, this contained many drawings and sketches by his wife and close collaborator Charlotte Hugonin, who has been credited with fostering Murchison's interest in geology. Further geological research in south-western England and the Rhineland helped to establish the Devonian system. He then embarked on an expedition to Russia which led him to elaborate the Permian system and resulted in a further publication, *The Geology of Russia in Europe* (1845). Murchison served two terms as President of the Geological Society of London and four as President of the Royal Geographical Society, of which he was a founding member. He was knighted in 1846 (having previously been decorated with the Russian Order of St Stanislaus). In 1855

London. In 1885, he was appointed Principal of the University of Edinburgh, where he endowed a Chair of Sanskrit and helped his brother John Muir establish the Muir Institute of Oriental Languages.

The collection contains correspondence relating to Muir's administrative career in the North-Western Provinces of India. Of particular importance is his intelligence correspondence during the Indian Rebellion of 1857, a vital historical source. Other papers include letters to Muir's wife from 1840 to 1895.
Coll-1037

Murchison, Roderick

The geologist Sir Roderick Impey Murchison (1792–1871), developed the modern classification of the Palaeozoic period.

Born in Tarradale, Easter Ross, Murchison attended the Military College at Great Marlow, Buckinghamshire, and

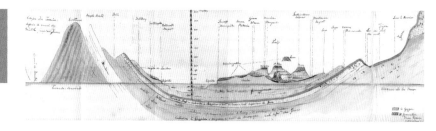

Geological cross-section drawn by Roderick
Murchison's wife Charlotte Hugonin

he was appointed Director of the Geological
Survey of Great Britain, and during the latter
part of his life conducted further geological
research in the Scottish Highlands. In 1871
he helped to found the Chair of Geology and
Mineralogy at the University of Edinburgh.
In his remarkable scientific career Murchison
published more than 180 papers.

The collection includes:
- Murchison's journal, 1792–1815
- personal papers, 1804–1870
- correspondence with Murchison's
  wife, his solicitor and Sir Andrew
  Crombie Ramsay, c.1820–1870.

There are also papers of Murchison's father
Kenneth Murchison (1751–1796), who
purchased the estate of Tarradale, Ross
and Cromarty, after a successful career
as a surgeon in India.

Coll-51

Murray, Kenneth

Sir Kenneth Murray (1930–2013) was a
molecular biologist who was one of the first to
join the University of Edinburgh's Department
of Molecular Biology after its formation

in 1967, becoming Professor of Molecular
Biology in 1976. He became widely known,
along with his wife Noreen, for his work
developing a vaccine against hepatitis B using
gene cloning technology. Murray was one of
the founders of Biogen, a technology company
specialising in drugs for neurological and
autoimmune disorders and cancer. Together
with his wife, Murray established the Darwin
Trust of Edinburgh, a Charitable Trust for
the promotion of research and education in
natural science. He was knighted in 1993.

The collection contains Murray's
laboratory notebooks, research data, diaries,
lecture notes, correspondence with students,
colleagues, societies and institutions, as well
as a personal collection of film and audio
recordings and school notebooks.

Coll-1527

Murray, Noreen

Noreen Murray (née Parker) (1935–2011)
was a molecular geneticist who became well
known for the work she conducted with her
husband Sir Kenneth Murray developing a
vaccine against hepatitis B using gene cloning
technology. She joined the University of
Edinburgh's Department of Molecular
Biology in 1968, becoming Lecturer, Senior
Lecturer and Reader before being appointed

to a personal chair in Molecular Genetics in 1988. She also served as President of the Genetical Society, Vice-President of the Royal Society and was a member of the UK Science and Technology Honours Committee.

The material includes her research papers, notebooks and correspondence with students, colleagues, societies and institutions.

Coll-1528

....

Murry, John Middleton

Writer and reviewer John Middleton Murry (1889–1957) was a prolific and controversial critic, editor and essayist on literary, religious and political themes.

Born in London, Murry studied Classics at Brasenose College, Oxford. His literary career began in 1911 as editor of *Rhythm*, a short-lived quarterly. In 1914, he met D H Lawrence and, the following year, they founded the journal *The Signature* together. Murry's first works were *Fyodor Dostoevsky: A Critical Study* and a novel *Still Life*, both published in 1916. Two further novels and four books of verse followed over the next

decade, but Murry's reputation rests on his work as editor, critic and essayist. As editor of *The Athenaeum* from 1919 to 1921, he published early work by the Bloomsbury Group. As founding editor of *The Adelphi* (later *The New Adelphi*) in 1923, he promoted a vision of modernism which embraced the legacy of Romanticism in opposition to the more classical approach of T S Eliot. His enthusiasm for Romantic verse found further expression in *Keats and Shakespeare* (1925) and *Studies in Keats* (1930). By the late 1920s, however, Murry's interests were shifting from literature to philosophy. In the 1930s he briefly converted to Marxism before slowly moving towards a radical Christian pacifism. Murry was the author of more than 60 books, ranging from further literary studies (John Clare, Jonathan Swift, William Blake) to works on philosophy, politics and religion. He is perhaps best remembered for his promotion of the work of his first wife Katherine Mansfield, and for his friendship with D H Lawrence, which inspired the controversial biography *Son of Woman: The Story of D. H. Lawrence* (1931).

The collection includes:
- manuscripts of monographs, essays, reviews, lectures and speeches
- notes and notebooks
- albums of press cuttings from 1939 to 1947
- letters and letterbooks
- diaries
- publishing contracts
- galley proofs.

Album of cuttings from *Peace News*, an anti-war journal edited by John Middleton Murry

There is also a collection of 32 books by or about John Middleton Murry, including his daughter Mary Middleton Murry's heavily annotated proof copy of her memoir *To Keep Faith* and her own annotated copy of Frank Lea's biography, *The Life of John Middleton Murry*. The majority of the books are presentation copies to Mary Middleton Murry or to her long-time companion Ruth Barker. They are to be found at shelfmarks SC 6965–6998 and JA 4085–4086. *Coll-62*

Nelson, Thomas

The Papers of Thomas Nelson & Sons are an outstanding publishing archive.

The British publishing firm of Nelson is still a prominent name. It began as a small bookselling business in the West Bow of Edinburgh in 1798, founded by Thomas Neilson (1780–1861). Neilson gradually extended his activities to include publishing, beginning with the appearance, in monthly parts, of Bunyan's *The Pilgrim's Progress*. Thus was established the formula of reprinting standard authors at low prices that would bring him international success. In 1818, the name of the firm was changed to Thomas Nelson due to customers' habit of misspelling Neilson. In 1835, Thomas was joined in the business by his son William and a little later by his younger son Thomas. The business continued to grow and branches were opened in London and New York.

In 1845–1846, the firm moved to larger custom-built premises at Hope Park just to the south of Edinburgh city centre. There, with a workforce of 600, all activities were carried out under one roof: printing, stereotyping, bookbinding, lithographing, engraving, woodcutting, warehousing and even dyeing of the plain white calico used in bindings. From 1856, colour-printing became a feature of their production and by 1860 the firm (now called Thomas Nelson and Sons) was the leading publisher of cheap colour-printed titles. From his earliest years with the firm, Thomas Nelson Junior exhibited a mechanical bent and in 1850 he invented a rotary press which was the forerunner of the presses used in the newspaper industry well into the 20th century.

Nelson's production focused on story books, religious books and books of travel and adventure by popular authors, particularly intended for young readers. A series of schoolbooks was initiated, and after the Education Act of 1871, which had prompted a demand for improved schoolbooks, Nelson's began its series of Royal Readers. In 1906 novelist John Buchan (1875–1940), became a partner and literary adviser and the firm also published his work. Other authors published include Walter Bagehot, Hilaire Belloc, G K Chesterton, Erskine Childers, Henry Newbolt, Mark Twain and H G Wells.

The papers include:
- general day books, general ledgers, account books, details of creditors, letter books and commission books for the years 1861–1915
- general correspondence, 1895–1960

- material from trade representatives and sales department material.

Within the Nelson Papers are more than 4,700 letters exchanged between John Buchan and Nelson's covering the years 1909–1929. The correspondence includes letters about manuscripts submitted from authors, illustrations for works, translations of works published, terms of contract and royalties, and new work published by other firms. The correspondence also deals with Buchan's own writing.

In 2012, the University received a donation of the file copies of more than 10,000 Nelson books from the late 19th century to the 1980s, from the successor company Nelson Thornes. These await listing.

Coll-25

New College Library

(For further description of the Library see entry
under Rare Books.)

New College Library holds rich and varied
theological collections mainly concerning:

- significant individuals or groups
  connected with New College 1843–
  1930 or Edinburgh University School
  of Divinity after 1930
- noteworthy individuals from the
  Church of Scotland or Free Church
  of Scotland, 1843–1930
- individuals or organisations significant
  to the religious life of Scotland.

There are also the archives of New College
itself including administrative records, class
photographs, student magazines, information
relating to student societies, as well as materials
relating to the history of the New College

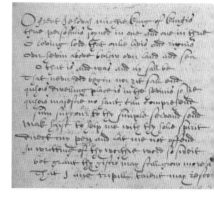

Sermon on Hebrews 11 by Robert Bruce,
Edinburgh, c.1590

building. Incorporating the collections of the
General Assembly of the Church of Scotland,
this is a valuable resource for theology, church
history and biblical history. The collection
extends to paintings and museum objects.

Paper catalogues for all of the collections
are kept in New College Library and some
catalogues are available online.

Thomas Chalmers Papers

The Reverend Thomas Chalmers (1780–1847),
Professor of Divinity at the University of
Edinburgh, made a stand against church
patronage resulting in the Disruption in
1843 when he led about one-third of Church
ministers to form the Free Church of Scotland.
He became the first Moderator of the General
Assembly of the Free Church of Scotland,
and was one of the founding fathers of New
College, Edinburgh. The majority of his
papers are held in New College Library,
comprising some 16,000 items, and are a
major archival source for British church

The grass withereth, the
flower fadeth; but the
word of our God shall
stand for ever.

Isaiah 40.8

Bible plants from Syria, presented to Reverend
Thomas Young, Ellon, Aberdeenshire, 1887

Illuminated manuscript of Rashi's commentary on Deuteronomy, undated

concern, who studied theology at New College and in Germany. He was organising secretary for the 1910 World Missionary Conference at Edinburgh, often deemed the start of modern ecumenism, and in 1912 founded the *International Review of Missions* which became the world's most prominent missionary periodical. A keen internationalist, Oldham advised the government on missions and German missionaries in particular during the First World War. He founded the International Missionary Council in 1921 and travelled widely, becoming an authority and mediator on issues raised by colonial administration in Africa. Oldham argued for greater cooperation between religious and secular groups, and his influence led to the formation of the World Council of Churches. During the Second World War he continued to encourage debate about lay responsibility in society. At his 'Moot' meetings with such figures as T S Eliot and John Baillie and through his Christian newsletter he initiated much new thinking about Christianity in modern society.

The papers comprise correspondence on his work in India, the 1910 World Missionary Conference, the 1937 Oxford conference and the World Council of Churches, German missionaries and Germany in the 1930s, Indian and African issues, publications and lectures. There are minutes, papers and reports relating to the Moot; drafts of books; extracts from journals by his secretary Betty Gibson (1889–1973) recording trips overseas; engagement diaries; photographs; and research notes by biographers on his life.
Coll-140

and social life during his lifetime. There are papers on his family's mercantile business in Anstruther, Fife; letters between family members; Chalmers' own correspondence including letters from significant figures of the day; professional papers on matters such as St John's, Glasgow, where he was concerned with people in poverty; his time at St Andrew's University where he was Professor of Moral Philosophy; the Convocation of 1842; and the Irish Famine. There are also journals, sermons, short-hand sermons, notebooks, essays, speeches and lectures.
MS CHA

J H Oldham Papers

Joseph Houldsworth Oldham (1874–1969) was a pioneer of ecumenism and social

Robert Baillie Papers

The Reverend Professor Robert Baillie (1599–1662) was a Church of Scotland minister and Principal of Glasgow University. The papers include letters and journals from 1637 to 1662, which covers his time as chaplain in the Covenanter army, appointment as Professor of Divinity at Glasgow, involvement in the Westminster Assembly of 1643, and his journey to the Netherlands in 1649 to persuade Charles II to accept the Covenant and the Crown. There are two manuscript copies of his letters and journals in different hands. There are also sermons, speeches and a list of his books.
MS BAILL

James Denney Papers

The Very Reverend James Denney (1856–1917) was born in Paisley, educated in Greenock, Glasgow University and the Free Church College in Glasgow. He was minister in East Free Church Broughty Ferry, Angus until he was appointed to the Chair of Systematic and Pastoral Theology at Glasgow Free Church College in 1897. He later became Professor of New Testament Language, Literature and Theology and then Principal of the College in 1915. His papers contain a substantial number of sermons and lectures, his own student notes and essays, and biographical notes on figures such as Thomas Chalmers (1780–1847).
MS DEN

James King Hewison Papers

The Reverend James King Hewison (1853–1941) was a parish minister in Rothesay for 40 years. His main interests were in the Covenanters, the history and lore of Dumfriesshire and Bute, church lands and freemasonry. He compiled several substantial scrapbooks on these topics which include printed pamphlets, articles, poems, illustrations and photographs. The collection includes manuscripts and correspondence relating to his publications including *The Covenanters*, *Ninian Winzet* and *Dalgarnoc: Its Saints and Heroes*. There are also personal papers.
MS HEW

James Kirkwood Papers

The Reverend James Kirkwood (c.1650–1708) was a Church of Scotland minister at Stair and in Minto who left for England in 1681 owing to the religious unrest of the time. His collection mainly deals with the provision of libraries in the Highlands and Islands and the distribution of Irish (Gaelic) Bibles in those areas, which also involved the physicist Sir Robert Boyle (1627–1691). There are also letters on charity schools and the Society for the Propagation of Christian Knowledge (SPCK).
MS KIR

Manuscript Sermons

A series of notebooks of sermons preached in Scotland from 1648 to c.1805, many of which were originally in the General Assembly Library. The sermons were mostly written by the preacher but in some instances they were recorded by another individual. The majority of the notebooks cover the Covenanting period and immediately thereafter and include sermons by Samuel Rutherford (1600–1661),

Last speech and testimony of
James Renwick, 13 February 1688

Donald Cargill (1619–1681), Richard
Cameron (c.1648–1680), James Renwick
(1662–1688) and Thomas Boston (1676–
1732). There are also shorthand sermons.
Similar sermon notebooks can be found
elsewhere in the University's collections.
MS SER

Robert Murray McCheyne Papers

The Reverend Robert Murray McCheyne
(1813–1843) was a Church of Scotland
minister. His papers include personal
and family correspondence; notebooks
of poetry; sermons and discourses; class
notes, including some delivered by Thomas
Chalmers (1780–1847); and papers on his
participation in the Kirk's deputation to
Palestine to investigate establishing a mission
to the Jews. Included in his Palestine papers
are a diary, sketches and poetry. He died aged
29, two months before the Disruption in
1843, and has subsequently been revered in
Presbyterian circles.
MS MACCH

John McIntyre Papers

The Very Reverend Professor John McIntyre
(1916–2005) was a minister of the Church
of Scotland and theologian. His academic
posts included Professor of Divinity in the
University of Edinburgh (1956–1986),
Principal of New College and Dean of
the Faculty of Divinity (1968–1974), and
acting Principal and Vice-Chancellor of the

University of Edinburgh (1973–1974 and
again in 1979). He was also Moderator of the
General Assembly in 1982–1983. His papers
include sermons, lectures, correspondence,
personal papers, papers and tapes relating to
broadcasts, publications and papers relating to
his time as Dean of the Thistle (1974–1980).
AA 4

Norman Walker Porteous Papers

Professor Norman Walker Porteous (1898–
2003) was Professor of Hebrew and Semitic
Languages at the University of Edinburgh,
Principal of New College and Dean of the
Faculty of Divinity. When he died he was
the University's oldest graduate and the last
surviving military officer of the First World
War. His interests lay in the Old Testament
and his papers contain correspondence with
many notable theologians including Karl
Barth (1886–1968), Rudolf Bultmann (1884–
1976), Walter Eichrodt (1890–1978) and
Otto Eissfeldt (1887–1973). He was involved
in the translation of the New English Bible.
MS POR 1, MS POR B1

Oliver Shaw Rankin Papers

The Reverend Professor Oliver Shaw Rankin (1885–1954) was Professor of Old Testament Language, Literature and Theology at New College. His collection includes lectures and sermon notes; lectures given in German at Berlin University; typescript for his posthumous work *Jewish Religious Polemic*; notes on the festival of Hanukkah; history of the religion of Israel; Old Testament theology and a European travel diary.
MS RAN

James S Stewart Papers

A minister in Aberdeen and Edinburgh, the Very Reverend Professor James Stewart (1896–1990) was Professor of New Testament Language, Literature and Theology at the University of Edinburgh from 1947 to 1966, and Moderator of the General Assembly in 1963. He was an influential preacher and author. His papers encompass his lectures, sermons, letters, parish ministry, broadcasts and the papers relating to his moderatorial year.
MS STE

Alexander Thomson of Banchory-Devenick Papers

Alexander Thomson of Banchory-Devenick (1798–1868) was an antiquarian and local laird. His substantial collection contains family papers; personal diaries which include accounts of travel around Europe; writings on antiquities such as the Newton Stone at Garioch; papers on prisons and industrial schools; papers on heritors and the Disruption of 1843, including preparation for creating a Free Church; and general correspondence from 1797 to 1868.
MS THO

John White Papers

The Very Reverend John White (1867–1951) was Moderator of the General Assembly of the Church of Scotland in 1925 and 1929, when the United Free Church reunited with the Kirk, a move which he had instigated. He had controversial views on Irish immigration to Scotland overseeing the report 'The menace of the Irish race to our Scottish nationality', which decades later was repudiated by the Kirk. His papers contain letters, sermons and speeches on these topics, his parish ministry and on the Church Extension Scheme to build churches in housing estates.
MS WHI

James Whyte Papers

The Very Reverend Professor James Whyte (1920–2005) was a leading Scottish theologian and Moderator of the General Assembly of the Church of Scotland in 1988–1989. His papers cover his parish ministries in Dunollie Road, Oban and Mayfield North, Edinburgh; his moderatorial year; and his time as Chair of Practical Theology and Christian Ethics at St Andrews University. His main interests were in liturgy, ecclesiastical architecture and pastoral care. As Moderator he preached at the memorial service for victims of the Lockerbie bombing and in 1996 he was called on to do the same for the victims of the Dunblane Massacre.
AA 5

Centre for the Study of World Christianity

The Centre for the Study of World Christianity (CSWC) archives are housed at New College and contain records relating to the history of world Christianity and the missionary movement. The collections include the records of missionary societies such as Latin Link (formerly the Evangelical Union of South America), the Regions Beyond Missionary Union, Sudan United Mission/Action Partners (now Pioneers); a substantial collection of private and missionary papers; and photographic material. Further details are given below.

Some CSWC catalogues are available online; and some lantern slides can be seen on the International Mission Photography Archive (c.1860–c.1960) website.

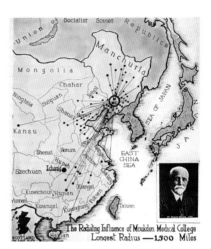

Map of the influence of Moukden Medical College, c.1935

CSWC: Church of Scotland Foreign Mission

The CSWC holds three collections originating from the Church of Scotland Foreign Mission Committee. The first concerns Manchuria, China, including records on Moukden Medical College, letters from missionaries, minutes, reports, photographs, maps and artefacts. The second contains slides and visual materials from the late 19th century to the 1980s, created by missionaries, often for educational purposes, in China, Asia, the Middle East, Africa and the Caribbean. The third collection is concerned with India and Nepal and contains minutes of missions in Rajasthan, Calcutta and Santhal; and records of Madras Christian College and Wilson College, Bombay.
CSWC40, CSWC41, CSWC47

CSWC: Regions Beyond Missionary Union

The Regions Beyond Missionary Union (RBMU) began in 1873, founded by Henry Grattan Guinness (1835–1910). It ran training colleges and sent missionaries to India, Nepal, Congo, Peru, Argentina, Kalimantan and Irian Jaya. The collection contains administrative records, letters from missionaries, reports, photographs, lantern slides, maps and audiovisual material from its establishment until the 1990s.
CSWC33

CSWC: Latin Link

Latin Link was previously known as the Evangelical Union of South America (EUSA), which was formed from three missions working in South America: Regions Beyond Missionary Union (RBMU) (Peru and Argentina), South American Evangelical

161

Mission (Argentina and Brazil) and Help
For Brazil. It later merged with the British
Andes Evangelical Mission and in 1990
merged with RBMU to form Latin Link. The
collection covers 1870–2012 and includes
minutes, circulars, records of committees,
correspondence, lantern slides, audiovisual
material and records of the mission's farms,
clinics and educational interests.
CSWC51

Nye, Robert

Robert Nye (1939–) is a versatile and
highly original poet, novelist and children's
writer, whose work draws on Celtic myth
and legend.

Born in London, Nye worked at a
variety of jobs – from milkman to newspaper
reporter – before moving to North Wales
in 1961 to devote himself fully to writing.
There he developed an interest in Celtic myth
and folklore which is reflected in many of his
own writings. Nye achieved critical acclaim
with his first two poetry collections, *Juvenilia
1* (1961) and *Juvenilia 2* (1963). At the same
time he began to contribute reviews to literary
journals and newspapers. He became poetry
editor for *The Scotsman* in 1967, and poetry
critic of *The Times* in 1971, besides regularly
reviewing fiction for the *Guardian*. While
continuing to publish poetry, Nye branched
out into children's writing in 1966 with *Taliesin*
and *March Has Horse's Ears*, both retellings of
Welsh legends. Over the following decades
Nye also became an acclaimed novelist for
adults with works such as *Doubtfire* (1967), the
Hawthornden Prize-winning *Falstaff* (1976),

Merlin (1978), and – for many critics, his
masterpiece – *The Life and Death of my Lord
Gilles de Rais* (1990). Nye has also published
plays, anthologies and editions of poets such
as Laura Riding, Ernest Dowson and Thomas
Chatterton. Nye lived in Edinburgh in the
1970s, serving as the University of Edinburgh's
Writer in Residence in 1976–1977.

The collection includes published and
unpublished manuscripts, drafts, working
notes, proofs, correspondence, source
materials and publishing house materials.
Coll-54

Oriental Manuscripts

The collection of more than 700 oriental
manuscripts includes some of the greatest
treasures of Edinburgh University Library.
The manuscripts are mainly Islamic, written
in Arabic or Persian, but there are also Jewish
Torah scrolls, Buddhist texts on palm leaves,
and Hindu manuscripts.

The Al-Bîrûnî, Rashid al-Din and
Mahabharata manuscripts (see Iconic

Pages from the *Mukhtasar Kitab al-Hisnul-Hasin*

Collections) are the best-known items. Other treasures include a beautiful Koran (Or.MS148) which belonged to Tipu-Sahib, Sultan of Mysore, AD 1749–1799, who was killed in the battle to defend his city, Seringapatam, against the British. Arabic manuscripts include commentaries on the Koran and works on subjects as diverse as traditions of the Prophet, prayers, law, general history and biography, medicine, mathematics, philosophy and ethics, grammar, rhetoric, poetry, prose, tales, dictionaries and controversy. Persian manuscripts cover theology, history, biography, travel, mathematics, astronomy, ethics, poetry, music, composition, proverbs, tales and romances, grammar, dictionaries, agriculture and war. Hindustani manuscripts deal with history, poetry, tales and astrology. Turkish manuscripts include material acquired in Astrakhan with several early Ottoman texts, diwans of Nava'i and items of dialect interest. There are also about 100 bundles or parcels of Buddhist works on palm leaves in Burmese, Pali, Sanskrit, Siamese,

Tipu-Sahib's Koran

Tamil and Tibetan. In addition, there are Sanskrit charters on copper plates. Other languages represented include Ethiopic/ Amharic, Armenian, Bengali, Cambodian, Hindustani, Javanese, Malay, Mon, Panjabi, Prakrit, Sinhalese, Syriac and Urdu.

The collection includes material gathered by Lieutenant-Colonel John Baillie of Leys and presented to the Library in 1876 by his grandson, Mr John B Baillie. Other donors to the collection were R M B Binning of the Indian Civil Service, George Bell MD, and the Reverend John Dickson who had been a missionary in Astrakhan. A number of manuscripts came with the David Laing bequest, including several fragments of a 9th-century Koran, at one time in the Mosque of Amr in Fustat — the first mosque in Egypt and indeed Africa (Or.MS.175).

In recent years, the collection has been augmented through further purchases,

including 40 manuscripts from the Ottoman provinces and Iran, dating mostly from the 18th and 19th centuries, and an illuminated prayer book from northern Nigeria, of 29 folios, each with lines of black stylised *maghribi*, with various illuminated panels and medallions.

The collection is not yet catalogued online. See Mohammed Hukk, *A Descriptive Catalogue of the Arabic and Persian Manuscripts in Edinburgh University Library* (Edinburgh, 1925) and R B Serjeant, *A Handlist of the Arabic, Persian and Hindustani MSS. of New College, Edinburgh* (London, 1942).

Coll-102

John Orr, photograph by Edward Drummond Young

Orr, John

John Orr (1885–1966) was a French medieval scholar who played a major role in the rebuilding of Caen after it was devastated by bombing in the Second World War.

Born in Cumberland but raised in Australia, Orr read Classics at the University of Tasmania. In 1905 he won a Rhodes Scholarship to Balliol College, Oxford, and graduated in 1909 with honours in Classical Moderations and in Law. A rest cure in France the following year stimulated an interest in medieval French and Romance linguistics. He went on to study Romance languages and literature at the Sorbonne and Florence before graduating BLitt at Oxford in 1913. After lecturing at Manchester University and East London College, he was seconded to the

Admiralty in 1916 and then to the Military Intelligence Corps in France. In 1919 he was appointed to the Chair of French at the University of Manchester. He published a number of significant articles before moving, in 1933, to the Chair of French at the University of Edinburgh.

In 1944 Orr played a key role in providing aid to the town and university of Caen, following bombardment by allied forces. He founded the Edinburgh-Caen Fellowship, which organised donations in the form of money, clothes, food and books for the university library. In recognition of his contribution, the reopened Caen University awarded him a doctorate *honoris causae* in 1945.

Orr continued his academic career after the war. He was instrumental in the creation of a new chair of French Literature in 1951 (which saw his own chair renamed as French Language and Romance Linguistics). From

Ragamala miniature

165

1951 until his retirement in 1955, he was also Dean of the Faculty of Arts. Between 1963 and 1966 he was President of the International Federation of Modern Languages and Literature. His many publications focused primarily on medieval Romance linguistics.

The papers consist of correspondence, lectures and other material mainly about Romance linguistics. There is a scrapbook of wartime newspaper cuttings, and photographic material relating to Caen. There are also rolled maps and linguistic charts.

Professor Orr also donated a large number of books to the University Library, some 300 of which have been reconstituted as a named special collection. They include early books in French, Italian and English, and annotated copies of his own works.
Coll-77

Papyrus fragment, Aratus, *Diosemeia*, 2nd century AD

Papyrus Manuscripts

Our oldest manuscripts

Towards the end of the 19th century, archaeologists discovered a rubbish dump near Oxyrhynchus in Egypt, where a vast number of ancient manuscript fragments were miraculously preserved. Primarily in Greek and Latin, the fragments provide information about many literary and theological works which are now lost or only known from later copies. They are now be to found in libraries all across the world. Edinburgh University Library has 18 fragments, the oldest being copies of tax receipts dating from about AD 17–19 (P.Oxy.309). One of the most important fragments is from the *Diosemia* ('Forecasts') of Aratus, dating from the 2nd century AD. Aratus (c. 315/310–240 BC) was a Greek didactic poet, whose work is a compendium of weather lore (P.Oxy.1807). All the fragments are catalogued in the online Gazetteer of Papyri in British Collections. They have been conserved and are mounted in glass for ease of study and display.
P.Oxy

Phrenological Society of Edinburgh

A popular pseudo-science, phrenology was the study of the structure of the human skull to determine an individual's character, inclinations and mental capacities.

George Combe, founder of the Phrenological Society of Edinburgh, photograph by D O Hill and Robert Adamson

in phrenology, and collected data that might 'improve and enlarge the boundaries of the Science'.

The records include:
- minute books for 1841–1870
- a letter-book covering the period 1820–1840
- a cash book
- catalogues of skull casts
- six notebooks including lecture titles, names of members and names of visitors who inspected the casts
- a memoir on the 'phrenology of Hindostan' read to the Society in 1823
- scrapbooks of newspaper cuttings
- printed items.

Coll-227

Its principles were established by Franz-Joseph Gall (1758–1828), Johann Gaspar Spurzheim (1776–1832) and George Combe of Edinburgh (1788–1858). Gall studied the heads of prisoners and inmates of lunatic asylums, and from his observations, mapped out where innate tendencies to 'murder', 'theft' or other crimes were seated in the brain. Spurzheim and Combe went on to divide the scalp into regions that were home to different traits: acquisitiveness, benevolence, combativity, self-esteem, wit, wonder, etc. Although now thoroughly discredited, phrenology remained popular and influential throughout the 19th century and is of significant historical and social interest.

Edinburgh was the British centre for phrenology. The Phrenological Society of Edinburgh was founded by George Combe on 22 February 1820. Its object was to hear papers and discuss questions connected with phrenology. It held correspondence with societies and individuals interested

Playfair, William Henry

Architect William Henry Playfair (1790–1857) is responsible for many of the neo-classical landmarks of Edinburgh's New Town and for completing the University of Edinburgh's Old College building.

Born in London, Playfair was the son of architect James Playfair (1755–1794), who died when William was four years old. He was sent to live with his uncle, John Playfair, Professor of Mathematics at the University of Edinburgh. After studying at the university himself, he embarked on an architectural career. His first public appointment was to lay out part of the New Town of Edinburgh in 1815. He fully established himself in the profession by winning the commission in 1817 to complete the unfinished new University building (leaving the front as designed by Robert and James Adam). The buildings now known as Old College include the sublime Playfair Library. He also designed the city's Royal Terrace and Regent Terrace, the unfinished National Monument on Calton Hill, the Royal Scottish Academy and the National Gallery on the Mound. Playfair's most important works in Edinburgh were executed in the Greek revivalist or classical style – confirming Edinburgh's title of 'Athens of the North' – but he was competent in other styles too. A later commission, New College, Edinburgh, is a jagged-lined rendering of the Gothic style. He also built country houses and mansions in the Italianate and Tudor styles.

After Playfair's death, his drawings were offered to the Library. The University expressed willingness to accept them, but requested that they be catalogued first. Playfair's trustees thus retained James A Hamilton, Playfair's clerk, to sort and catalogue the drawings. More than 5,000 drawings were eventually presented to the University. However, an almost equal amount of material was apparently discarded by Hamilton as unsuitable.

The drawings range from Playfair's student drawings, through sketch designs and preliminary schemes, to many presentation drawings in watercolours. The earliest catalogued plans, elevations and sections relate to the commission to complete the new University building from 1817 onwards. In total there are 5,062 drawings.

Coll-13

Elevation of the Royal College of Surgeons by William Henry Playfair, 1832

Pollock, Martin Rivers

Martin Rivers Pollock (1914–1999) established molecular biology as a distinct discipline at the forefront of the genetic engineering revolution of the late 20th century.

Born in Liverpool, Pollock attended Winchester College and Trinity College, Cambridge, where he studied medicine. He completed his medical training at University College Hospital Medical School, qualifying MB, BChir in 1940. Pollock held hospital appointments at University College Hospital and Brompton Chest Hospital 1939–1941 before joining the Emergency Public Health Laboratory Service as a bacteriologist in 1941.

In 1943 he was seconded to a Medical Research Council unit to work on infective hepatitis. In 1945 Pollock was formally taken onto the staff of the Medical Research Council. He worked at the National Institute for Medical Research (NIMR), Mill Hill, London, initially under Sir Paul Fildes before being appointed Head of the Division of Bacterial Physiology in 1949. He remained at the NIMR to 1965, spending two periods (1948 and 1952–1953) studying in the laboratory of Jacques Monod at the Institut Pasteur, Paris.

Pollock looked to establish a unit for teaching and research in molecular biology, which would bring together bacterial genetics and biochemistry, and a number of possible locations had been evaluated. Michael Swann, the Dean of the Faculty of Science at the University of Edinburgh, persuaded Pollock to move north, and in 1965 Pollock was appointed Professor of Biology at the University of Edinburgh. Shortly afterwards, his colleague William Hayes moved from the MRC Unit for Bacterial Genetics at Hammersmith Hospital in London. Together they established at Edinburgh the Department of Molecular Biology, the first such teaching department in the world. Pollock took early retirement in 1976, moving to Dorset. He took no further active part in scientific research but maintained his growing interest in the relationship between science and art, organising a major conference on the subject in 1981. Pollock's 30 years of scientific research from the end of the Second World War, both at the NIMR and the University of Edinburgh, focused on enzyme induction in bacteria. He studied the mechanism by which beta-lactamase enzymes (particularly penicillinase) are involved in the development of bacterial resistance to antibiotics. For his contributions in this area Pollock was elected to the Fellowship of the Royal Society in 1962. In the 1970s Pollock became interested in developments in biotechnology and artificial intelligence, encouraging interdepartmental cooperation in these areas.

The collection reflects all aspects of Pollock's work and covers the whole of his adult life. It is divided into the following sections:

- biographical
- Medical Research Council
- University of Edinburgh
- research
- drafts and publications
- lectures and broadcasts
- societies and organisations
- politics
- tape recordings of conferences
- correspondence.

Coll-1586

Robertson, Jeanie

The Scottish traditional folk singer Jeanie Robertson (1908–1975) was from a travelling family from the north-east of Scotland. Robertson sang in the old style, having learned most of her songs through the oral tradition of her family. Her singing was introduced to a wider public on a self-titled 1959 LP. Widely regarded as a seminal figure in the music culture of Scotland's travelling people Jeanie was a contemporary of Jimmy McBeth, Belle Stewart and Flora MacNeil. In recognition of her services to traditional music she was awarded the MBE in 1968.

The collection is largely composed of some 160 letters from Robertson to the folklorist and poet Hamish Henderson (1919–2002). It also contains her Equity card and a recording contract.

Coll-725

Robison, John

John Robison (1739–1805) was a scientist and mathematician, who invented the siren and worked with James Watt on an early steam car.

Robison studied at Glasgow Grammar School and Glasgow University, where he graduated MA in 1756. He then travelled to Canada as a private tutor to the son of Admiral Charles Knowles and made surveys of the St Lawrence Rover and neighbouring territory. In 1762, he was commissioned by the Board of Longitude to take charge of John Harrison's chronometer on its trial voyage to Jamaica. Returning to Glasgow, he conducted experiments with James Watt, and in 1766 was appointed Lecturer in Chemistry at Glasgow University. In 1770 he went to Russia as private secretary to Admiral Knowles, who had been charged with reorganising the Russian navy. Two years later, Robison was appointed Professor of Mathematics at Kronstadt, the training college for the imperial sea cadet corps. He returned to Scotland in 1773 to take up the Chair of Natural Philosophy at Edinburgh.

Robison's writings were varied and influential. Between 1793 and 1801 he contributed well over 40 articles to the third edition of the *Encyclopaedia Britannica* (1797) and its supplement on topics ranging from 'Resistance of Fluids' to 'Seamanship'. In 1803 he produced his edition of Joseph Black's *Lectures on the Elements of Chemistry* and the following year he published his own *Elements of Mechanical Philosophy* (1804). Robison's most widely read work, however, was of a less scientific nature: *Proofs of a Conspiracy against All the Religions and Governments of Europe, Carried on in the Secret Meetings of Free Masons, Illuminati, and Reading Societies* (1797).

John Robison (1798)
Sir Henry Raeburn
© The University of Edinburgh

Trans. Roy. Soc. Edin.　　　　　　　　　　　Vol. LIX.

J. P. Chu : "Studies on Plumage in the Male Brown Leghorn Fowl."—Plate IV.

J. P. Chu, photo.

Plate from J P Chu, 'Studies on Plumage in the Male Brown Leghorn Fowl'

The collection consists of lecture notes from Robison's tenure as Professor of Natural Philosophy at the University of Edinburgh. They cover the sciences of mechanics, hydrodynamics, astronomy, optics, electricity and magnetism; and also touch on a wide range of other subjects, including musical chords, canals and gunpowder.

Coll-204

Roslin Institute

To many, the word 'Roslin' is synonymous with modern advances in animal genetics, above all the cloning of Dolly the sheep in 1996. Since the Institute was founded as an independent entity in 1993, it has been a major international centre for genetics and genomics research and its collections have outstanding significance.

The Roslin Institute has its roots in the University of Edinburgh's Institute of Animal Genetics, established in 1919, and its many related bodies and research units. In 1986, two of these, the Poultry Research Centre and Animal Breeding Research Organisation (ABRO) combined with the Institute of Animal Physiology based at Babraham, Cambridge, to form the Institute of Animal Physiology and Genetics Research (IAPGR), with twin sites in Cambridge and in Roslin, outside Edinburgh. In 1992, the Agriculture and Food Research Council opted to develop Roslin and Babraham as two independent institutes, and on 1 April

1993, the Roslin Institute was established as an independent institute of the Biotechnology and Biological Sciences Research Council with Professor Grahame Bulfield as its first director. After the success of Dolly the sheep, cloned at Roslin in 1996, several separate companies were formed to exploit the potential of the new technologies. The Roslin Institute merged with the University of Edinburgh in 2008.

This collection consists of:

- books from the Roslin Institute Library
- bound offprints from the Roslin Institute and its various predecessor bodies (the Animal Breeding Research Organisation, the Poultry Research Centre and the Edinburgh Research Station of IAPGR) (Coll-1362)
- a large amount of archival material, including annual reports, press cuttings, information concerning research projects and commercial partnerships, and the departmental papers of the Institute Director and Secretary (EUA IN23).

Roslin Slide Collection

This collection of 3,465 glass positive slides was acquired from the Roslin Institute (see page 171). The slides, which date from the 1870s to the 1930s, cover a wide range of subjects: photographs of indigenous peoples from around the world and scenes documenting research trips; personal portraits (frequently of figures connected with the natural or veterinary sciences); photographs and drawings of domestic animals and illustrations and extracts from books, articles and newspapers. The majority of the slides are black and white, although some are hand-coloured or tinted.

It is thought that at least part of the collection was created for teaching purposes by James Cossar Ewart and Robert Wallace, who were respectively Professor of Natural History and Professor of Agriculture and Rural Economy at the University of Edinburgh. Both Ewart and Wallace appear (separately) in the slides, as do colleagues and other persons known to both or either of the men. While some of the slides appear to be directly associated with Ewart or Wallace, it is supposed that a portion of the collection may have been sent to them by colleagues from around the world. The collection is fully catalogued and digitised. *Coll-1434*

'Maori Man', Roslin Slide Collection

Salvesen, Christian

Based in Leith, Christian Salvesen became one of the biggest whaling companies in the world.

The extensive business archive of Christian Salvesen Ltd was formally transferred to the University of Edinburgh in 2012. The firm was founded in 1872 by Norwegian-born Christian Fredrik Salvesen who set up in Bernard Street, Leith as a shipbroker and shipowner. This was the golden age of the steamship and maritime commerce was booming. In the 1880s, Salvesen was joined by three of his sons who continued the business after his death in 1911. By then the firm's vessels were trading with ports on the Baltic, and in Norway and Sweden, and were servicing whaling stations in the Arctic, Iceland and the Faroe Islands. Cargo lines were also opened up between Leith, Malta and Alexandria, and then into the Black Sea. In the early decades of the 20th century, whaling came to dominate Salvesen's business, with interests extending as far as the Falkland Islands and South Georgia. Indeed the firm led the whaling industry at a time when the Antarctic was considered a boundless resource. As stocks began to diminish after the Second World

War, however, it was prominent in urging conservation. The firm diversified into other areas of commerce, emerging as a major frozen food merchant. In October 2007, it became a wholly owned subsidiary of the French-based transport and logistics provider Norbert Dentressangle.

The archives cover the period from the 1850s to the 1960s. They contain ledgers, private journals, cash books, invoice books, letter books, day books, station records, stock books and accounts, correspondence, order books and records of telegrams. There is material relating to Salvesen ships, including voyage books, photographs and ledgers. There are particulars of ports arranged alphabetically. The collection also includes material on whaling including sales and purchases of whale products, catch records and scientific results of marine biological research. Material on the Salvesen partners themselves includes financial papers, investment registers, personal papers, diaries, notebooks, letter books, letters, and estate matters and staff material. There are also Salvesen family papers.

The papers of Sir Gerald Elliot, former Chairman of Salvesens, were acquired in 2012 (Coll-1357).

Coll-36

Sang, James Henderson

James Henderson Sang (1912–2002) conducted research into the genetics of the fruit fly, which has enhanced our capacity to combat disease.

Born in Aberdeen, Sang was educated at Robert Gordon's College and the University of Aberdeen, where he graduated in zoology in 1933. Following postgraduate research at St John's College, Cambridge, he was appointed Assistant Lecturer in Natural History at the University of Aberdeen in 1938. After serving in the Ministry of Aircraft Production during the Second World War, Sang joined the staff of the Institute of Animal Genetics at the University of Edinburgh in 1947. In 1951, he transferred to the adjacent Poultry Research Centre, where he conducted important work on the nutrition and population growth of the fruit fly *Drosophila*, developing a synthetic culture medium which became an essential tool for physiological genetics. In 1965 Sang was appointed to a professorship in the School of Biology at the University of Sussex where he established a research centre dedicated to the study of *Drosophila* development.

'Prospecting Cruise to South Georgia and Antarctica, 1913–1914', photograph by David Ferguson

173

Here he discovered methods of manipulating early embryos, using molecular biology to tackle problems which he had uncovered over the course of his research. Sang was elected Fellow of the Royal Society of Edinburgh in 1959 and was a life member of the Genetics Society of Great Britain.

The papers cover the period 1948–1951, when Sang was employed at the Institute of Animal Genetics, and are mainly connected with an Agricultural Research Council enquiry into staffing and personal tensions within the Institute which eventually led to the creation of separate units for animal breeders and experimental geneticists. *Coll-1391*

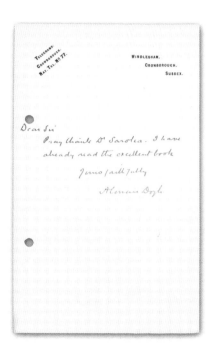

Letter from Arthur Conan Doyle to Charles Sarolea

Sarolea, Charles

Charles Sarolea (1870–1953) was a prolific and controversial commentator on a wide range of political, philosophical and literary topics.

Born in Tongeren in the Belgian province of Limburg, Sarolea was educated at the University of Liège, graduating in Classics and philosophy. In 1894 he was appointed to the newly founded lectureship in French at the University of Edinburgh and in 1918 he became the University's first Professor of French. He held the Chair of French until his resignation in 1931. Although Sarolea published important works on French language and literature, his interests extended well beyond academia. He wrote thousands of articles on a wide range of political, philosophical and literary subjects, and was a tireless lecturer and campaigner. An exceptionally gifted linguist, he was reputed to speak more than 20 languages. Sarolea became a naturalised British citizen in November 1912, but for over 50 years he represented Belgium as its Consul, latterly Consul-General, in Edinburgh. He was also primarily responsible for the Collection Nelson, the successful French-language publishing venture by Nelsons of Edinburgh (see page 154). An avid book-collector, his private library of some 200,000 works was one of the largest private libraries in Europe. In the 1930s, Sarolea's fierce anti-communism led him to sympathise with European Fascist movements, which has coloured the recent reception of his work.

The collection covers the years 1897–1952 and contains material relating to all of Sarolea's many activities and interests.

It consists of four main divisions:

- papers relating to the weekly literary journal *Everyman*, which Sarolea founded and edited
- papers and correspondence relating to his work at the University of Edinburgh
- his writings, comprising drafts of books, chapters, articles for journals and newspapers, university lectures, speeches and radio talks
- miscellaneous papers, including family letters and correspondence relating to various foreign countries.

Particularly significant tranches of correspondence concern Sarolea's relations with the Belgian royal family and Czechoslovakia, 1919–1942 (including letters from prominent Czech politicians Eduard Beneš and Jan Masaryk).

Coll-15

Scottish Anthropological and Folklore Society

In 1922, the Council of the Royal Anthropological Institute in London authorised 12 of its fellows to found an Edinburgh and Lothians branch. Its inaugural meeting was held in the Royal Scottish Geographical Society meeting rooms in Edinburgh on 6 February 1923. In 1932, a number of its members founded a self-standing Scottish Anthropological Society, with which the branch formally merged in 1933. The Scottish Anthropological Society first met in June 1932 at the Royal Scottish Museum and established its aim as the furtherance of the study of anthropology, in general, but with particular emphasis on the anthropology of Scotland. The provisional council met on 8 November and set up committees to deal with an anthropometric survey of Scotland, folklore, dialect, comparative religion, general ethnology and propaganda. The society organised a series of meetings and lectures and published its *Proceedings* as a journal. In 1936 the Society changed its name to the Scottish Anthropological and Folklore Society. In the post-war years, however, membership dwindled and the Society was wound up in 1960.

The collection includes minute books of the Edinburgh and Lothian Branch of the Royal Anthropological Society, the Scottish Anthropological and Folklore Society and the Standing Committee of Anthropological Teaching. There are also various papers relating to the winding up of the Scottish Anthropological and Folklore Society.

Coll-262

Minutes of the Inaugural Meeting of the Scottish Anthropological Society, with press cuttings

Scottish Marine Station

The Scottish Marine Station for Scientific
Research was located on a floating barge,
known as the 'Ark', near Granton, on the
Firth of Forth. It was a joint initiative of the
Meteorological Society of Scotland and the
Royal Society of Edinburgh. Oceanographer
John Murray (1841–1914), a prominent
member of both societies, and Director of
the Challenger Office (see HMS *Challenger*,
page 73), played a particularly prominent
role in establishing the project. Opened for
scientific work in April 1884, the station was
a floating laboratory with accommodation
for seven scientists who carried out extensive
and varied biological experiments. They
also performed a series of observations on
the temperatures of the water in the Firth
of Forth and investigated the nature of the
sea-bed and its marine life. The station
was provided with a steam launch fitted
for dredging purposes and for making
hydrographic observations, plus two small
Norwegian skiffs. It also possessed a complete
library of works on marine biology and physics.

Among those who worked at the station
were future polar explorers William Speirs
Bruce and Fridtjof Nansen. The station was
eventually towed to Millport, Cumbrae,
in the Firth of Clyde, where it became an
annex of the Millport biological station
(future headquarters of the Scottish Marine
Biological Association).

The collection consists largely of
notebooks containing details about the
experiments conducted at Granton, 1888–
1901. They show calculations, water and
other analyses, notes on chemical deposits,

Experiment at the Scottish Marine Station,
November 1896

photographs, sketches, and tables both
written and printed. There are also invoices
and receipts for payment, 1883–1887 and
papers relating to accounts, 1884–1901.
Coll-263

School of Scottish Studies Archives

The School of Scottish Studies was established
at the University of Edinburgh in 1951
to collect, archive, research, study and
publish material relating to the cultural
traditions of Scotland. It was initially funded
by the Carnegie Trust for the Universities
of Scotland and by the University of
Edinburgh. Early fieldworkers included
Calum Maclean (previously of the Irish
Folklore Commission), followed by Hamish
Henderson and Francis Collinson, with
Basil Megaw being appointed the first full-
time director in 1957. Over the following
decades they and their colleagues undertook
ambitious and pioneering work in field
recording, helping to establish the School

of Scottish Studies as an internationally acclaimed research institute. The School of Scottish Studies Archives remain central to teaching and research and are a vital repository of Scottish culture.

The Collections

The collections are composed principally of sound, image and manuscript material. The sound archive contains more than 33,000 items, the core of which is the fieldwork recordings made by staff, students and associates since 1951. The subject matter covers cultural life, folklore and traditional arts and recordings originating from Scotland and its diaspora. Collections continue to grow via the fieldwork of students and staff and through donations. Donated material includes the John Levy collection of original fieldwork of mainly religious music from Asia along with various oral history projects dating from the 1970s to the present.

The photographic archive, containing more than 80,000 items and dating from the 1930s, complements the sound archive in documenting life in Scotland. Notable collections include images of the Hebrides taken by Werner Kissling and Robert Atkinson. Material relating to tales, tradition, folklore, song and music, dating from the 19th century onwards, in Gaelic, Scots and English can be found across the small complementary collection of manuscripts. The archives also hold the Linguistic Survey of Scotland and the Scottish Place-Name Survey, the latter with a substantial holding of more than 5,000 maps. A substantial collection of supporting and contextualising books and journals has been built up alongside the archives to form the Scottish Studies Library.

Serjeant, Robert Bertram

See main entry under Rare Books.
Coll-1062

Shepperson, George Albert

George Albert Shepperson (1922–) is a leading historian of modern Africa and a great benefactor of Edinburgh University Library.

Born in Peterborough, Northamptonshire, Shepperson was educated at King's School, Peterborough, and St John's College, Cambridge. His studies were interrupted

Duncan Matheson on stilts, Kintail, 1988
Ian MacKenzie, School of Scottish Studies Archives

by the Second World War, when he served in East Africa, India and Burma, but he subsequently completed a history degree. Shepperson joined the staff of the University of Edinburgh in 1948 as Lecturer in Imperial and American History. He became a Senior Lecturer in 1960 and a Reader in 1961. In 1963 he was appointed to the William Robertson Chair of Commonwealth and American History. Shepperson's greatest academic interest lay in the African diaspora and the history of the African peoples and their spread across the world. His key publications include *Independent African: John Chilembwe* (1958; written in collaboration with Tom Price), and *David Livingstone and the Rovuma* (1964).

The collection contains publications, correspondence and personal items, including:

- articles, addresses, tapes, talks and correspondence on nationalism in Nyasaland (present-day Malawi), and particularly relating to Hastings Banda and John Chilembwe
- papers relating to missionaries in Africa and African ethnological artefacts
- pamphlets, papers and cuttings relating to federation and independence in post-colonial Africa
- correspondence and materials on the University College of Rhodesia and University of East Africa
- material on the tea trade
- material on Tanganyika (present-day Tanzania) and Uganda, including correspondence with Julius K Nyerere.

In addition there are miscellaneous items acquired later, such as letters to Lady Tweedsmuir about her husband John Buchan's novel *Prester John*.
Coll-490

Smith, Norman Kemp

Norman Kemp Smith (1872–1958) was one of 20th-century Scotland's leading philosophers.

Born and schooled in Dundee, Smith read Classics and philosophy at the University of St Andrews, and pursued further studies at Jena, Zurich, Berlin and Paris. He was a Lecturer in Philosophy at Glasgow University from 1897 to 1906 when he went to Princeton, New Jersey, as Professor of Psychology, then, from 1914, as Professor of Philosophy. During the First World War, he returned to Britain and, between 1916 and 1918, served with the Department of Information in London. In 1919, Kemp was appointed to the Chair of Logic and Metaphysics at the University of Edinburgh and occupied the post until his retirement in 1945. His major published works include *Commentary to Kant's Critique of Pure Reason* (1918), *Prolegomena to an Idealist Theory of Knowledge* (1924), a translation of Kant's *Critique of Pure Reason* (1929), *The Philosophy of David Hume* (1941) and *New Studies in the Philosophy of Descartes* (1952).

The collection contains notebooks, papers and letters from correspondents including Woodrow Wilson and Max Born. There are also notes towards philosophical lectures, offprints of articles, drafts, pocket diaries, testimonials and photographs.
Coll-1038

Smith, Sydney Goodsir

Sydney Goodsir Smith (1915–1975) played a major role in the 20th-century Scottish Literary Renaissance and was a vital presence on Edinburgh's post-war literary scene.

Born in Wellington, New Zealand, Sydney Goodsir Smith arrived in Scotland in 1928, when his father Sir Sydney Alfred Smith (1883–1969) became Professor of Forensic Medicine at the University of Edinburgh. Smith began a medical degree at the University of Edinburgh, but abandoned it to read modern history at Oriel College, Oxford, graduating in 1937. Due to chronic asthma, he was turned down for active service in the Second World War. He worked instead for the War Office, teaching English to Polish troops. Smith began writing poetry in English in the 1930s but, under the influence of Hugh MacDiarmid, soon turned to Scots. His early collections *Skail Wind* (1941), *The Wanderer and Other Poems* (1943) and *The Deevil's Waltz (*1946) established him as the leading poet in the second wave of the Scottish Renaissance Movement. These were followed by his masterpiece *Under the Eildon Tree* (1948), a 24-part cycle on romantic love. Later collections included *Orpheus and Eurydice* (1955), *Figs and Thistles* (1959) and *Kynd Kittock's Land* (1965). Smith also experimented with Scots prose including the riotous novel *Carotid Cornucopius* (1947). In the following decades, he turned increasingly to drama and to writing for broadcast, including two radio poems commissioned by the BBC: *The Vision of the Prodigal Son* (1959) on Robert Burns'

bicentenary and *The Twa Brigs* (1964) on the opening of the Forth Road Bridge. His play *The Wallace* (1960) was commissioned for the Edinburgh International Festival.

An active critic and editor, Smith also published *A Short Introduction to Scottish Literature* (1951) and edited *Robert Fergusson, 1750–1774: Essays by Various Hands* (1952), *Gavin Douglas: A Selection from his Poetry* (1959) and *Hugh MacDiarmid: A Festschrift* (1962). His most significant editorial project is perhaps Robert Burns' *The Merry Muses of Caledonia* (with James Barke) for the Burns bicentenary in 1959. An accomplished painter and caricaturist, Smith was also long the art critic of *The Scotsman*.

The collection includes manuscripts, typescripts, and proofs of poetry, drama, fiction, criticism and broadcast materials. There are galley proofs and an actor's prompt copy of *The Wallace*, 1960. There is a small amount of correspondence including letters from Norman MacCaig and Hugh MacDiarmid. There are also artworks, including sketches and caricatures.
Coll-497

....

Sprigge, Timothy

Timothy Lauro Squire Sprigge (1932–2007) was a British idealist philosopher, keenly interested in animal rights and the ethical treatment of animals.

Born in London, Sprigge studied at Gonville and Caius College, Cambridge and at University College London (UCL) where he worked on the manuscripts of

Jeremy Bentham. In 1961 he submitted his dissertation entitled 'The Limits of Morals Defined' and was awarded the degree of PhD (Cantab). From 1979 to 1989 he held the Chair of Logic and Metaphysics at the University of Edinburgh. Sprigge was President of the Aristotelian Society, 1991–1992, and in 1993 he was elected a Fellow of the Royal Society of Edinburgh. His publications include: *Facts, Words and Beliefs* (1970), *Santayana: An Examination of his Philosophy* (1974), *The Vindication of Absolute Idealism* (1983), *The Rational Foundations of Ethics* (1987) and *James and Bradley: American Truth and British Reality* (1993). Sprigge's own philosophy combined elements from Spinoza, Hegel, William James and Francis Herbert Bradley. It 'emphasises the reality of the absolute, the larger unity that binds us together'.

The collection includes:

- unpublished papers including 'What I Believe'
- further manuscripts, papers, notebooks and computer disks
- material relating to Thomas Aikenhead (1676–1697), the last person in Britain to be executed for blasphemy
- lecture notes
- letters from fellow philosophers, 1967–2003
- further correspondence, 1960–1998
- offprints
- personal documents including a diary and photographs.

Coll-1154

Stewart, Dugald

See main entry under Rare Books.

Tait, Peter Guthrie

Physicist and mathematician Peter Guthrie Tait (1831–1901) made major contributions to the science of thermodynamics, graph theory and topology.

Born in Dalkeith, Tait studied at Edinburgh Academy, the University of Edinburgh and Peterhouse, Cambridge, where he graduated BA in 1852 and became a Fellow the same year. He was appointed Professor of Mathematics at Queen's College, Belfast, 1854, and held the post there until 1860 when he became Professor of Natural Philosophy at the University of Edinburgh. Tait came to know William Thomson (Lord Kelvin) (1824–1907) around this time and they both worked on the *Treatise on Natural Philosophy* (1867) which encapsulated new views on the science of energy and long remained a standard work in the field. Other significant publications include *An Elementary Treatise on Quaternions* (1867), *Sketch of Thermodynamics* (1868), *Lectures on Some Recent Advances in Physical Science* (1876), *Heat* (1884) and *Dynamics* (1895). In total, Tait published nearly 400 papers or articles and more than 20 books. Tait investigated the properties of ozone and verified Kelvin's discovery of the latent heat of electricity. He also conducted research into the flight of the golf ball. He was a lifelong friend of physicist James Clerk Maxwell.

The collection includes:

- notes of Tait's lectures on natural philosophy taken down by students, 1881–1882 and 1885–1886
- manuscript notes by Tait about the Tay Rail Bridge disaster
- correspondence with Michael Faraday, Lord Kelvin, Sir Archibald Geikie and other individuals.

Thomson, Godfrey

Godfrey Hilton Thomson (1881–1955) was a pioneer of intelligence testing. Born in Carlisle, in 1925 he became both Professor of Education at the University of Edinburgh and Director of Studies at the Edinburgh Provincial Training Centre, Moray House. Thomson and his team formulated the Moray House Tests, which were used throughout the UK for school selection. In 1931, the Scottish Council for Research in Education set up the Scottish Mental Survey, a unique test of the entire nation's intelligence. Thomson was at the centre of this project. On 1 June 1932, almost every Scottish child born in 1921 was tested (87,498 children). In 1947, the exercise was repeated for school children born in 1936. Thomson published prolifically and was committed to teaching and citizen development. The papers, which are catalogued online, include biographical and personal papers, publications by Thomson and unpublished material. A full description of the papers' discovery can be found in I J Deary, 'An intelligent Scotland: Professor Sir Godfrey Thomson and the Scottish Mental

Surveys of 1932 and 1947', *Journal of the British Academy*, 1, July 2013, pp.95–131. *Coll-1310*

Tovey, Donald Francis

See main entry under Rare Books.
Coll-411

Urquhart, Fred

Frederick Burrows Urquhart (1912–1995) is widely considered to be the finest Scottish short-story writer of the 20th century, known for his ear for the spoken language and sensitive depiction of female experience.

Urquhart was born in Edinburgh but spent much of his early childhood in Fife, Perthshire and Wigtownshire, where his father worked as a chauffeur to a succession of wealthy families. On returning to Edinburgh, he attended Broughton Secondary School, leaving at the age of 15 to work as a bookseller's assistant for several years. From the early 1930s onwards, Urquhart had short stories published in journals and broadcast on the radio. By 1935, he was able to write full time. His first published volume was *Time Will Knit* (1938), a novel of working-class Edinburgh life. It was followed in 1940 by his first collection of short stories, *I Fell for a Sailor*. At the outbreak of war, Urquhart's pacifist convictions led him to become a conscientious objector. He was first sent to work as a farm labourer at Laurencekirk in the Mearns, which was to inspire many of his finest short stories. He was later assigned to Woburn Abbey, the estate of the Duke

Conrad Hal Waddington

of Bedford, where he got to know George Orwell and the Scottish painters Robert Colquhoun and Robert MacBryde.

In the immediate post-war years, Urquhart published five acclaimed collections of short stories: *The Clouds are Big with Mercy* and *Selected Stories* (both 1946), *The Last G.I. Bride Wore Tartan* (1947), *The Year of the Short Corn* (1949) and *The Last Sister* (1950). In the 1950s, however, the market for short stories declined rapidly, leading Urquhart to take up work as literary agent, editor, reviewer, reader for a number of publishers, script-reader for Metro-Goldwyn-Mayer, and scout for Walt Disney. Only in the 1980s was Urquhart able to publish three new books of short stories: *Proud Lady in a Cage* and *A Diver in China Seas* (both 1980), and his final collection *Seven Ghosts in Search* (1983).

Urquhart was also highly regarded as a novelist. His debut *Time Will Knit* won praise from both Edwin Muir and Neil M Gunn; *The Ferret Was Abraham's Daughter* (1949) and *Jezebel's Dust* (1951) are among Scotland's major novels of the Second World War; his final novel, *The Palace of Green Days* (1979), drew on childhood memories of Perthshire and was his first published novel with an overtly homosexual theme. There are other complete novels in our collection which remained unpublished due, at least in part, to their more explicit depiction of homosexuality.

The papers contain manuscripts and typescripts of short stories, novels, plays, poetry, essays and introductions for works edited by Urquhart. There are readers' reports and correspondence with publishers such as Cassell, and J. M. Dent, and film companies such as MGM and Walt Disney. There is correspondence with Urquhart's parents, with many Scottish writers, and with his literary agent Herta Ryder. Finally there are diaries, juvenilia and other personal documents.

Coll-49

Waddington, Conrad Hal

Conrad Hal Waddington (1905–1975) was an embryologist and developmental biologist who laid the foundations for systems biology.

Born in Evesham, Worcestershire, Waddington attended Clifton College and Sidney Sussex College, Cambridge, where he took the Natural Sciences Tripos. After graduating, he was elected a Fellow of Christ's College, Cambridge and lectured in zoology. During the Second World War, he was an operational researcher for the Royal Air Force and subsequently scientific advisor to the Commander-in-Chief of Coastal Command.

In 1947, he came to Edinburgh to occupy two posts in tandem: the University's Buchanan Chair of Animal Genetics and Chief Geneticist of the Genetics Section of the Agricultural Research Council's National Animal Breeding and Genetics Research Organisation (NABGRO, later ABRO), housed within the Institute of Animal Genetics. Waddington was responsible for attracting many prominent scientists to the Institute, and helped to consolidate Edinburgh's major role on the genetics world stage. He founded the School of the Man Made Future at the University of Edinburgh in 1972 and pioneered an interdisciplinary approach to the environment, which was continued by the Centre for Human Ecology. Waddington gave widespread currency to the concept of canalisation (concerning the course of developmental processes) and epigenetics, establishing an Epigenetics Research Group at the Institute in 1963. He wrote a standard textbook, *Principles of Embryology* (1956), and also helped to popularise science in such general books as *The Ethical Animal* (1960).

The collection includes:
- Waddington's scientific notebooks
- manuscripts and typescripts of essays, articles and books
- material relating to lectures
- illustrative material for publications
- correspondence relating to Waddington's writings
- material relating to meetings, conferences, societies and organisations.

The papers date from Waddington's early student days at Cambridge to his death in 1975, and reflect the full breadth and scope of his interests and knowledge, which extended beyond science to art, philosophy and sociology. There is a separate collection of Waddington's offprints.

Coll-41

Wain, John Barrington

Writer John Barrington Wain (1925–1994) remains best known for his 1953 novel *Hurry on Down*, which captured the scepticism and irreverence of the post-war generation.

Wain was born in Stoke-on-Trent and educated at the High School, Newcastle-under-Lyme, and then St John's College, Oxford. He was a Lecturer in English Literature at the University of Reading, 1947–1955, but resigned his post to become a freelance author and critic. He later became the first Fellow in Creative Arts at Brasenose College, Oxford (1971–1972)

Manuscripts by John Barrington Wain

and was subsequently appointed to the five-year post of Professor of Poetry at Oxford in 1973. Like contemporary figures Kingsley Amis, Philip Larkin and John Braine, Wain began publishing just as Britain was recovering from the Second World War. It was a time when writers were reacting against the orthodoxies of modernism. As a novelist, Wain was associated with the Angry Young Men school and, as a poet, with the 'Movement'. His fictional works included *Hurry on Down* (1953); *Living in the Present* (1955); *The Contenders* (1958); *A Travelling Woman* (1959); *Nuncle and Other Stories* (1960); *Strike the Father Dead* (1962); *The Young Visitors* (1965); *Death of the Hind Legs and Other Stories* (1966); *The Smaller Sky* (1967); *A Winter in the Hills* (1970); *The Life Guard and Other Stories* (1971); *The Pardoner's Tale* (1978); *Lizzie's Floating Shop* (1981); *Young Shoulders* (1982); *Where the Rivers Meet* (1988); *Comedies* (1990); and *Hungry Generations* (1994). In addition he published nine volumes of poetry and three plays and worked prolifically as an editor, critic, biographer, anthologist, reviewer and broadcaster.

The collection includes manuscripts and typescripts of most of Wain's novels, short stories, poetry, plays and criticism. There is also extensive correspondence. *Coll-29*

Walker, John

John Walker (1731–1803), natural historian and Church of Scotland minister, had a major impact on the establishment of geology as an academic subject.

Walker studied at the University of Edinburgh and was licensed to preach in 1754. He was ordained minister of Glencorse in 1758 but transferred to Moffat in 1762 where, with support from his sponsor, Henry Home, Lord Kames, he was able to explore his interest in natural history. Between 1764 and 1786, he made four journeys to the Hebrides which formed the basis for his posthumously published *An Economical History of the Hebrides* (1808). Influenced by William Cullen, Walker was drawn to chemistry and mineralogy. He realised that the classification of minerals had been neglected and travelled throughout the British Isles, sometimes with Cullen, collecting minerals from mines and outcrops. Using his own personal collection as well as the Edinburgh University Museum, he had

'An Epitome of Natural History', MS by John Walker

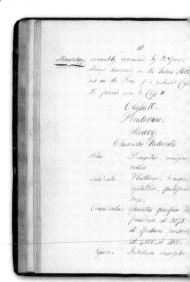

established an *Elementa Mineralogiae* by
the 1750s, and this classification was later
modified to include 323 genera. Among the
most interesting minerals that he collected
in the 1760s was strontianite, from the mines
of Leadhills.

In 1779 John Walker was appointed
Professor of Natural History and Keeper of
the University Museum at the University of
Edinburgh. Besides dealing with all aspects
of natural history, his lectures focused on
agriculture's place in national improvement,
and on the history and geography of the
Scottish Highlands.

Walker was a member of the Highland
Society of Scotland and the Edinburgh
Natural History Society and played an
instrumental role in the establishment
of the Royal Society of Edinburgh.

The collection consists of papers on
natural history, geography, agriculture,
Scottish history and parish management.
Coll-205

Robert Wallace at the World's Dairy Congress,
Washington, DC, October 1923

Wallace, Robert

Robert Wallace (1853–1939) played a
major role in establishing agriculture as
an academic discipline.

Wallace was born into a farming family
in Dumfries and Galloway. After study at
the University of Edinburgh, and a period of
private farming, he was appointed Professor
of Agriculture at the Royal Agricultural
College in Cirencester. In 1885 he returned
to the University of Edinburgh to take up
the Chair of Agriculture and Rural Economy.
Wallace was committed to the application
of scientific standards to agriculture, and
throughout his career he sought to improve
the standard of agriculture in Britain
and the Commonwealth. He added

courses in forestry and agricultural entomology to the Edinburgh curriculum. He also established the Edinburgh Incorporated School of Agriculture which led to the official recognition of Edinburgh by the then Board of Agriculture as an agricultural teaching centre. In the pursuit of his studies and interests, he travelled to Canada, Australia, New Zealand, India, Southern Africa and Malaysia, as well as the USA, Egypt, Greece, Mexico and Japan. Towards the end of his career, between 1914 and 1917, Wallace engaged in correspondence with Woodrow Wilson, President of the USA, on the treatment of prisoners and hostages in Germany. His publications include *Farm Live Stock of Great Britain* (1889), *The Rural Economy and Agriculture of Australia and New Zealand* (1891), *Argentine Shows and Live Stock* (1904) and *Heather and Moor Burning for Grouse and Sheep* (1917).

The papers consist of notes on agriculture, c.1900–1920, together with many leaflets, pamphlets and newspaper cuttings. There are also copies of his letters to President Wilson along with relevant documents.

Wallace was also one of the creators of the Roslin Glass Slide Collection (see page 172). *Coll-87*

Wilmut, Ian

Sir Ian Wilmut (1944–) led the research team responsible for cloning Dolly the sheep.

Wilmut was born in Warwickshire and studied embryology at Nottingham University, receiving his BSc in 1967 and a doctorate from the University of Cambridge in 1971. He remained in Cambridge at the ARC Unit of Reproductive Physiology and Biochemistry, working to develop the first methods for the deep-freeze storage of mammalian embryos. This led to the birth in 1973 of Frosty the calf, the first mammal to be born following the transfer of frozen and thawed embryos.

In 1973 Wilmut joined Edinburgh's Animal Breeding Research Organisation. By 1985, Wilmut was co-leader of a project to produce transgenic sheep that could express human therapeutic proteins in their milk. The first sheep to produce clinical amounts of such a protein successfully was Tracy, born in 1990. Wilmut and colleagues went on to examine the factors influencing the development of cloned embryos, which led in 1995 to the birth of Megan and Morag, the first mammals to be cloned from differentiated embryos grown in culture. In 1996, Wilmut led the team that produced Dolly the sheep, the first animal to be cloned from an adult body cell. This research has led to biomedical applications, including developing organs for xenotransplantation, and cloning and modifying animals for agricultural benefit.

In 2005 Wilmut was made Professor of Reproductive Science at the University of Edinburgh. In 2006, he founded and directed the MRC Centre for Regenerative Medicine at the University of Edinburgh (which in 2011 became part of the Scottish Centre for Regenerative Medicine), and was also given the title Professor Emeritus by the University. Wilmut was awarded the OBE in 1999 and was knighted in 2008.

The collection spans the dates 1969–2011 and consists of Wilmut's published papers, funding applications for different experiments, licence and patent applications, press cuttings, media enquiries and correspondence.

Coll-1320

Wright, Gordon

As a publisher and photographer, Gordon Wright (1942–) has been a tireless and inspirational presence on Scotland's literary scene.

Born in Edinburgh in 1942, Wright served an apprenticeship in the photographic department of mapmakers John Bartholomew after leaving school, then went on to work for the Edinburgh printers W & A K Johnston and Banks & Co. In 1967, he was asked to provide photographs for the literary and political magazine *Catalyst*, edited by poet William Neill, and soon assumed full responsibility for its design and illustration. This brought Wright into contact with many leading and emerging Scottish writers and inspired him to set up as a publisher in his own right.

Wright's first publication was *Scotland's Castle* (1969), a poetry booklet by William Neill. Subsequent publications included *Four Points of a Saltire*, an anthology of poems by Sorley Maclean, George Campbell Hay, William Neill and Stuart MacGregor, and Liz Lochhead's debut collection *Memo for Spring*. He made a significant contribution to the publication of new Scottish talent besides bringing many neglected writers (Helen Cruickshank, Flora Garry, Fionn MacColla) back into public view.

The archive contains extensive correspondence with authors Flora Garry and George Mackay Brown; original manuscripts and proofs of works by people including Hugh MacDiarmid, Sorley Maclean and Duncan Glen; business records and promotional materials.

There is also a separate collection of photographs of Scottish writers taken by Wright between 1968 and 1979. The subjects include Helen Cruickshank, Hugh MacDiarmid, Norman MacCaig, Liz Lochhead, Billy Connolly, George Mackay Brown, Hamish Henderson and William McIlvanney.

Coll-1070

'Towards Dolly' exhibition, 2015

¶Breuiarij Aberdonēsis ad per
celebris ecclie Scotorū potissimuz
vsum et consuetudinē Pars hye-
malis de tpe et de scis ac dauitico
psalterio congruenter per ferias
diuiso: cum Inuitatorijs hymnis
Antiphonis capitulis Responso-
rijs horis feriarū cōmēoracionibs
p āni curriculū necnō cōe scōrz plu
rimarzqz virginū ⁊ matronarz ac di
uersorz scōrz ... q sparsim in
incerto antea vagabantur: cum
Kalendario et mobiliū festorum
tabula ppetua varijsqz alijs adiū
ctis ⁊ de nouo additis sacerdotibs
plurimū qq necessarijs i Ediburgē-
si oppido walteri chepmā merca
toris ipēsis impressa Februarijs
idibus. Anno salutis nre ⁊ gre. ix
M. supra et quigētesimū.

iii. Rare Books

The University of Edinburgh holds some 400,000
rare books, many found nowhere else in the world.
These include books printed before 1900, but also
more modern books, such as those annotated by
important writers or produced by private presses,
using traditional skills and high-quality materials.

Aberdeen Breviary, 1509–1510

Abercromby, Lord John

Archaeology, folklore and travel

John Abercromby, 5th and last Lord
Abercromby of Aboukir and Tullibody
(1841–1924), left this collection to the
Library. Abercromby entered the army
in 1858, retiring in 1870 with the rank of
lieutenant in the Rifle Brigade. He served
as Vice-President of the Folklore Society
and President of the Society of Antiquaries
of Scotland. He succeeded his brother to
the title in 1917. His publications included
A Trip through the Eastern Caucasus (1889);
Pre- and Proto-Historic Finns (2 vols, 1898);
and *A Study of the Bronze Age Pottery of
Great Britain and Ireland* (2 vols, 1912).
Dying without male heirs, he endowed the
Abercromby Chair of Archaeology at the
University of Edinburgh and bequeathed us
some 2,500 volumes and 400 pamphlets on
archaeology, ethnology and linguistics, and
a substantial body of correspondence and
papers. The collection reflects his interests. It
is rich in material relating to Asia, particularly
the Caucasus, plus folklore and early pottery,
particularly in Britain and Finland. Most of
the books are 19th century, with some
18th-century material.

The books are all listed in the
pre-1985 typescript catalogue and there
are rudimentary online records for some
of them. The shelfmark is L.A.B.

The manuscript collection includes
material that relates to Abercromby's
publications as well as to his personal life.
There are a large number of letters and
postcards spanning the years 1881 to 1916. The
collection also includes notebooks; drawings of
archaeological artefacts; bundles of studies for
The Pre- and Proto-Historic Finns; material on the
tabulation of Finnish folk tales; printed items,
notes, photographs of the Canary Islands;
material including photographs, press cuttings,
notes on *A Study of the Bronze Age Pottery of Great
Britain and Ireland*. There are inventories of
household effects at several addresses, and a box
containing material relating to the Hon Ralph
Abercromby (John Abercromby's brother). In
addition to a number of photograph albums
of views, features and acquaintances, there are
five plan chest drawers of unsorted material,
mainly illustrative. A handlist is available.
Coll-55

G Perrot, *A History
of Art in Chaldaea and
Assyria*, vol. 2, 1884
Abercromby Collection

Appleton, Edward

See main entry under Archives and Manuscripts.
Coll-37

....

Auden, Wystan Hugh

**Leading collection of one of
the 20th century's greatest poets**

Modern poetry is one of the strengths of the
Library's collections. The Auden Collection
is particularly important and there is no
comparable collection in Scotland. It is a
scholarly collection of the writings of possibly
the greatest 20th-century poet in English.

The collection does not come from
Auden (1907–1973) himself, although there
are a number of signed copies. Many of the
books were purchased in 1982 from Barry
Bloomfield, Auden's bibliographer. The
collection formed the basis of *W.H. Auden; a
Bibliography*, 1924–1969, by B C Bloomfield
and E Mendelson (Charlottesville, 1972),
and contains copies of the majority of items
listed in that work. Annotated copies of the
bibliography are found at Auden.514–515.
Both Bloomfield and Mendelson have donated
books to the collection over the years, and we
make occasional purchases in this area.

In the collection are many first editions
in their original dust jackets, privately printed
pamphlets and ephemera, and a comprehensive
assembly of later editions and critical works.
There are also portraits and large framed items
including some explicit material.

In total there are some 800 volumes,
all with shelfmarks starting 'Auden'. The
collection is fully catalogued online.

The manuscript collections include
autograph letters and typescript poems
corrected in Auden's hand; there is also
Auden material in the A H Campbell
Collection. A detailed listing is available.
There is a further collection of material
connected with the compilation of
Bloomfield and Mendelson's bibliography.
Coll-45

....

Bindings

Fine, important and interesting bookbindings
are found throughout Special Collections.
There are early Scottish bindings, including
a contemporary binding on the copy of John
Bellenden's *Hystory and Croniklis of Scotland*,
printed on vellum about 1540 (Df.2.11). The
collection is particularly strong in holdings of
the late 16th- century shield binder, believed
to have worked in Edinburgh. The slightly
later work of Andro Hart of Edinburgh is
also represented. During the 18th century,
Scotland developed an outstanding tradition

Scottish herringbone binding. Holy Bible, 1719

Presentation thesis binding. George Abercromby, *Disputatio juridica*, 1794

tourist souvenir bindings and theses bound in 'Dutch' gilt decorated papers. Later examples of attractive publishers' cloth bindings and designer dust jackets can also be found.

We have a good number of royal and armorial bindings, many now described in the online British Armorial Bindings database, produced by John Morris and Philip Oldfield (http://armorial.library.utoronto.ca). These include books from the library of Henry Sinclair, Bishop of Ross (1508–1565).

There are also many fine foreign bindings showing a wide range of styles, materials and colours.

Many of our early bindings are described in W S Mitchell, *A History of Scottish Bookbinding* (1955); another useful source is John Durkan and Anthony Ross, *Early Scottish Libraries* (1961). Manual files and rubbings are available in the Centre for Research Collections.

Books that are acquired for their binding features are now kept together at shelfmark Bdg.

of decorative bookbinding, particularly on Bibles and prayer books, which were often given as wedding or christening presents. We have examples of distinctive Scottish wheel and herringbone bindings, plus bindings identified as the work of master binder James Scott. There are also examples of school prize bindings, Mauchline-style

Collection of legal theses with decorated paper wrappers

E Pagkosmos Ekthesis, 1852

was a charismatic and popular national figure and his death led to a day of national mourning.

This bequest consists of about 250 books, mainly in Greek. Most are 19th century but there are some earlier items, including a French textbook printed in 1709. It is a strong resource for the history of education, particularly in the classical languages.

The books are all listed in the pre-1985 typescript catalogue and there are rudimentary online records for many of them. The shelfmark is Bl.Coll.

The manuscript collection includes 23 letters and a number of poems, at various locations.

....

Blackie, John Stuart

Greek scholarship and Scottish nationalism

John Stuart Blackie (1809–1895) was Professor of Greek at the University of Edinburgh from 1852 to 1882. He translated various works from German and Greek into English, and was also interested in the reform of Scottish universities. Blackie was a keen promoter of Scottish identity and raised funds for the establishment of a Chair of Celtic. He

Blöndal, Sigfus

Iceland and its literature

Icelandic studies are well represented in Edinburgh, particularly in this collection of

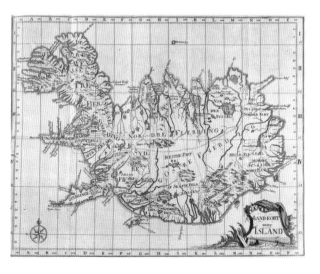

Tilforladelige Efterretninger om Island med et nyt Landkort, 1752

some 3,000 books, pamphlets and journals. It was purchased by the Library from the Icelandic scholar Sigfus Blöndal in 1950.

In the same year the Icelandic Government presented about 250 items on Icelandic topics. They are shelved beside the Blöndal Collection (shelfmark LL.108). The combined collection is strong on Iceland's literature and the sagas, its history, topography and natural history, both printed in Iceland and elsewhere. The material is mainly 19th century with some 18th-century material.

The books are all listed in the pre-1985 typescript catalogue and there are online records for many of them. All have shelfmarks in the range LL.100.5.3–LL.108.7.65. The Centre for Research Collections maintains listings of other Nordic material in the library, including the correspondence of Grímur Thorkelin in the David Laing collection. We continue to make occasional purchases in this area.

....

Brown, Gerard Baldwin

See main entry under Archives and Manuscripts. Coll-314

....

Bruce, William Speirs

Oceanic and polar exploration

This major collection about the oceans and polar exploration was bequeathed by Dr William Speirs Bruce, explorer and oceanographer (1867–1921). Bruce studied at the Granton Marine Station and at the University of Edinburgh, and took part in numerous expeditions looking at the meteorology, botany and zoology of the polar regions. In 1902, Bruce organised and led the Scottish National Antarctic Expedition to the Weddell Sea, returning home in 1904. This expedition took some of the earliest cine film of Antarctica.

The collection contains some 1,000 volumes, 2,000–3,000 pamphlets and offprints, and 30 albums of pictures and news cuttings, all on oceanography or Arctic and Antarctic exploration. The volumes include famous early 19th-century travel accounts, annotated research publications and scientific reports.

The books are all listed in the pre-1985 typescript catalogue and there are online records for about 350 of them. The pamphlets and other printed material are not catalogued. The shelfmark is Bruce Coll.

Papers of William Speirs Bruce, 1902–1904

The manuscript part of the collection includes notebooks, annotated typescripts, postcards, photographs, maps, diaries, correspondence and lists of specimens. Topics include the *Balaena*, fish and fisheries, Franz Josef Land, the Jackson-Harmsworth Expedition, meteorology, oceanography, Repulse Bay, the Seychelles, soundings, South Georgia, Spitzbergen and whaling.

Related materials include a volume of newspaper cuttings relating to the Scottish National Antarctic Expedition, and a set of album material from the Scottish National Antarctic Expedition. The collection complements the Challenger Expedition records and the Christian Salvesen archive in its depiction of travel and life across the polar oceans.

Coll-72

G Symeoni, *La vita et Metamorfoseo d'Ovidio*, 1559
Buchanan Collection

Buchanan, Thomas Ryburn

Fine books from a collector's library

Thomas Buchanan (1846–1911) was born in Lanarkshire but educated in Oxford where he took charge of the great Codrington Library at All Souls College. He entered politics as a Liberal, and was first elected to Parliament as MP for Edinburgh in 1881. He ended his career as Parliamentary Under-Secretary for India.

His widow gave 116 volumes to the Library in 1941. The collection is that of a bibliophile, and all the items exemplify fine printing, fine binding and/or distinguished provenance. These are some elegant editions of the classics in superb condition.

There are basic online listings for many of the books. The Centre for Research Collections maintains a detailed author and shelf catalogue with further details of provenance, bindings and imprints.
Shelfmarks: JA 2170–2246; JY 704–725; Inc.197.5

Cameron, Alexander

Celtic and Scottish studies

The collection was formed by Dr Alexander Cameron (1827–1888), Celtic scholar and minister of the Free Church at Brodick in Arran. It was given to the Library in 1889 by shipowner and colonialist Sir William Mackinnon of Balinakill (1823–1893),

T Pennant, *A Tour in Scotland*, 1769
Cameron Collection

who had purchased the library on
Cameron's death.

It contains about 3,500 volumes, mainly
on Celtic studies and Scottish theology. There
are many 19th-century, some 18th-century
and a few 17th-century works. Among them
are some extremely rare works in Gaelic.

The books are all listed in the pre-1985
typescript catalogue and there are online
records for most of them. The collection
is mainly kept together at shelfmarks
beginning 'C.R.'

....

Campbell,
Archibald Hunter

Poetry of the thirties

One of our strongest collections in literature
of the 1920s and 1930s is the library of
Archibald Campbell (1902–1989). Educated
at Edinburgh and Oxford, Campbell was a

leading scholar of the law, with an interlude
as a code-breaker at Bletchley Park. He
was Regius Professor of Public Law in the
University of Edinburgh, 1945–1972.

The library was presented in 1984,
and reflects Campbell's literary connections
formed at Oxford. He was a contemporary
and friend of Stephen Spender, Christopher
Isherwood and W H Auden; his library contains
much English literature and secondary material
of the 1930s with large holdings of Auden,
Spender, Pound, Forster and Norman Douglas.
There is also a smaller group of early legal and
classical texts and miscellaneous other literary
material. Professor Campbell subsequently
bequeathed to the Library his copy of Auden's
Poems, 1928, a famous rarity.

The book collection is mainly catalogued
online. Shelfmarks: SC 5076–5339, JA
3936–3951 SD 4421–4459, SD 4652–4677.

The manuscript collection includes nine
metres of material, some unsorted, including
correspondence and three photograph
albums. Highlights are letters from Auden,
Spender and Humphrey Carpenter.
Coll-221

Campbell, Colin

See main entry under Archives and Manuscripts.
Coll-38

....

Carmichael–Watson

See main entry under Archives and Manuscripts.
Coll-97

....

Cleghorn, Hugh

Trees and India

In 1895 some 383 volumes on forestry, land use and botany, in particular relating to India, were presented from the library of Dr Hugh F C Cleghorn of Stravithie (1820–1895). The collection consists mainly of 19th-century publications.

International Forestry Exhibition, Edinburgh, 1884, Official Catalogue

The books are all listed in the pre-1985 typescript catalogue and there are online records for some of them. The books have shelfmarks in the ranges Att. 64–67 and Xf.1–2. See H J Noltie, *Indian Forester, Scottish Laird: the Botanical Lives of Hugh Cleghorn of Stravithie* (Edinburgh, 2016).

....

Collinson, Francis

See main entry under Archives and Manuscripts.
Coll-90

....

Coltness Papers

See main entry under Archives and Manuscripts.
Coll-17

....

Corson, James

Walter Scott, from Waverley to souvenirs

We have one of the leading collections of books by and about Sir Walter Scott, which was formed by Dr James C Corson (1905–1988). Corson was a Scott bibliographer and former Deputy Librarian of Edinburgh University Library.

Corson was dedicated to the pursuit of Scotland's first great historical novelist from an early age. He had begun collecting printed editions of Scott in the secondhand bookshops of Edinburgh while he was still at school. Eventually his collection expanded to fill the old church at Lilliesleaf, near Melrose, in the old manse of which he lived and died. His zeal was recognised by his appointment as Honorary Librarian of Abbotsford in the 1950s.

Engraving after C R Leslie for Walter Scott,
The Heart of Midlothian, 1833

The collection was purchased by the
Library in 1975 and transferred here in 1989
on Corson's death; his widow Ada Corson
bequeathed funds to ensure its upkeep
and development.

There are now some 7,000 printed
items comprising editions of Scott in
English and translation, biographical and
critical material, an estimated 10,000
illustrations and newscuttings, 60 framed
pictures, some original manuscript material
and an assortment of miscellaneous Scott
memorabilia. The Corson Collection is the
basis of the Walter Scott Digital Archive,
which the Library maintains.

Dr Corson's own typescript catalogue
and index slips can be consulted in the
Centre for Research Collections. The printed
books are catalogued online with shelfmarks
starting 'Corson'.

Crew, Francis Albert Eley

Foundations of modern genetics

Francis Albert Eley Crew (1886–1973), a
qualified medic and poultry geneticist, was
the first director of what became known
as the Institute of Animal Genetics from
1920 as well as occupying the Buchanan
Chair of Animal Genetics at the University
of Edinburgh from 1928. Crew held both
these posts until the Second World War, after
which he transferred to the Chair of Public
Health and Social Medicine. In his role as
Director of the Institute, Crew attracted
a wide variety of researchers and funding,
helping to make it one of the foremost
centres of genetics research in the world.
In his own research, he contributed greatly

F A E Crew by Drummond Young, Edinburgh

to the fields of intersexuality and sex transformations in mammals and birds, particularly the domestic fowl. Crew was also the organising secretary and Chairman of the 7th International Congress of Genetics in Edinburgh in 1939, which was interrupted by the outbreak of war.

The collection consists of 87 bound volumes and one box of unbound offprints, and includes offprints authored by Crew himself as well as by others, covering the dates 1900–1940. Many of the offprints are autographed by well-known geneticists such as William Bateson, Arthur Darbishire and H J Muller, and cover a range of subjects from animal and poultry breeding, social history and eugenics. The offprints are partly catalogued online. Books from Crew's library were also donated and are awaiting cataloguing.

Dante, *La divina commedia*, 1491

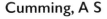

Cumming, A S

Dante and Italy

This collection of some 200 items on Italian studies, particularly Dante, was bequeathed to the Library by Dr A S Cumming in 1939. Most of the books are 19th or 20th century, but the collection includes a copy of Dante's *La divina commedia* printed at Venice in 1491 (Inc.113*).

The books are all listed in the pre-1985 typescript catalogue and there are online records for some of them. All books have shelfmarks starting 'Cum. Coll.'

Heiskell Darwin Collection

In 2012 the University received a loan of early editions of the works of Charles Darwin from the Heiskell Bibliographical Foundation, via the University of Edinburgh USA Development Trust, being the collection of Charles L Heiskell, MD, from California. This includes some great rarities in excellent

On the Origin of Species, set of editions from Darwin Collection

condition, including two fine copies of the first edition of *On the Origin of Species* (1859). The library already possessed a number of important early editions, so we now have a collection of more than 100 volumes of lifetime editions of Darwin's works. All the books are catalogued online with shelfmarks starting 'Darwin'.

....

Horst W Drescher Collection

Henry Mackenzie's *The Man of Feeling* and 18th-century sentimental literature

Mackenzie (1745–1831), alumnus of the University, was both a lawyer, in Edinburgh and London, and a successful literary author. *The Man of Feeling*, first published

in 1771, is the epitome of the sentimental novel. Mackenzie wrote other novels and plays, and was the editor of the literary periodicals *The Lounger* and *The Mirror*, which followed in the tradition of Addison's *Spectator*.

The collection was part of the library of Professor Horst W Drescher, of the University of Mainz, and Honorary Research Fellow of the Institute for Advanced Studies in the Humanities in the University of Edinburgh, who studied and published on Mackenzie over a long period. It was donated by his widow in 2014. There are 224 volumes of works by Mackenzie and by

Henry Mackenzie,
The Man of Feeling, 1791

contemporaries: Steele, Addison, Smollet, Edgworth, Inchbald, and some works on Scottish history from the same period.

The collection is fully catalogued online with shelfmarks starting 'Drescher'.

....

Drummond, William

Our first literary collection

One of the most important gifts ever presented to the Library, the collection was given by a former student, William Drummond of Hawthornden (1585–1649), the laird, poet and man of letters. More than 600 books were donated, mostly in 1626 but some in later batches up to 1636. A number of items with the Drummond provenance have been acquired since.

Drummond was friend of poets Michael Drayton and Sir William Alexander, Earl of Stirling, an acquaintance of Ben Jonson and a supporter of King Charles I. He graduated from the Tounis College (now the University of Edinburgh) in 1605 before proceeding to further study at Bourges and Paris in 1607 and 1608. He published various works of verse as well as some political pamphlets.

Drummond began collecting books soon after he graduated, and amassed a superb private library. It has provided the University Library with some of its greatest treasures, especially in the fields of literature, history, geography, philosophy, theology,

James VI on horseback, in William Drummond, *Poems*, 1616

science, medicine and law. They include two Shakespeare quartos, and works by Jonson, Spenser, Drayton and Sir Philip Sidney. There is also a complete copy of John Derrick's *Image of Irelande* (1581), and two early pamphlets encouraging the colonisation of Nova Scotia.

There are now about 700 volumes (including a few manuscripts) in Latin, Italian, French and Spanish, as well as English. A printed catalogue was issued in 1627 after Drummond's first large donation: *Auctarium Bibliothecae Edinburgenae, sive catalogus librorum quos Guilielmus Drummondus ab Hawthornden Bibliothecae D.D.Q. anno. 1627*. It was reprinted in 1815. The most thorough investigation of

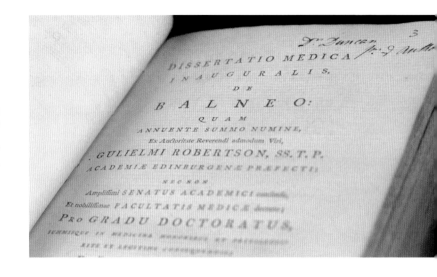

B Parr, *De Balneo*, 1773
Duncan Collection

Drummond and his books will be found in Robert Macdonald's *The Library of Drummond of Hawthornden* (Edinburgh, 1971), which lists and discusses all Drummond's known books, some 1,400 titles, not just those given to the University of Edinburgh. See also John Scally, *'A Labyrinth of Delight': The World of William Drummond of Hawthornden 1585–1649* (Edinburgh, 2005).

The books are all listed in the pre-1985 typescript catalogue and there are online records for most of them. All have shelfmarks starting 'De'.

....

Duncan, Andrew (the elder)

Medical theses

Dr Andrew Duncan (1744–1828), also known as Andrew Duncan the elder, was a professor of the University of Edinburgh and a leading figure in the Edinburgh medical world. He founded a public dispensary, an institution for giving free medicines and medical advice to the poor. This afterwards became the Royal Public Dispensary. Moved by the tragic death of the poet Robert Fergusson (1750–1774), Duncan was instrumental in the foundation of the Edinburgh Lunatic Asylum, which was built in 1807.

This is a collection of more than 1,900 medical theses, mostly presented to Duncan by grateful students. It has recently been reconstructed and is fully catalogued online. All the theses have shelfmarks starting 'Duncan'. This is just a small part of the University's vast collection of medical theses which continues to grow today.

The manuscript collection includes numerous lecture notes and correspondence, at various locations.

Coll-199

East Asian Studies

The East Asian Studies Collection was set up in the mid-1960s with the establishment of the Chinese and Japanese departments in the former Faculty of Arts. It comprises about 60,000 items published mainly in China (including Taiwan) and Japan, and a small amount in Korea, in their languages. The collection is traditionally strong in arts, philosophy, literature, history and religion in Chinese and Japanese, both as reprints of classics and modern publications. Over the last 50 years, the collection has grown into a regional centre of resources for multidisciplinary studies of East Asia. It is the only such collection in Scotland. In recent years, the subject coverage has extended to social sciences, international relations, film studies and translation studies. The East Asian Studies Collection is supplemented by a large amount of material in Western languages in the General Collections and by a growing number of electronic resources in Chinese and Japanese languages.

Imperial Summer Palace, Peking, 1860
ECA Rare Book Collection

Edinburgh College of Art Rare Book Collection

Large, illustrated books on art, architecture and design

(For the history of ECA, see entry under Edinburgh University Archives.)

In 2011 Edinburgh College of Art merged with the University of Edinburgh. Later that year the ECA rare books collection was transferred into the Centre for Research Collections where it is now fully catalogued. The collection includes some 1,500 items, among them some outstanding items on the history of architecture, art and design.

Many of the books came to ECA from the institutions that preceded it, the drawing academy of the Board of Trustees for Manufactures in Scotland, and the School of Applied Art: the collection thus reflects the teaching practices of art in both the 19th and 20th centuries. This affected collecting policy: for example, the ECA Typography Department had a number of examples of early printing and bindings; the Trustees' Academy collected very expensive illustrated works on classical architecture and design, which would otherwise have been unavailable to any ordinary student. It also affected use: for example in preferring to acquire the unbound, portfolio edition, where one was available, and possibly sometimes dis-binding volumes to allow separate use of individual plates. However, overall the condition of the items – particularly the rarer volumes such as the sets of Piranesi's works – is good.

Some of the books are unrecorded or unique. Of particular importance are the

hand-painted shawl designs and the volumes of textile samples. The collection also includes photographs, examples of Japanese books and foreign maps. Some 37 items are British or English-language books printed before 1801. The earliest book in the collection is an edition of the sermons of St Bernardine of Siena printed before 1489.

All the items are catalogued online, with shelfmarks starting 'RECA'.

Edinburgh University Press

Edinburgh University Press (EUP) was founded in the 1940s and remains one of the world's leading academic imprints. It became a wholly owned subsidiary of the University of Edinburgh in 1992. Today the main subject areas across the books and journals programme include American studies, Classics and ancient history, critical editions, film and media studies, history, Islamic and Middle Eastern studies, language and linguistics, law, literary studies, philosophy, politics and Scottish studies. *The Innes Review* is an example of a leading scholarly journal published by EUP.

The Library receives copies of EUP publications for archival preservation and the collection currently includes some 4,000 items. All are catalogued online, the books with shelfmarks beginning 'EUP', the journals with shelfmarks beginning 'EUP Per'; there is also a subsection of Polygon books with shelfmark Poly.

Faculty of Actuaries

Finance and mathematics

The Scottish Faculty of Actuaries built up an extensive and important library of works relating to economics, mathematics and finance. Although the strength of the collection is in 19th-century publications, it includes some significant early works such as an edition of John Napier's *Logarithmes* printed in 1616. There are many pamphlets and a few manuscripts.

There are 1,476 books. The collection is on deposit in Special Collections, and is largely catalogued online with basic records. All books have shelfmarks starting 'FAct'.

Fairbairn, William Ronald Dodds

Pioneering psychiatry

William Fairbairn (1889–1964) was born and educated in Edinburgh and became a pioneering psychiatrist and psychoanalyst. He served in the army during the First World War and in 1915 he visited Craiglockhart, where W H R Rivers was pioneering psychotherapeutic work with shell-shock victims. By the end of the war he had decided to become a psychotherapist. His work has recently started to attract considerable attention, particularly his sensitive studies of child abuse.

His library of about 400 books was presented to the Psychiatry Library by Nicholas H Fairbairn, and subsequently passed to Special Collections. The collection includes many key texts from the golden age of early 20th-century psychiatry, some with annotations.

The books are fully catalogued online with shelfmarks starting 'Fairbairn'. Fairbairn's manuscripts are in the National Library of Scotland.

....

Forbes, Daniel Macintosh

This collection of about 200 items on the Philippines was bequeathed in 1917 by Dr Daniel Macintosh Forbes. There are some outstanding examples of early printing in Manila and some fine Spanish books about the islands.

The collection is scattered across the General and Special Collections. The books are all listed in the pre-1985 typescript catalogue and there are online records for some of them. The Centre for Research Collections maintains files which allow the collection to be reconstructed virtually.

J Maldonado, *Religiosa hospitalidad*, 1742
Forbes Collection

Freshwater Collection

Decorated publisher's bookbindings

Peter Freshwater, former Deputy Librarian of the University Library, presented his collection of books with decorated bindings in 2014.

There are 180 volumes; the majority are examples of the mass-produced decoration of the 19th century, ranging from blind-stamped cloth and leather of

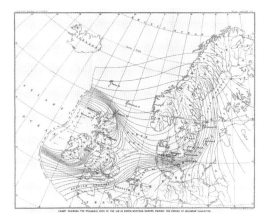

the 1820s–1840s, to the gilt
and multicoloured illustrated
cloth from the later decades of
the 19th century and the early
20th century. All are catalogued
online, with brief descriptions of
the bindings.

....

Geddes, Patrick

See main entry under Archives and Manuscripts.
Coll-1167

....

Geikie, Archibald

See main entry under Archives and Manuscripts.
Coll-74

....

Geikie, James

Geology and history

James Geikie (1839–1915) was the leading
British authority on Pleistocene geology.
He originated the still currently held belief
that human habitation continued in Europe
throughout the glacial period. This substantial
collection reflects his geological interests.

In 1861 Geikie took up a position with
the Geological Survey, mapping glacial drift
deposits in central Scotland. Geikie made

his reputation with the book *The Great Ice
Age and its Relation to the Antiquity of Man*
(1874). In 1882 he succeeded his brother,
Sir Archibald Geikie (1835–1924), as the
second Murchison Professor of Geology and
Mineralogy at the University of Edinburgh,
which post he held until 1914. He was
President of the Royal Society of Edinburgh
when he died.

Edinburgh University Library purchased
this material from his heirs shortly after his
death. There are about 5,000 pamphlets in
200 volumes, mostly offprints on geology,
many with manuscript notes and insertions.

Items whose authors' surnames lie
between A and Foo are listed in the pre-1985
typescript catalogue and there are online
records for some of these. The Centre for
Research Collections maintains manual
files listing the whole collection. All have
shelfmarks starting 'He'.

The manuscripts of James Geikie and
his family include correspondence, lecture
notes, photographs, reprints and maps. There
is a detailed online manuscripts catalogue.
Coll-99

Gibb, Forbes

Forbes Gibb Collection

Edinburgh is in some ways the birthplace of the genre of crime writing. This is a collection of books, pamphlets and journals about the reception of Arthur Conan Doyle's Sherlock Holmes stories. There are also some examples of other 20th-century detective fiction.

Professor Forbes Gibb, an information scientist at the University of Strathclyde, donated this collection in 2001. It currently contains 1,565 volumes, all fully catalogued with shelfmarks starting 'Forbes Gibb'.

....

Gibbon, Lewis Grassic

Library of leading Scottish novelist

Lewis Grassic Gibbon, whose real name was James Leslie Mitchell (1901–1935), is now regarded as one of the most important Scottish writers of the early 20th century. His reputation has risen steadily and his trilogy *A Scots Quair* has been adapted for various different media. The books he collected in his lifetime, however, are very much the working collection of a man with broad interests and little money.

The collection was presented by his daughter, Mrs Rhea Martin, in 1988, with a second part following in 1992. There are about 300 volumes, mainly of English and Scottish literature, a few with presentation or ownership inscriptions. They contain classics of English and Scottish literature, works on history and culture, and may provide evidence about the sources for his historical and social novels.

The collection was reconstituted in 2009–2010, and the books are catalogued online with shelfmarks starting 'Gibbon'. Gibbon's manuscript collection is preserved in the National Library of Scotland.

....

Guthrie, Douglas

See main entry under Archives and Manuscripts. Coll-52

Halliwell-Phillipps, James Orchard

William Shakespeare and early drama

The Library's rich holdings of early English drama include the majority of editions of William Shakespeare published before 1660, mainly through the Halliwell-Phillipps Collection. Halliwell-Phillipps (1820–1889) was a prolific and controversial literary scholar, who built up vast collections on Shakespeare and English literature.

Halliwell-Phillipps established a relationship with the Library through David Laing, who had arranged for Halliwell-Phillipps to have access to our rare copy of *Titus Andronicus* (London, 1600).

Over a number of years starting in 1872, Halliwell-Phillipps donated some 1,000 printed volumes on Shakespeare. The University was able to secure another collection, consisting mainly of Jacobean, Restoration and early 18th-century plays, which Halliwell-Phillipps had gifted to Penzance Library in 1866, by purchase at auction in 1964. The impetus for that purchase came from the recently formed Friends of Edinburgh University Library. This second collection includes 600 volumes of 17th- and 18th-century English drama.

The books all appear in the pre-1985 typescript catalogue and there are online records for many of them. Other files are available in the Centre for Research Collections which would allow the collection to be reconstructed virtually. Many have shelfmarks in the range Hb.–Hd., although the more important items have been transferred into the JA sequence.

The overall collection includes 16th-century works by Italian, French and Spanish authors. Its strength lies in English books, especially English drama of the 17th and 18th centuries. The plays include works by Ben Jonson, Beaumont and Fletcher, George Chapman, Thomas Middleton, John Webster, John Dryden, Philip Massinger and William Wycherley. Several are playhouse copies with contemporary stage directions added in manuscript.

Halliwell-Phillipps bequeathed a further 100 volumes of notebooks and diaries, as well as 300 volumes of literary correspondence. The latter contain about 15,000 letters of authors. There are manual indexes to the Letters of Authors.

Coll-103

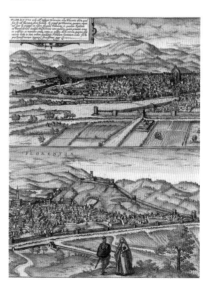

Halliwell-Phillipps scrapbook: map of Florence, from G Braun, *Civitates Orbis Terrarum*, 1572

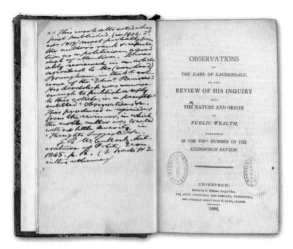

Earl of Lauderdale, *Observations on the Review of his Inquiry into the Nature and Origin of Public Wealth*, 1804, with W B Hodgson's annotations

Hodgson, William Ballantyne

Babbage, the invention of the calculating machine and economics

William Hodgson (1815–1880) was Professor of Political Economy at the University of Edinburgh and a leading educational reformer. Educated at the University of Edinburgh, in 1871 he was appointed as the University's first Professor of Commercial and Political Economy and Mercantile Law. His classes were popular, even though his subject was not part of any degree curriculum.

His collection of some 1,000 books on the history of political economy, trade and finance were gifted to the Library by his widow in 1880. They include 32 items from the library of Adam Smith, and others from the library of Charles Babbage, the mathematician and inventor of the calculating machine that presaged the computer. Hodgson annotated many of his books.

These books all appear in the pre-1985 typescript catalogue and many have online catalogue records. Originally all items had shelfmarks beginning 'Zo.' and 'Zp.', although some items have now been moved to other sequences. Many are to be found at shelfmarks SD 2440 onwards.

There are also two volumes of manuscripts on political economy and phrenology.

....

Incunabula

Our earliest printed books

Incunabula, from the Latin for 'swaddling clothes', are books from the infancy of printing – anything printed using moveable type before 1501. These books are among the most precious items in any library and the University of Edinburgh is privileged to have a significant collection of nearly 300 such books.

These early books have mostly been brought together from other sequences and other collections, although some remain in other locations to keep collections intact. Many have numerous provenances. There

Bible, Nuremberg, 1483

are some particularly beautiful books with hand-colouring and early bindings. A copy of the *Decretals* of Gratian, printed in 1472, was reputedly the favourite printed book of its owner, William Morris (Inc.4.4). Most of the books are continental imprints, including a copy of the first book printed at Venice in 1469. There are two papal indulgences printed by Wynkyn de Worde in 1497 and 1498, and an imperfect copy of Caxton's *Polychronicon*.

The books are listed in Frank Nicholson's *List of Fifteenth-Century Books in the University Library, Edinburgh* (Edinburgh, 1913). Annotated copies of Nicholson's catalogue in the Centre for Research Collections record additions and corrections. An online listing is in progress. All the books have shelfmarks starting 'Inc.'

S Brant, *Stultifera Navis*, Strasbourg, 1497

Johnson-Marshall, Percy

See main entry under Archives and Manuscripts.
PJM

Keith, Arthur Berriedale

The library of Arthur Berriedale Keith (1879–1944), Regius Professor of Sanskrit and Comparative Philology here from 1914 to 1944, was given by his sister to the Library on his death. The third son of an Edinburgh newsagent, Keith was educated at the Royal High School and the University of Edinburgh before going on to study at Balliol College, Oxford. He was called to the English Bar and served in the Colonial Office for 14 years before being appointed to the Regius Chair of Sanskrit in 1914. He made great contributions to Vedic and classical Sanskrit scholarship. He was also called in to advise the Government during the abdication crisis in 1936.

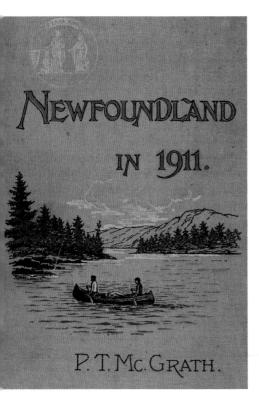

The collection includes some 1,600 books and well over 1,500 pamphlets, mainly on Sanskrit and other Indian literature, history and politics, and the constitutional history of the British Empire. All material appears in the Library's pre-1985 main catalogue and there are basic online records for many items. There is also a shelflist available from staff.

The manuscript collection includes:
- papers and correspondence including Colonial Office correspondence, 1901–1914
- correspondence about constitutional matters, 1908–1939
- correspondence with political figures such as R Stafford Cripps and Herbert Samuel
- material relating to the Government of India Bill, 1931–1935, and to the Peace Treaty, 1919
- material on Malta, 1924–1940
- material on the Beaverbrook Case
- material including correspondence with Muriel Blundell and Sylvia Pankhurst on British policy towards Italy after the invasion of Ethiopia
- correspondence on the subject of Keith's revision of *The Law and Custom of the Constitution*.

There is also material relating to Keith's career and to general family matters. The papers are listed in the *Guide to Arthur Berriedale Keith Papers and Correspondence, 1896–1941* by Ridgway F Shinn Jr (1981). *Coll-34*

PT McGrath, *Newfoundland in 1911*
Keith Collection

Kennedy-Fraser, Marjory

See main entry under Archives and Manuscripts.
Coll-1036

....

Koestler, Arthur

See main entry under Archives and Manuscripts.
Coll-146

....

Laing, David

See main entry under Archives and Manuscripts.
Coll-1

....

Litill, Clement

See also Iconic Special Collections.

The foundation collection

The 276 volumes bequeathed by Clement Litill (or Little) in 1580 were the first books in the University Library. The books cover both Catholic and Protestant theology and humanist scholarship. There are outstanding individual items such as the unique copy of the Sarum breviary printed at Rouen in 1496 (Dd.1.24) and the first book printed at St Andrews (the *Catechisme* of Archbishop John Hamilton, 1552, Dd.2.33). Many of the books have fascinating provenances, having been owned by Scottish bishops such as

Litill Collection book stamp

Henry Sinclair or William Scheves, and have early manuscript annotations.

A manuscript catalogue of the books was drawn up in the 1580s and is printed in the *Miscellany of the Maitland Club*, vol. 1 (Edinburgh, 1834), pp.285–301. A catalogue with full bibliographical details is in Charles P Finlayson, *Clement Litill and his Library; the Origins of Edinburgh University Library* (Edinburgh Bibliographical Society and the Friends of Edinburgh University Library, 1980). The Library contains 243 of the original volumes. All appear in the Library's pre-1985 main catalogue and all are now catalogued online. The collection was reconstructed in the early 19th century by David Laing and all the books now have shelfmarks beginning 'Dd'.

....

MacCaig, Norman

See main entry under Archives and Manuscripts.
Coll-69

....

MacDiarmid, Hugh

See main entry under Archives and Manuscripts.
Coll-18

Macdonald, George

About 200 items on classical archaeology
were bequeathed by Sir George Macdonald
(1862–1940), numismatist, classical scholar
and archaeologist. He was an expert on
Romano-British history and this is reflected
in the collection. All items are in the Library's
pre-1985 main catalogue. Many have basic
online catalogue records and there is a
manual author catalogue of the collection
available via staff.

Shelfmark: MacD Coll.

F Haverfield, *Roman London*, 1911
Macdonald Collection

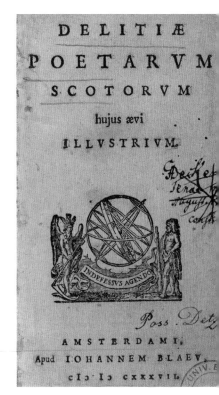

Mackay, Aeneas

This is an excellent and wide-ranging
antiquarian collection bequeathed
by Aeneas J G Mackay (1839–1911).
Educated at the Edinburgh Academy, at
King's College London and the Universities

Delitiae Poetarum Scotorum, 1637
Mackay Collection

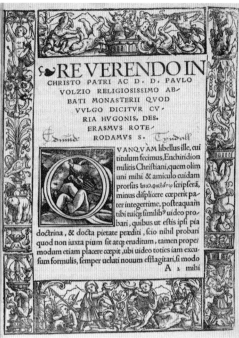

Erasmus, *Enchiridion*, 1518
Malkiewicz Collection

of Oxford, Heidelberg and
Edinburgh, he held the Chair
of Constitutional History at
the University of Edinburgh
from 1874 until 1881. He
was awarded an LLD by the
University in 1882 and founded
the Scottish History Society in
1885. He devoted the rest of
his life to the practice of law,
notably as Sheriff of Fife and
Kinross from 1886 until 1901,
as well as farming and forestry.

The collection includes
some 4,000 volumes mainly on
history, literature and law as well
as items on many other subjects.
Scottish books feature strongly but there
are also key works in French and English
literature, including a copy of Spenser's
1611 *Faerie Queene*.

All books appear in the Library's
pre-1985 main catalogue where they are
identified as coming from the Mackay
Bequest, and there are online records for
many of them. Shelflists for the material with
shelfmarks in the range Hf.–Hh. are available
in the Special Collections, but the rest of
the collection has always been scattered,
including open access locations.

....

MacKinnon, Donald

See main entry under Archives and Manuscripts.
Coll-98

Malkiewicz, Andrew

**From incunabula to
the French Revolution**

Andrew Malkiewicz lectured in history at
the University of Edinburgh, during which
time he collected a remarkable number of
rare books and manuscripts. He generously
presented this collection to the University
in 2013. There are some 300 printed items,
with particularly strong holdings of pamphlets
produced during the French Revolution. The
earliest item is an edition of Sallust printed
in Venice in 1474. There are also more than
40 manuscripts, ranging from a letter signed
by Charles IX of France in 1568 to orders of
Napoleon Bonaparte. The collection is fully
catalogued online.
Shelfmark: Malk.

Maps

A wide range of atlases, plans and early maps can be found across Special Collections. There are particularly strong collections of maps of Scotland and particularly Edinburgh, including Post Office maps and a remarkable volume of fire insurance plans which was in use from 1892 to 1960 (RB. FF.156). Early foreign maps include three attractively decorated 'portolan' pilot charts

drawn by Franciscus Oliva in Marseille in 1650 (Dc.1.40). There is also a significant number of Blaeu maps of Scotland, all catalogued online with shelfmarks beginning 'Blaeu'. There are many maps in printed books – travel literature being one of the collection's strengths – and in the archives and manuscripts, particularly in the collections relating to town planning or exploration. An annotated checklist of atlases is available.

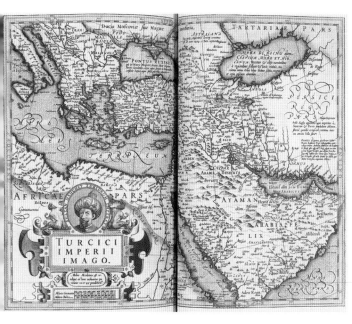

The Ottoman Empire, from G Mercator, *Atlas*

The Arctic, from G Mercator, *Atlas*

McCall Smith, Alexander

Alexander McCall Smith (1948–) was Professor of Medical Law at the University of Edinburgh, but has become an outstandingly successful novelist through his *No. 1 Ladies' Detective Agency* series. He is now one of the world's best-known writers for both adults and children.

This is a collection of translations of his works, donated by the author, which continues to receive additions. Languages represented include Korean, Swedish, Arabic and Japanese. The collection shows a good selection of examples of modern foreign fiction publishing. It also testifies to the influence of Scottish literature around the world.

At present there are more than 200 works in the collection. All are catalogued online with shelfmarks starting 'AMS'.

....

McPherson, Karin

This is a collection of 1,640 books published in and about the former country of East Germany, donated by lecturer Dr Karin McPherson. It includes many books not available elsewhere in Scotland and is a unique resource for the study of the culture, history and politics of the German Democratic Republic (GDR). It has been described as a time capsule, giving a comprehensive overview of the GDR's literary (and sometimes broader) culture from its inception to its end (1949 to 1989), with the main focus on the period from 1960 to 1989.

The collection includes prose by authors who gained recognition beyond the GDR. There are works by female authors who contributed substantially to an alternative approach to social issues in the GDR, including Anna Seghers, Brigitte Reimann, Irmtraud Morgner, Kerstin Hensel, Brigitte Burmeister and Sarah Kirsch. There is fiction by leading authors and poets who left the GDR under silent protest against political censorship, including Erich Loest, Reiner Kunze, Peter Huchel, Jurek Becker and Sarah Kirsch. There are major works by playwrights, including Peter Hacks and Heiner Müller. Finally, there is also poetry by figures who became leading influences in the establishment while at the same time upholding a critical stance within the socialist society. Foremost among them are Georg Maurer, Erich Arendt, Bertolt Brecht and Volker Braun.

All the books are catalogued online with shelfmarks starting 'KMP'.

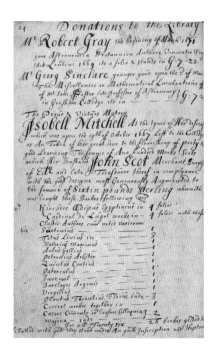

Mitchell, Isobel

In 1667 Isobel Mitchell, widow of John
Scott, Treasurer of the City of Edinburgh,
gave 26 books to the Library to the value of
£30. These included a Hebrew Bible printed
in Amsterdam in 1657. Thomas Craufurd,
regent in the College 1626–1662 and the
first historian of the University, described
her donation as 'the more esteemed because
it is from a worthy matron and lover of
learning, a good example to all others
of her sex'. Mitchell was the first woman
recorded as a donor to the Library, and
her books can still be located today using
manual finding aids.

Library Donations Register 1667–1824

Moon Collection

Brenda Moon, chief librarian of the
University 1980–1996, the first woman
to hold the post, bequeathed a selection of
books from her library to the University in
2011. The collection of 79 volumes reflects
her personal interests and research in travel,
Egypt, botany, natural history, poetry and
book illustration. Among them is a copy of
John Lylie's *Euphues: The Anatomy of Wit* from
1636, several works beautifully decorated
with woodcuts by Agnes Miller Parker, and
a copy of the first edition of *The Hobbit*.
The collection is fully catalogued online,
with shelfmarks starting 'Moon'.

T Allom, *Cornwall
Illustrated*, 1831
Moon Collection

iii. Rare Books

Moray House Library

The special collections of Moray House, the University's School of Education, include some important works in the history of education.

The Gilchrist Collection

This lifetime collection by Sandy Gilchrist, a retired headteacher from Lanarkshire, Scotland, of 2,500 Scottish school textbooks dating from 1700 to 1965, covers all parts of the Scottish curriculum. It includes texts used by pupils and teachers, Scottish local education authority and school schemes of work, and pamphlets and handbooks on classroom and school management directed at teachers and headteachers, published commercially or by local authorities or government bodies. This is one of the few collections available to education researchers studying Scotland's distinctive education system.

Aunt Judy's Magazine, 1866–1885

219

Children's Fiction collection pre-1960

A collection of children's novels, fairy tales, collections of stories and annuals, mostly from the 1850–1930 period, together with a number of reference books on the subject of children's fiction of that period, this contains about 400 books.

Ladybird Books collection

A collection of Ladybird books on every available subject, currently about 320 in number. There are also a number of Ladybird books in the Gilchrist Collection.

Selection of items, Moray House Library

Scottish Schools collection

Currently about 45 books on the history of individual Scottish schools.

Scottish Education Reports

Official reports on Scottish education from the years 1841–1978 including annual reports from the Scottish Education Department and its predecessors from approximately 1872 to 1978.

Murry, John Middleton

See main entry under Archives and Manuscripts.
Coll-62

....

Nairne, James

**Most significant donation
of the late 17th century**

James Nairne, or Nairn (1629–1678), left
the Library 1,840 items, mainly theological,
but also including scholarly works on history,
philosophy, literature, Classics, medicine
and science.

The son of an Edinburgh merchant,
Nairne entered the Tounis College in 1646,
graduating in 1650. Two years later he was
appointed to the post of librarian of the
College which he held until December 1653,
when he resigned to become Chaplain to
the Countess of Wemyss. He held charges
in a number of parishes near Edinburgh, in
Lothian, and finally in Wemyss in Fife. Among
his friends he numbered Robert Leighton,
who became Bishop of Dunblane where his
own library remains, and Gilbert Burnet,
Bishop of Salisbury and author.

Nairne's bequest increased the size of the
Library by one-third. It is one of the largest
surviving Scottish private libraries of its time,
and presents a picture of the intellectual
interests of an educated Scotsman of the
day. He was clearly receptive to current
developments in European thought and the
collection contains books that were widely seen
as revolutionary, such as the works of Spinoza.

A catalogue was printed at the time of the
donation: *Catalogus librorum quibus Bibliothecam
Academiae Jacobi Regis Edinburgenae adauxit R. D.
Jacobus Narnius* (Edinburgh, 1678). A detailed
modern listing is contained in Murray CT
Simpson, *Catalogue of the Library of the Reverend
James Nairn* (Edinburgh University Library,
1990). Some 133 items appear to have gone
astray over the years. All the books known to
survive are listed in the Library's pre-1985
main catalogue and many are now catalogued
online. Locations are scattered but the
collection can be reconstructed virtually
using Murray Simpson's catalogue.

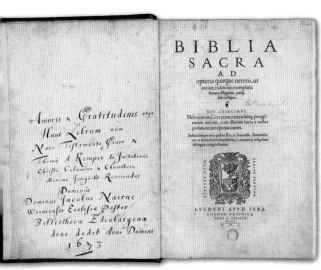

Biblia Sacra, 1550

Nelson, Thomas

See main entry under Archives and Manuscripts.

Coll-25

....

New College Library

New College Library began in 1843, with the formation of the Free Church of Scotland's New College. The original Library was founded upon donations, including many rare books from libraries, churches and individuals across Europe. The Library also grew by amalgamation, incorporating, for example, the library of the United Presbyterian Church in 1900 and the library of the General Assembly in 1958. In 1962, an agreement was ratified by the General Assembly of the Church of Scotland in which New College Library's collections were presented to the University of Edinburgh on permanent loan. Over its five floors, New College Library holds more than 250,000 volumes, of which approximately 90,000 are held in the Special Collections.

New College Library's rare book collections reflect its heritage as a centre of learning for Presbyterian ministry. Treasures from the Reformation include the first edition of John Calvin's *Institutes of the Christian Religion*, the progenitor of all subsequent Presbyterian doctrinal treatises, published in 1536, and the 1637 *Book of Common Prayer* with which Charles I attempted a unification of worship, which was driven out after the triumph of the Covenanters in 1638. Early Bibles in Latin, Greek and Hebrew as well as English form a rich seam throughout the collections, which also includes more modern Bibles in languages from throughout the globe. However the rare book collections also demonstrate more catholic interests, including more than 100 incunabula, and a complete set of the *Acta Sanctorum*, 68 volumes of the lives of saints, begun in 1643. The inclusion of the first edition of James Hutton's *Theory of the Earth* (1795) bears witness to the early teaching and debate about theology and science which continues in the School of Divinity today.

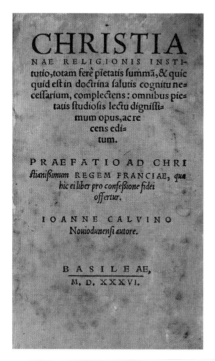

Jean Calvin, *Christianae religionis institutio*, 1536

Fructumꝗ vꝛ
ctoꝛie ſgentē
ꝓpłs roman⁹
ẹxcipere po=
ſcet hoꝛū. ꝛc.

℟ Symeon at Cryſtes cyrcunciſion
Theſe woꝛdes vnto the iewes dyde tell
Myn eyen bcholdeth your redempcyon
The lyght and gloꝛy of yſraell.

 Eus in adiutoꝛiū meū intēde
Dñe ad adiuuādū me feſtina
Gloꝛia pꝛi ⁊ filio: ⁊ ſpūi ſctō.
Sicut erat in pꝛincipio ⁊ nūc
et ſemper: ⁊ in ſecula ſeculoꝛ amē.

Hoſtiū vo du
ces et captiui
nobilioꝛes āte
victi duceban
tur vt ipoꝛ. ꝛc.

E iiij

Robert Louis Stevenson, *Prayers written at Vailima*, 1910

New College Library also holds significant archive and manuscript collections, with the general sequences holding many early items such as the last speech and testimony of covenanter James Renwick in 1688. (See separate entry under Archives and Manuscripts.)

With the help of the Funk Donation, considerable progress has been made in cataloguing the rare book collections online, but sheaf catalogues for the historic collections are also available in the New College Library Hall.

Dalman-Christie & Hebrew Collections

Jewish sacred texts, biblical scholarship and devotional works in Hebrew can be discovered throughout New College Library's Special Collections. These include the Dalman-Christie Collection, originally transferred to New College Library in 1946 from the Church of Scotland Hospice in Jerusalem. This contains early printed Jewish texts and volumes of prayers and festival devotions.

The study of Biblical languages to allow first-hand engagement with scriptural texts has always been a feature of the New College curriculum. This is reflected in the Hebrew Collection, which contains dictionaries, language primers and textual commentaries from the 17th to the 20th centuries.

Ieha-Rav rabenu Mosheh bar Naḥman. *Perush ha-Torah.* Pisa: Bene Sontsino, 1514

Jakob Breyne, *Exoticarum aliarumque minus cognitarium plantarum centuria prima*, 1678
Dumfries Presbytery Library

the Royal College of Physicians of Edinburgh (1681–1682), and court physician to King William III and Queen Mary (1688–1702).

Early Bibles

The Bible is at the heart of New College Library's rare books collections, just as it was in the Scottish Reformation. More than 600 early Bibles, many in large folio editions designed to be read from the pulpit, form one of the most heavily used Special Collections.

Dumfries Presbytery Library

The Dumfries Presbytery Library is a collection of 16th- and 17th-century books first documented in 1710, with the acceptance of a substantial donation of books from Dr John Hutton. Originally used as a lending library for the ministers of Dumfries, it was transferred to the General Assembly Library in Edinburgh in 1884, and then to New College Library in 1958. The New College librarian John Howard took a particular interest in the Dumfries Presbytery Library and reassembled 1,500 volumes from the collection in their original pressmark order. The books are inscribed from the library of John Hutton, first Treasurer of

Serenissimi et potentissimi Principis Iacobi, Dei gratia, Magnae Britanniae, Franciae, et Hiberniae Regis, fidei defensoris, opera… [Works of King James I & VI], 1619
Dumfries Presbytery Library

The Bible [Geneva Version], 1583   *The Byble in Englyshe* [Cranmer's Version], 1541

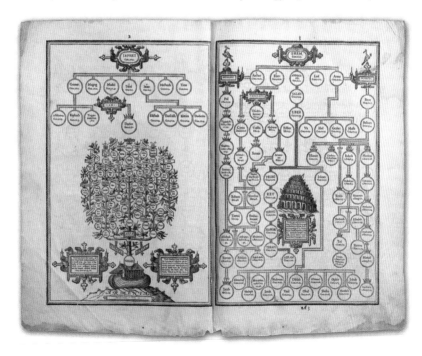

The Holy Bible [Authorised Version], 1611

Lactantius, *Diuinarum Institutionum libri VII*, 1532, formerly owned by Archbishop Thomas Cranmer

dictionaries, grammars, poetry and periodicals covering the language, history and culture of the Scottish Highlands. Many works are from limited print runs or known to be rare items. They can be identified using the shelfmark Gaelic Coll.

Hymnology Collections

At the heart of the Hymnology Collections in New College Library are 2,000 hymnbooks gifted in the 1880s by James Thin, the founder of the famous Edinburgh bookshop. This was added to by gift, purchase and the reorganisation of other library books to create this collection of more than 5,000 items. The collection includes psalms, sacred songs and poetry as well as hymns, including items intended for children, both for Sunday school and home use. There is much 19th-century material representing the Scottish Protestant

Predominantly English, but also including Latin, Greek and polyglot editions, this collection of rare Bibles ranges from the 16th to the 19th centuries.

Gaelic Collections

Just over 400 items form New College Library's Gaelic Collections of monographs and pamphlets, dating from the 18th to the 20th centuries. Much of the collection is religious or sacred verse, such as the poems of Dugald Buchanan and the hymns of Peter Grant, but it also includes history,

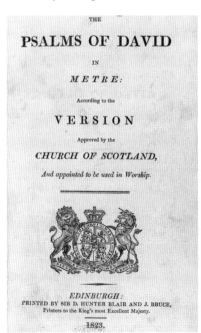

THE

PSALMS OF DAVID

IN

METRE:

According to the

VERSION

Approved by the

CHURCH OF SCOTLAND,

And appointed to be used in Worship.

EDINBURGH:
PRINTED BY SIR D. HUNTER BLAIR AND J. BRUCE,
Printers to the King's most Excellent Majesty.

1823.

The Psalms of David in metre, according to the version approved by the Church of Scotland, 1823

Decorated bindings from
the Hymnology Collection

Names of your Notes

John Playford, *The whole book of Psalms: with the usual hymns and spiritual songs,* 1707

tradition, but the collection also includes rare 17th- and 18th-century titles as well as works from other countries and denominations.

Incunabula Collection

New College Library possesses about 100 incunabula, or books printed between the birth of print in 1475 and the year 1500. These include a beautiful copy of Euclid's *Elements of Geometry,* one of the first printed books in which geometrical figures occur. Notable donor Frederick Sargent gave New College Library this 1481 edition of Platina's *Vitæ Pontificum.*

Inglis Collection

More than 40 items form the Inglis Collection, given to New College Library

Platina, *Historici Liber de Vita Christi ac Pontificum Omnia*, 1481

Euclid, *Elementa Geometriae*, 1482

in 1921 by the Reverend James W Inglis, missionary to Manchuria for the United Free Church of Scotland. The collection primarily contains Chinese Bibles and catechism, including an early printed edition of the Chinese New Testament produced by Robert Morrison (1782–1834).

Longforgan Free Church Ministers Library

The Longforgan Free Church Ministers Library came into New College Library in 1962 together with custom-made glazed bookcases. Online cataloguing has revealed a collection of 2,000 patristic and theological books, the earliest of which was printed in 1618. It reflects its origins as a manse library, a gift to the Free Church at Longforgan, Dundee by David Watson (1835–1904), owner of Bullionfield Paperworks at Invergowrie. Most of the items are in custom-made bindings, and several were found in mint condition with uncut pages.

Publication Committee of the General Assembly, Standard Documents Connected with the Free Church of Scotland, 1847

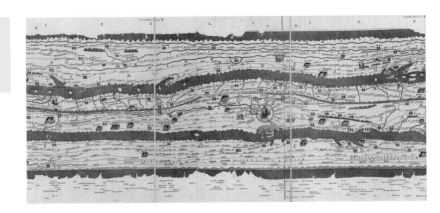

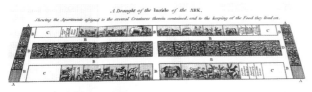

Conrad Miller, *Castori Romanorum Cosmographi: Tabula quae Dicitur Peutingeriana*, 1888
Longforgan Collection

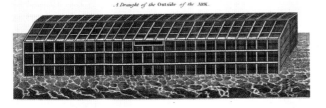

Edward Wells, *An Historical Geography of the Old and New Testament*, 1809
Natural Science Collection

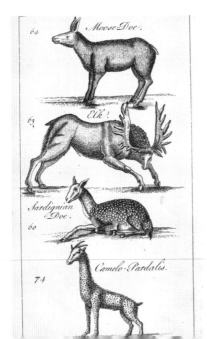

Natural Science Collection

New College Library's Natural Science Collection dates from the early days of New College, where 'natural science' was taught until the 1930s, when the College merged with the University of Edinburgh. Many of the books have bookplates and marks indicating their use with the Natural Science class. The collection covers the 19th-century controversies over evolution and natural selection, with geology also well represented.

Richard Brookes, *A new and accurate system of natural history*, 1763

Pamphlets

New College Library has an exceptional pamphlets collection of more than 35,000 items, possibly because when Professor David Welsh called for donations to found New College Library, he singled out pamphlets as of particular importance. Spanning the development of the Scottish Church from the time of the Reformation to the present century, the sermons, theological debates and reports of Church government and discipline which are contained in this collection are a reflection of the parallel development of Scottish history, and of the establishment and disestablishment of a national Scottish Church. Cheaply printed and distributed, pamphlets made current issues and debates of all kinds accessible in print to the ordinary reader. These flimsy publications were bound together to gather up the threads of religious and political argument, from 17th-century controversies to the present day. The Funk Donation enabled more than 12,000 items to be catalogued to complete the online cataloguing of this collection, which has revealed hundreds of items to be unique.

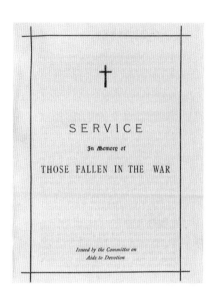

Church of Scotland Committee on Aids to Devotion. *Service in memory of those fallen in the war*, 1918

The Life and Prophecies of
Mr. Alexander Peden, Late Minister
of the Gospel at New Glenluce,
in Galloway, 1783

Ralph Erskine, *Faith's Plea upon God's Word and Covenant on a Preparation Day.* Edinburgh: Printed, and sold in Moriso's-closs, 1771

Paterson Collection

Containing approaching 300 items, largely
Bibles, in a huge variety of languages and
scripts, the Paterson Collection represents
the interests and life's work of John Paterson
(1776–1855). The National Bible Society
received this library in 1957 and gifted it
to New College Library in 1991.

Paterson was a Glasgow-trained
missionary for the Congregational Church,
who translated and printed the scriptures
into Finnish, Georgian, Icelandic, Sami,
Latvian, Moldavian, Russian, Samogitian
and Swedish. First based in Sweden, where
he founded the Finnish Bible Society, in
1812 Paterson moved to St Petersburg,
where he was involved in the work of
what became the Russian Bible Society.
In later life he returned to Scotland where
he continued to be active in the Scottish
Congregational Church.

Meije Issanda Jesusse Kristusse Wastne Testament
[Estonian New Testament], 1686

TESTAMENTE NUTAK

Kaladlin okauzeennut

nukterſimarſok, nar'kiutingoæn-
niglo ſukuïarſimarſok.

KIÖBENHAVNIME,
Uliarſuïn igloænne pingajuekſſinik nakittarſimarſok
1 7 9 9 .
C. F. Skúbartimit,

Testamente nutak: Kaladlin okauzeennut nuktersimarsok
[Eskimo Bible], 1799

Shaw Collection

Nearly 500 items form the Shaw Collection
on the Catholic Apostolic Church at New
College Library. Further research is required
to verify the history of this collection, but
it may have been put together by P E Shaw,
author of *The Catholic Apostolic Church,
Sometimes Called Irvingite: A Historical Study*
(New York, 1946). Several items in the
collection bear his inscription.

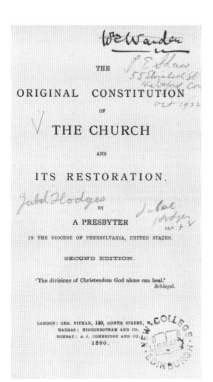

The Original Constitution of the Church and its Restoration, 1890

The Catholic Apostolic Church movement was inspired by Edward Irving (1792–1834), who began his career as a Church of Scotland minister who worked with Thomas Chalmers on his urban ministry projects. Irving moved to London where he became a strikingly popular preacher, holding charismatic services that included controversial spiritual phenomena such as speaking in tongues. The collection covers the liturgy, doctrines and government of the Catholic Apostolic Church movement, along with sermons and addresses by prominent figures in the church.

New Zealand collection

Our largest single Commonwealth collection

This major specialist collection includes some 7,000 volumes on all topics relating to New Zealand. The collection was formed in 1991 when the Government of New Zealand presented the historical volumes of the Library of the High Commission in London to the University of Edinburgh. The New Zealand House Library in London was the largest in New Zealand's overseas posts, and had been in existence for over a hundred years.

M Pomare, *Legends of the Maori*, 1930

Now known as the New Zealand Studies Collection, it includes extensive sets of New Zealand official publications, especially the Parliamentary series. It covers most aspects of New Zealand's life, history and development, with particular emphasis on history, exploration, literature, anthropology and Maori studies. Most titles were published before 1975.

The collection is dispersed, fully catalogued and available for standard loan. Some 200 books have been transferred to Special Collections, including numerous pre-1850 books and rare emigrants' books, ornithological books and early travel guides.

Orr, John

See main entry under Archives and Manuscripts.
Coll-77

Private Press Collections

Modern books in the great tradition
Edinburgh University Library holds a notable number of private press books in its Special Collections, with approximately 150 known titles from 24 British private presses. Produced in small numbers by craftsman of the print trade during the 19th, 20th and 21st centuries, these private press books have considerable artistic and literary value. The early 19th-century private press with the greatest number of works in the Library's collection is the Lee Priory Press, with 22 titles in the catalogue. There are also six examples of the late

19th-century Kelmscott Press, including William Morris's own *The Well at the World's End* (JY611).

The Nonesuch Press is the best-represented press from the 20th century with 35 titles in the collection, a number which also makes it the largest single private press holding in the Library. Between the world wars, the Nonesuch Press produced books in the Kelmscott tradition of fine printing between the world wars and the Main Library holds treasures such as the Nonesuch *La Divina Commedia*, the *Miscellaneous Poems* of Andrew Marvell, the *Paradoxes* of John Donne and *The Complete Works of William Shakespeare* (RECA.F.275, SC 933, RECA.S.117 and Hb.5.51). The Old Stile Press, a contemporary private press, has a significant showing in the Library's collection with over 20 stunningly illustrated books in Special Collections.

Edinburgh University Library also has select holdings of books from the Doves, Ashendene, Eragny, Gregynog, Vale, Essex House, Golden Cockerel, Shakespeare Head, Hogarth, Hafod, Signet, Tragara, Cranach, Fanfrolico, Brewhouse, Hawthornden, Mandrake, Beaumont, Rampant Lion and Shoestring Presses. Many of these books came to the Main Library's collection from Edinburgh College of Art, the library of Archibald Hunter Campbell and the Alan F Stark bequest.

These books are not physically kept all together, but all can be located through the online catalogue.

Publishers' Collection

Penguin paperbacks and the 20th-century explosion of print

Penguin Books had its beginnings in 1935, when the publisher Allen Lane found himself with nothing to read at an Exeter train station. The result was the Penguin paperback, which spearheaded the drive for quality mass-market publishing in the 20th century. This collection includes many early examples and first editions of what are now fragile books, giving an excellent overview of these developments in publishing.

The basis of the collection was a collection of more than 500 Penguin titles published before 1960, which were bequeathed to the Library by Kenneth Swanson Ryrie in 1979. Ryrie was a native of Thurso, who graduated from the University of Edinburgh in 1942 (MA Hons in Mathematics and Natural Philosophy). He worked on radar and navigational aids during the closing years of the Second World War, and spent the rest of his engineering career at Ferranti Ltd. He was a devoted Freemason and historian of the Craft, and collected books.

The collection has developed through donation, exchange and purchase to include various series such as Pelicans, Puffins, King Penguins and Penguin Specials. There are also examples of the work of other publishers who like Penguin sought to bring good literature to the masses, such as Gowans & Gray, Père Castor, Insel Bücherei, Stead's Books for the Bairns, Zodiac and Albatross. It is particularly interesting to see how the Second World War impacted on publishing in terms of titles, content and aspects of physical production such as paper quality.

There are now some 2,300 volumes, which are not yet catalogued, but a listing is available from staff.

Ramage, David Goudie

French and English poetry

Ramage (1907–1986) was a leading bibliographer and librarian, and one of his memorials is the ongoing collection purchased with funds he left to the University. Born in Leith, he graduated from the University of Edinburgh in 1929 with a first-class honours degree in English literature and language. A scholar in French and English, a minor poet and an historical bibliographer with particular interests in early printed books and private presses, he was appointed deputy librarian (1930–1936), and later librarian of the University of Durham (1945–1967), spending the intervening years as deputy librarian of the University of St Andrews. He compiled a *Finding-list of English books to 1640* (1958) and was editor of *The Durham Philobiblon*, a charming, eclectic and occasional bulletin of bibliography which ran from 1949 until 1969.

In 1987, under the terms of David Ramage's will, Edinburgh University Library received over £99,000 'towards the acquisition of a research collection of editions of French and English poetry'. The interest on this endowment provides for the purchase of books of poetry in French and English. Some of these volumes are on open access; rarer and more fragile pamphlet items are kept in Special Collections with shelfmarks starting 'Ramage'. Among the particularly rare and ephemeral items is a fine set of the subversive and elusive 1960s periodical *The English Intelligencer*. There are about 3,000 items in the collection, many of which are in the online catalogue.

T Moore, *Poetical Works*, 1840
Ramage Collection

Ransford Collection

Contemporary poetry, from the founder of the Scottish Poetry Library

Tessa Ransford (1938–2015), was born in India, returning to Britain with her family as a child. She wrote poetry from an early age, but was first encouraged to take it seriously while studying German at the University of Edinburgh. She published a number of collections of poetry from the mid-1970s onwards, and, inspired to create a centre in Scotland to provide a resource and support for poets, was the instigator, founder and first director of the Scottish Poetry Library. Shortly before her death in 2015 she donated nearly 850 volumes of her collection of contemporary poetry, much of it by Scottish poets, and many of the volumes with inscriptions and notes from the authors. After her death a further 100 volumes were donated by her executors. The collection is fully catalogued online.

Reid, John

A general immortalised in collections of music, rare books and manuscripts

John Reid (c.1721–1807) was a general and founder of the Reid Chair of Music at the University of Edinburgh; through his bequest some of the finest illustrated books were acquired.

The son of Alexander Robertson of Straloch in Perthshire, John Robertson was educated at the University of Edinburgh and received a commission in Lord Loudon's

Reid Bequest binding stamps, on Juvenal, *Satyrae*, 1644

regiment of Highlanders in 1745; he subsequently adopted his mother's maiden name as his own, she being a Reid of Straloch. He served with the regiment on the Hanoverian side during the 1745 rebellion, and afterwards in the Netherlands, Martinique and British North America. He purchased some 35,000 acres in Vermont, some of which was seized by settlers from New England in 1773, and he lost his claim to them following the American War of Independence.

He returned to London, where he was promoted to the rank of general, and died in 1807. A good flautist and composer, especially of music for wind bands, his best-remembered tune today is 'In the Garb of Old Gaul'.

In spite of his losses he left a sum of £68,876 for the founding of a Chair of Music at the University of Edinburgh, the money to be further applied to the purchase of a library or for any other proper purpose. The chair was established in 1839, after the death of his daughter who had a life interest in the estate, and from 1841 £400 per annum was used for the purchase of rare and costly books for the University Library. These have included early printed and finely illustrated books and medieval manuscripts. Originally these were shelved in the Reid Room in Old College, which was reserved for the use of professors and senior lecturers. This was the first fund available to the Library for purchasing historical research volumes that were not simply textbooks.

The purchases are scattered but many of the early books have shelfmarks beginning 'Re.' or 'Rq.'

Reid Music Library

From Boethius to Beethoven

The collections of early and special printed and manuscript music, in Special Collections since 2003, are some of the finest in the UK. The nucleus of the library was the books bequeathed by General John Reid, whose name the collection retains.

Rare highlights from the collection include an edition of Boethius on the theory of music printed at Venice in 1499 (C.204), and Sebastian Virdung's *Musica Getutscht* (Basel, 1511, C.186) – the first printed book on Western musical instruments. There are many first and early editions of composers such as Handel.

More recent printed material maintained as sub-sections of the Music Library include the Tovey and Weisse Collections, described separately. A more recent music accession is the Reid Concert Hall Collection of scores and other performance copies, many handwritten. The library of Frederick Niecks, Professor of Music before Tovey, is also distributed across library collections.

The earlier holdings are listed in the catalogue by Hans Gal, *Catalogue of Manuscripts, Printed Music, and Books on Music up to 1850 in the Library of the Music Department at the University of Edinburgh* (Edinburgh, 1941). Plans are underway to reorganise and recatalogue the whole music collection.

For the separate collection of English madrigal books, see W Beattie, 'The English Madrigal Books in the University Library', *University of Edinburgh Journal*, 4 (1930–1931), pp.12–17.

....

Roslin Institute

See main entry under Archives and Manuscripts.

....

Royal College of Surgeons

In 1763, the Royal College of Surgeons of Edinburgh, founded in 1505, gave its library to the University of Edinburgh, in return for borrowing privileges in the University Library. There are some 560 books, mainly medical but with some English literature and history. The earliest books are a copy of the *Hortus Sanitatis* (Strasbourg, c.1490, Inc.20) and a copy of Argellata, *Cirurgia* (Venice, 1497, Inc.119) but most are 17th-century continental publications. Some have manuscript notes which indicate they were bought by students abroad.

Sebastian Virdung, *Musica Getutsch*, 1511

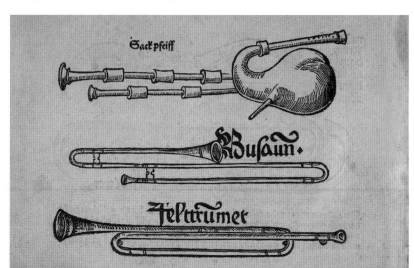

Petrus de Argellata, *Chirurgia*, 1497
Royal College of Surgeons Collection

The collection was scattered, but a list by size was drawn up at the time, and this has provided the basis for a recent listing by author, available via staff.

....

Royal Medical Society

The Royal Medical Society of Edinburgh, a student society founded in 1727, built up an impressive library over the centuries and still maintains substantial collections, particularly of manuscript dissertations. However, the great bulk of the library was sold at auction in 1969. Some 59 items not otherwise in Edinburgh were retained and are now on deposit in Edinburgh University Library. All items are fully catalogued online to a high standard. The shelfmarks begin with 'R.M.S.Coll'.

Ryrie, Kenneth Swanson

See Publishers' Collection.

....

School of Scottish Studies Library

See main entry under Archives and Manuscripts.

....

Serjeant, Robert Bertram

Islam and the Yemen

Robert Serjeant (1915–1993) was educated at the University of Edinburgh, where he graduated with an MA in Semitic Languages, and at Trinity College, Cambridge, where he gained his PhD in 1936. He was the Tweedie Fellow at the University of Edinburgh in 1939; during his fellowship he catalogued the Oriental manuscripts in New College Library, publishing his *Handlist of the Arabic, Persian and Hindustani MSS of New College, Edinburgh* (London, 1942), before moving to the School of Oriental and African Studies to engage in research on South Arabia. He saw war service in Aden before returning to England to teach at SOAS. He moved to the Middle East Centre, University of Cambridge in 1964, eventually retiring as Director, and as Professor of Arabic, in 1982. He was a prolific author and editor of publications on a wide range of Middle Eastern subjects.

In 1995 his widow Mrs Marion Serjeant gifted his library of some 5,000 volumes on Islam and the Yemen, together with his manuscripts, to the University. Most of the book collection is kept together as a specialist

(نأظر السراي)   (رئيس الموسيق)   (السيد منصب بن علي)   ومعهم صاحب السياحة

iii. Rare Books

collection; it is catalogued online and available on open access. It complements and is located beside other Middle Eastern collections such as the Watt and Smith collections.

There are also 11 boxes of manuscript material, mostly received in 2005, containing notebooks, typescripts and copies of Arabic documents.

Coll-1062

....

Session Papers

This collection of proceedings in the Scottish Court of Session contains an estimated 25,000 individual printed items in 600 volumes, all giving a fascinating insight into social conditions and domestic life in the 18th and 19th centuries. The importance of the law courts in Edinburgh is reflected in the collections around the city – the National Library of Scotland having begun life as the Advocates' Library to take just one example. The Law Library in Old College continues

to maintain rich collections of early and historical law, particularly in the Gordon Duncan room.

The Session Papers are not catalogued, but are arranged chronologically from 1744 to 1860, and may be consulted in the Centre for Research Collections. The series has shelfmark E.B. 346(41)4 Cou.

JULY 4th, 1766.

Unto the Right Honourable the Lords of Council and Se

THE

PETITION

OF

Mrs. ELIZABETH DUNBAR, lawful Daugh of, and general Difponee, and Executrix c firmed, to the deceafed Sir *Patrick Dunbar Northfield*, Baronet, and of *James Sinclair Durin*, Efq; her Hufband, for his Intereft,

Humbly fheweth,

THAT *George* Vifcount of *Tarbat*, afterwards of *Cromerty*, having purchafed Part of the La and Eftate that belonged to the deceafed Sir *Je Sinclair* of *Mey*, at a judicial Sale before y Lordfhips, was decerned, by the Decreet, dividing the P to pay to thofe having Right to two Decreets of Apprif to be hereafter mentioned, affecting that Eftate, the two lowing Sums, *viz.* the Sum of 5154 *l.* 15 *s.* 10 *d.* and of 331 *l.* 9 *s.* 10 *d.* both *Scots*, with Intereft from *Whitfur* 1694, and in Time coming, during the Not-payment.

The Perfons who had originally Right to thefe Apprifi which were both compleated by Charter and Seafine in 16 were *Alexander Cuthbert*, Provoft of *Invernefs*, and *Alexar*

A   *Dun*

Petition, July 4th, 1766

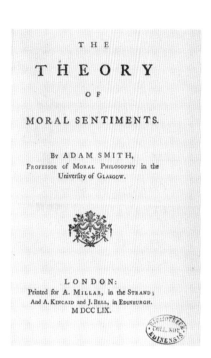

Smith, Adam

**Scotland's greatest economist –
and a great book collector**

The library of the great Scottish economist
Adam Smith (1723–1790) is one of our
landmark printed collections. There are about
850 works in 1,600 volumes, including some
great treasures such as a fine copy of the first
edition of Copernicus' *De revolutionibus* (1543).

We hold about half the original library,
with other significant portions in Glasgow
and Tokyo. The bulk of our collection was
given to the library of New College in the
19th century by David Douglas Bannerman
(1842–1903), grandson of David Douglas,
Smith's heir. The collection was transferred to
the Main Library in 1972. Smaller groupings
and individual items have been acquired
subsequently, such as 32 books in the
Hodgson Collection. We acquire books from
Smith's library whenever possible.

The collection is unsurprisingly strong in
politics, economics, law and history, but there
are also many literary works, particularly
French literature, and books on architecture
by Vitruvius and Palladio. The condition of
the volumes is generally good and there are
numerous examples of fine bindings from
the 18th century and earlier.

The books are fully catalogued online.
In 2010 the books were reconstituted as a
distinct special collection, with shelfmarks
starting 'Smith'. A published catalogue of
Smith's library is available: Hiroshi Mizuta,
Adam Smith's Library, 2000.

....

Gray–Steinbeck Collection

John Steinbeck first editions

The collection of John Steinbeck material,
consisting of almost 150 items, including
first, early and significant editions of his
works, examples of reprinted editions and
biographical and bibliographical works, was
collected by Robert P Gray, an alumnus
of the University, and honorary OBE, and
donated to the University of Edinburgh USA
Development Trust in 2015.

Particular highlights include a copy of
the first edition of Steinbeck's first novel
Cup of Gold, with the dustwrapper, published
shortly before the American stockmarket
crash of 1929, and first editions of *The Grapes*

of *Wrath*, *Of Mice and Men*, and *East of Eden*. The books are fully catalogued online, with shelfmarks starting 'Steinbeck'.

Gaspar Plautius, *Nova typis transacta navigatio*, 1621
Dugald Stewart Collection

....

Stewart, Dugald

Enlightenment philosophy in Edinburgh

Dugald Stewart (1753–1828) studied at the University of Edinburgh and was Chair of Moral Philosophy here from 1785. He taught political economy and a 'common sense' philosophy in opposition to the scepticism of David Hume.

Dugald Stewart's library included the books of his father Matthew Stewart (1717–1785), Professor of Mathematics at the University of Edinburgh. The collection passed into the hands of Dugald's son Colonel Matthew Stewart (c.1784–1851), who bequeathed it, along with many of his own books, to the United Service Club in London. In 1910 the whole collection, with books

from all three collectors, was transferred to the University of Edinburgh.

The collection contains 3,432 titles in some 4,000 volumes. It is a rich and broad collection covering many topics but particularly strong in political economy, moral philosophy and mathematics. It is particularly rich in French publications from the Revolutionary period. There is a large number of presentation copies reflecting Dugald Stewart's wide circle of acquaintances and admirers, for example from Jefferson, Byron and Maria Edgeworth. The younger Matthew Stewart added some early printed books (there are 33 incunabula in the collection) and works on oriental subjects.

For a short description of the collection, see the article by K C Crawford in *The Bibliotheck*, 10 (1980), pp. 31–34. A short-title catalogue by former Rare Books Librarian

Sheila Noble is available for consultation in the Centre for Research Collections. All the books appear in the Library's pre-1985 Guardbook catalogue and many are catalogued online. Most have shelfmarks beginning 'D.S'.

There are also some 21 manuscript volumes including letters, lecture notes and Dugald Stewart's diary of journeys in England and Scotland, 1797–1803. There are also papers of Helen D'Arcy Stewart, his wife (1765–1838).

....

Sussex, Duke of

In 1845 the University purchased some 1,000 early tracts relating to the Reformation from the library of Augustus Frederick, Duke of Sussex (1773–1843), sixth son of King George III. These greatly strengthen the Library's holdings of works by Luther and other 16th-century German reformers.

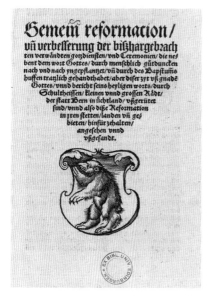

Gemein Reformacion

The books all appear on the pre-1985 Guardbook catalogue, with shelfmarks starting 'Dh'.

....

Theses of the University of Edinburgh

The unique record of student work

The rare book collections contain a remarkable body of student theses going back to the early 17th century. The collection allows us to trace the development of the thesis from an oral examination conducted in Latin, published as a single sheet that could be pasted on the wall – to modern scholarly research, now frequently supplemented with databases and digital images. The bulk of the thesis collection from the 18th and 19th centuries is medical; during the later period theses become increasingly substantial and illustrated with photographs and original drawings. A surprising number of medical students seem to have found reason to conduct their research in sunny locations such as the West Indies. During the 20th century the breadth of disciplines which could be examined for a PhD widened considerably, and early in the 21st century it became a requirement to submit an electronic as well as a paper version for the Library. In total there are now some 25,000 theses in the collection.

The 4,000 pre-1830 theses are mainly catalogued online to a high standard. They are scattered across various locations in Special Collections, and can be located by

Theses candidates and topics, Edinburgh, 1699

keyword searches. The 1830–1985 theses are mainly not catalogued online and can be located using manual lists. Since 1985 all new theses received have been catalogued online with shelfmarks starting 'Theses' and then arranged by year.

....

Tovey, Donald Francis

The theory and practice of music

Sir Donald Francis Tovey (1875–1940) was Reid Professor of Music at the University of Edinburgh and a brilliant musicologist and composer.

Tovey was privately educated by music teacher Miss Sophie Weisse (1851–1945) and then at Balliol College, Oxford. The young Tovey soon achieved fame as a pianist, scholar, composer and organiser of concerts in Britain and in Europe. This brought him into contact with many of the major music figures of the day, with whom he corresponded extensively and who held him in high regard. He was appointed to the Reid Chair of Music at the University of Edinburgh in 1914, in succession

Donald Francis Tovey

iii. Rare Books

to Frederick Niecks, and held the chair until his death. During his tenure his output of compositions and research publications continued unabated. His opera 'The Bride of Dionysius' was produced in Edinburgh in 1929, and his cello concerto was performed and recorded by Pablo Casals. He created the University's professional Reid Orchestra which brought together orchestral performers from the worlds of the University and professional music. He was knighted in 1935.

He bequeathed to the University his substantial library of printed and manuscript scores and books on music, and later brought a substantial archive of his correspondence and papers to join them. There are some outstanding items in the collection such as the manuscript of 'The Edinburgh Symphony' by Julius Röntgen. The books are arranged alphabetically by composer and are mainly catalogued online.

There are also over 20 metres of archival material, ranging from notes and drafts of lectures to accounts and administrative material, drafts of broadcasts to photographs and diaries, cuttings and reviews. There is also extensive correspondence between Tovey and Weisse, and other leading musical figures. The correspondence is catalogued online.

Coll-411

....

Turner, William Price

William Price Turner (1927–1998) was a poet, critic and editor who spent much of

his life in Glasgow or Yorkshire. In 2001 the University of Edinburgh acquired some 400 poetry pamphlets from Turner's library. They are all catalogued online with shelfmarks beginning 'Turner'.

....

Veterinary Library

See also Archives and Manuscripts.

Landmarks in the history of animal health

The Royal (Dick) School of Veterinary Studies was founded in 1823 by William Dick (1793–1866) and is the second oldest veterinary school in the UK. Following its merger with the University of Edinburgh, the Dick Vet's archives and rare books have been transferred to Special Collections over several years. The collection of 944 books that were formerly in the School's War Memorial Library suggests the breadth and depth of teaching and research. It contains many great highlights in the history of veterinary medicine, with particular but not exclusive strengths in farriery. There is an excellent copy of George

245

Stubbs' *The Anatomy of the Horse* (London, 1766). A number of books are unrecorded elsewhere. The dates range from 1537 to 1993.

George Stubbs, *The Anatomy of the Horse*, 1766

The collection also includes various sub-collections, particularly the 123 books relating to horses and ponies collected by lecturer James Grant Speed (1906–1980) who was an anatomist at the Veterinary School.

A total of 208 volumes transferred in earlier years are catalogued, with shelfmarks in the ranges SD 4783–4931, SCF 771–780, SC FF 95–102. Some 736 items transferred in 2011 are not yet catalogued. Plans are underway to recatalogue the whole collection as a distinct sequence with shelfmarks starting 'Vet'.

....

Wallace, Alfred Russel

The theory of natural selection

Alfred Russel Wallace (1823–1913) was a naturalist, explorer and writer. Born in Monmouthshire, he started his career as a collector of natural history specimens. He did extensive fieldwork first in the Amazon River basin, and then in the Malay Archipelago, where he identified the Wallace line dividing the fauna of Australia from that of Asia. In the Malay expedition he obtained 126,500 specimens, among them more than 200 new species of birds and more than 1,000 new insects. He also did important work on the orangutan. Wallace is best known for independently proposing a theory of natural selection which prompted Charles Darwin to publish his own more developed and researched theory sooner than intended. He became one of the world's most famous scientists. He is also known for espousing opinions now seen as scientifically eccentric, such as his opposition to vaccination and his interest in spiritualism and the paranormal.

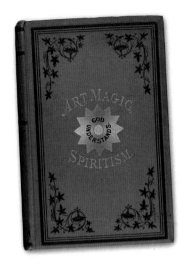

Emma Britten, *Art Magic*, 1876
Wallace Collection

His interests were wide, including a commitment to social progress and women's rights as well as science. These interests are reflected in his personal library of some 470 books, donated in 1993 by the University of Oxford Museum. They are now catalogued online, with provenance information, and located at shelfmarks SD 8270–8742.

....

Watt, William Montgomery

Islam and Christianity

William Montgomery Watt (1909–2006) was a priest in the Scottish Episcopal Church, and Professor of Arabic and Islamic Studies at the University of Edinburgh. Educated at the Universities of Edinburgh, Jena, and at Balliol College, Oxford, he held various lectureships at this University. In 1964 he accepted the chair, from which he retired in 1979. Ordained in 1939, he was an active priest who reflected and wrote on the relationship between Christianity and Islam for much of his life.

His collection contains some 1,400 titles and is strong in several areas, notably Islam, and particularly in Quranic commentary. Other subjects covered include mysticism and Islamic law, Islam and medieval philosophy, the relationship between Islam and Christianity, the history of the Arab world, and Arabic literature.

The collection is mainly catalogued online and is on open access, along with the related Serjeant and Smith collections.

....

Weisse, Sophie

Beethoven at Edinburgh

Sophie Weisse (1851–1945) was the piano teacher of composer Donald Francis Tovey (1875–1940), who became Reid Professor of Music at the University of Edinburgh. Her influence over Tovey was considerable and she maintained a close relationship with him from his childhood until his death.

Beethoven, *Briefe*, 1909

Her collection of some 600 books and scores relating to Beethoven was purchased in 1948.

The collection is not catalogued, but has recently been reassembled as a prelude to listing, with shelfmarks starting 'Weisse'.

....

White, James Cathcart

Gifts of books and money: a continuing tradition

James Cathcart White (1853–1943), an Edinburgh graduate and advocate, left the Library a fine collection of some 360 works and a significant sum of money which is still used to purchase books and manuscripts today.

The collection includes incunabula, including a copy of Cicero's *Epistolae ad Familiares* printed on vellum in 1469 (Inc.76.5), which happens to be the first

Book of Hours, possibly English, 15th century

book printed in Venice. There are other early printed works and modern titles, mainly of English literature, history and biography, which are scattered throughout the Library.

Cathcart White also bequeathed 14 late medieval manuscripts, including 11 magnificent Books of Hours. These are described in N R Ker, *Medieval Manuscripts in British Libraries*, vol. 2 (Oxford, 1977).

For further information, see:
Donaldson, Robert, 'Nine incunabula in the Cathcart White Collection in Edinburgh University Library'. *The Bibliotheck*, 2, 1959, pp.66–69.
University of Edinburgh Journal, 12 (1942/1943), p.72.

Book of Hours, Flanders, 15th century

iv. Musical Instrument Collections

The University's musical instrument collection is unsurpassed in the UK, and comparable to prestigious collections worldwide in Paris, Brussels, Berlin and New York. The collection contains many instruments which are the 'oldest', 'rarest' or 'best' examples of instrument-making in the world. The collection is also one of the first to achieve the status of Recognised Collection of National Significance from the Scottish Government in 2007, having been accredited under the Museums Accreditation Scheme since 1998.

Double-manual harpsichord, Jacob Kirckman, London, 1755

Double-manual harpsichord, Joannes Ruckers, Antwerp, 1638

Double-manual harpsichord by Pascal Taskin, Paris, 1769

The collection has its origins in the late 1840s when Professor John Donaldson started to collect objects expressly for the study of musical instruments and acoustics. It was partly because of the instrument collection that the teaching of music moved from Old College to the newly built Reid School of Music in Bristo Square in 1859. From comparatively small beginnings, the collection has grown over the years, in particular since the late 1960s. This increase can be attributed in part to the gift of the Raymond Russell Collection of Early Keyboard Instruments (and the decision by the University to purchase St Cecilia's Hall to display the collection) and the 1968 Galpin Society Exhibition, held during the Edinburgh Festival and displayed at the Reid Concert Hall. Presently the

collection numbers about 5,270 objects, covering all musical instrument traditions. Many of the instruments came to the University as part of collections of private individuals – often the world authorities in their particular instrument type.

Musical instruments form an unusual category of object in being primarily made as tools for making music, while also often decorative objects in their own right. Instruments were highly prized, and the surviving examples

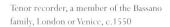

Tenor recorder, a member of the Bassano family, London or Venice, c.1550

Tenor trombone,
Anton Schnitzer II,
Nuremberg, 1594

from earlier centuries say much
about cultural connections, particularly
throughout Western Europe. Some of the
larger instruments – keyboards and some
stringed instruments – also serve a research
purpose in the general field of decorative
arts, as they are dated. Other objects
(often unsigned pieces) can be compared
stylistically, enabling a greater understanding
of decorative art developments.

Violin without sides, a member of the Bassano
family, London, probably second half of the
16th century

A significant number of the instruments
are maintained in playing condition, and
are regularly played in concert series,
demonstrations and for teaching.

Among the most prestigious items in the
collection are:

- the only double-manual harpsichord
  by the Ruckers family, produced in
  1638, with its original unaligned
  keyboards
- a harpsichord by Pascal Taskin, dated
  1769, which is the most reproduced
  harpsichord in the world (and, indeed,
  the model for the first 'reproduction'
  harpsichord)
- a solid ivory recorder made in England
  by a member of the Bassano family
  (probably in the mid-16th century)
- violins by members of the
  Bassano family
- a trombone by Schnitzer, Nuremburg,
  dated 1594
- an early *cornett*, probably dating from
  the 17th century
- a very early clarinet made only
  a generation after the instrument
  was invented
- two full sets of early saxophones made
  by Adolph Sax himself
- a unique contrabass serpent (known as
  the 'anaconda' because of its size)

Quarter of instruments made by Adolph Sax,
Paris, all dating between 1856 and 1861

- guitars by all the leading makers
  from the early 19th century –
  Lacote, Staufer, Fabricatore,
  Panormo and Pages
- four Italian baroque guitars from
  the early 17th century.

A particularly remarkable instrument is the
Blades tam-tam. One of the common sights
when viewing films from the mid-20th century
is the opening credits of films made by the Rank
Organisation. A well-built minimally dressed
man uses a large hammer to strike a gong
of almost the same size as himself. However
everything is not as it seems – the pictured
gong is, in fact, a papier mâché model that is

twice the diameter of the real instrument. Had
it been genuine the performer might well have
been deafened. The actual instrument used to
record the sound belonged to James Blades,
whose collection we hold.

Tam-tam, unsigned,
China, c.1930

Five 19th-century
guitars. From left:
René Lacôte, Paris,
c.1830; Louis
Panormo, London,
c.1845; Josef Pages,
Cadiz, 1813; Gennaro
Fabricatore, Naples,
1822; Johann Georg
Stauffer, Vienna, 1829.

Anne Macaulay Collection

Anne Macaulay had a particular interest in fretted stringed instruments, in particular those of the guitar and lute family. A member of the Fife-based Russell family of paper-makers and a professional pilot, she started collecting in the 1960s at a time when interest in these instruments was particularly limited, and was able to amass a collection of fine examples. She was an active amateur player and was particularly interested in examples that were in, or could be restored to, playing condition.

Her collection is wide ranging, in particular in relation to instruments of the guitar family. It includes a number of early baroque guitars from Germany, France and Italy (including examples attributed to

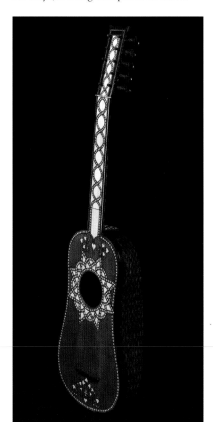

Matteo Sellas of Venice; Pfanzelt, which was converted in the historical period from gut to metal strings; and Pietro Railich with the back, sides and neck decorated in very fine parquetry work). Later guitars feature a six-course Spanish example by Josef Pages of Cadiz (with the finest decoration of its type), and a range of early 19th-century guitars by other leading makers such as Fabricatore, Panormo and Lacote, and later instruments by C F Martin, and Manuel Ramirez – the last built at the time the workshop was near its pinnacle, having one of its instruments used by the then-young Andrés Segovia.

Other instruments of particular note include several English *guittars* (wire-strung instruments of the 18th century), including examples by Hintz and Gibson, the latter with an ivory fingerboard and beautifully elegant tuning machine-heads with an enclosed gearing.

C H Brackenbury Memorial Collection

The Brackenbury Collection is wide ranging and was built up over many years. It includes examples of many types of instrument. The collection is particularly strong in stringed instruments of various types. There are some unusual specialisms within the collection, for example several early gut-strung mandolins and a number of English *guittars*.

Objects other than complete instruments have also been collected, including a presentation

Baroque guitar by Pietro Railich, Venice, c.1650

Milanese or Lombardic mandolin, Michel Angelo
Bergonzi, Cremona, 1755

box containing hundreds of parts from
viols and violins such as end-pins, scrolls,
bridges and tailpieces. Such a collection
is rare as these items are often lost once
removed from the original instrument but
are often finely made or highly decorative.

....

John Donaldson Collection

It is to John Donaldson, Professor of Music
at the University of Edinburgh from 1845 to
1865, that we owe both the Reid Concert
Hall and the nucleus of the instruments that
has become the present musical instrument
collection. He was very forward-thinking in
his approach to teaching, and to the needs
of music within the University as a whole.
His work and tenure included the building of
the Reid Concert Hall as a teaching building

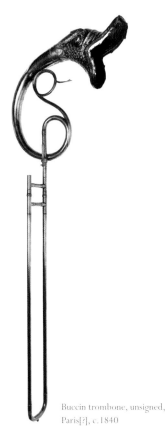

Buccin trombone, unsigned,
Paris[?], c.1840

for music and for housing the music library and museum of instruments. Money for building the hall and for acquiring objects for the collection came from the bequest of General Reid – a military man who was a keen musician and amateur composer. A series of photographs survive from the late 19th century showing the collection *in situ* as Donaldson intended it, and from these the importance which collections played in the day-to-day teaching and education of music students during this period is very apparent.

The collection was not, unlike other general musical instrument collections, amassed out of any personal interest in particular types of instrument, but rather as a collection which was to be used in University teaching. It includes apparatus for the teaching of acoustics and illustrating general principles of instrument construction and physics. In many ways Donaldson appears to have been attracted to the more unusual – examples include a violin without sides (then catalogued as 'old', and now believed to have been made by a member of the Bassano family in London during the second half of the 16th century), an English *guittar* with a piano-key mechanism and several *pochettes* – small dancing-master's violins which, as the name suggest, fit into the master's pocket when not in use.

Sir Nicholas Shackleton Collection

Professor Sir Nicholas Shackleton was a highly distinguished geoscientist at Cambridge University whose work was groundbreaking and award-winning. His approach to forming and refining his musical instrument collection – principally one of clarinets – was undertaken in the same scholarly manner, and is one of the world's most outstanding woodwind collections (in both size and scope), which he amassed over a 40-year period.

The clarinets range in date from about 1740 – not long after the invention of the instrument – to comparatively modern times. The collection represents the clarinet in all of its forms (as well as a number of other woodwinds), including outstanding examples by the finest historical makers. There are also instruments that are in some way unusual – perhaps in their choice of material or key mechanism. The collection includes clarinets made, unusually, from brass, ebonite (a black-coloured early plastic) and clear plastic.

The collection consists of some 880 instruments, including 817 clarinets and basset horns, along with 42 flutes and examples of oboes, bassoons and French

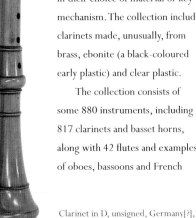

Clarinet in D, unsigned, Germany[?], c.1740

Clarinet in D, unsigned, Germany[?], c.1740

Rodger Mirrey Collection of Early Keyboard Instruments

Dr Rodger Mirrey started his collection in the mid-1960s at a time when interest in early keyboard instruments was increasing year by year. As a collector he was less concerned with instruments that were highly decorative, and concentrated on those which were of clear importance to the history of early keyboard instruments as individual examples. In doing so, he put together specific groups which are highly important to several traditions of early keyboard history.

One particular area in which this collection is unrivalled is the early English harpsichord, where Mirrey was able to acquire examples by Thomas Barton, Benjamin Slade, John Crang and John Wilbrook. Together these form a group which amounts to about one-third of the surviving instruments of their type, and in which each individual instrument has its own great importance. The Crang instrument, in particular, has an ownership history which can be traced from new in 1745, and its casework is in a style somewhat removed from the (by then) standard veneered and cross-banded decoration.

A second area of particular note is the collection of Italian harpsichords, including an instrument of 1574 by Bernardinis de Trasuntinis (the oldest dated instrument in the whole University instrument collection), and examples of the work of Cresci, Muccardi, Fransiscus di Paulinis and Migliai. Each of these instruments is unique and important in the history of Italian instruments.

horns. The clarinets cover all sizes from the largest contrabass instruments to the smallest examples in high A (essentially an octave above the 'normal' clarinet). All major traditions are represented, usually by the finest examples of their kind.

The scientific approach by which the collection was formed shows the clarinet scholar the development of the instrument over the centuries. It also allows the scholar, in the case of important makers such as Simiot, to examine a relatively large number of a maker's examples side by side and to trace the similarities and changes that can be found in the finest workshops.

Double-manual harpsichord, Luigi Baillon, Cyteux, 1755

Other important instruments in the collection include the unsigned Flemish clavichord of c.1620 and an unfretted small-compass Saxon clavichord from the first half of the 18th century (contemporary with J S Bach). The double-manual harpsichord by Baillon is an important and rare example of a French-made instrument built outside Paris. It has many Saxon influences, the maker probably having learnt there, and is an outstanding example of historical significance.

....

Raymond Russell Collection of Early Keyboard Instruments

Raymond Russell was a man of independent means and with a passion for knowledge. It is his collection and legacy to the University that has provided the focus for the acquisition, study and performance of early keyboards at the University of Edinburgh. His book *The Harpsichord and Clavichord*, first published in 1959, is still used as the standard introductory textbook on early keyboard instruments. Russell started his collection in the late 1940s at a time when there was a general lack of interest in early keyboards, which, combined with his knowledge and resources, allowed him to create a private collection which was unrivalled in scope.

All of the major keyboard traditions are represented within the collection, including particularly rare examples such as a harpsichord by Johann Adolph Hass from Hamburg, along with a clavichord by the same maker dating to

Unfretted clavichord, Johann Adolph Hass, Hamburg, 1763

the previous year, and a musically unaltered harpsichord by Joannes Ruckers (the 'Stradivarius of the harpsichord world') along with three other examples from the same family's workshops.

There are also two late 18th-century French double-manual harpsichords, both of which are very popular models as the basis for modern reproduction instruments. One is by Pascal Taskin and the other by Goermans, which was altered by Taskin some 20 years after it was built. This process included altering the initials in the decorative rose to make it appear that it was made by Joannes Couchet, a member of the Ruckers family, greatly increasing the value of the instrument. A highly decorated double-manual harpsichord by Jacob Kirkman of London has an interior featuring walnut and sycamore marquetry designs, the exterior with panels of burr walnut and half-cabriole

claw-and-ball legs. The instrument is a superb example of Georgian woodworking in addition to a fine-sounding harpsichord.

Russell's interest extended to smaller examples as well, including virginals by Bertolotti (a Venetian-made instrument from the late 16th century) and Stephen Keene (the largest surviving English virginal), clavichords, and various English-made instruments covering much of the 18th century.

....

Frank Tomes Collection

Numbering some 63 items, the Frank Tomes Collection is small, but shows a high level of connoisseurship in its compilation. Although it does not represent everything that Tomes himself collected, the selection best represents the intentions of Tomes as a collector. The quality of the objects shows the eye of a collector who was also a highly skilled professional brass-instrument maker.

The collection is not restricted to a single type of instrument, although brass instruments are predominant. They span the range of examples, including the bugle, serpent, ophicleide, cornopean, cornet, vocal horn, saxhorn, clavicor, tuba, trumpet and trombone. Non-brass objects include instruments of world cultures: wind instruments, the clarinet, and a Turkish crescent – a large percussion instrument with numerous bells that went by the popular name of the 'Jingling Johnny'.

Of especial interest to researchers are the larger, less conventional brass instruments such as the Russian bassoon, *serpent forveille* and ophicleide – all of which share a kinship and a position among instruments which never quite made it into the long-term musical mainstream, for all their individual characteristics and attractions.

The collection also includes brass instrument mouthpieces. Mouthpieces, like bows, may often be considered to be somewhat ephemeral, but in fact have a bearing on the tone the instrument produces.

....

James Blades Collection

The James Blades Collection brings together the multitude of instruments that were owned by James Blades, the leading London-based orchestral and studio percussionist of the

Ophicleide in C by Charles Pace, London, 1849–1858

mid-20th century. Perhaps the most important job that Blades held was also the most simple: every few months he would go into a studio with his tam-tam – one of several he owned – and strike it (see page 254).

Perhaps no musician has to cover as wide-ranging collection of instruments as a percussionist. Composers of orchestral music make use of both tuned (xylophone, glockenspiel, tubular bells, tuned timpani) and untuned (cymbals, kettledrums, side-drums, bass drum, triangle) instruments, and will frequently call for a wide variety of sounds according to the piece of music. A typical orchestra will often require more than one percussionist to comply with the composer's intentions. Even percussionists who play other types of music are required to play numerous objects, frequently needing both hands and feet to be employed simultaneously.

The collection includes other objects such as kettledrums, gong drums, tom-toms, side drums, cymbals, glockenspiels, tubaphone, and a variety of instruments made by Blades himself. It was common practice for percussionists to devise and make their own instruments in order to achieve a sound that was particularly desired.

Bagpipe Collection

In 2008 the musical instrument collection was awarded a grant by the Heritage Lottery Fund through its *Collecting Cultures* stream. This five-year project saw the purchase, display and publication of a new collection of bagpipes for the University. The bagpipe is traditionally thought of as a Scottish instrument, immediately conjuring images of players dressed in tartan pipes marching (often in bands) at the Edinburgh Tattoo and numerous other events. Although this image is, of course, legitimate, it represents only one aspect of the British pipe tradition.

Whereas the Highland pipes are particularly associated with Scotland and its musical heritage, numerous other types have co-existed with the Highland pipes, usually for use in vastly different contexts. Scotland has several types such as the Lowland pipes and Border pipes – smaller chamber instruments

that have a more limited, but thriving, following. Outside Scotland, the Northumbrian pipes have a solid tradition, while other parts of the British Isles can also lay claim to pastoral pipes and even perhaps the Union pipes which are particularly well known in Ireland.

The remit of the acquisitions project was to collect examples of the British pipe and interpret them in a wider context. As a result, instruments of all the piping traditions were collected and exhibited. Some of the instruments came from the collection compiled by Andreas Hartmann-Virnich, including six sets of pipes and seven chanters made by the Glen family of Edinburgh.

The acquisition project resulted in addition of some 18 sets of pipes and nine practice chanters to the collection.

Pastoral Pipes, probably by Hugh Robertson, Edinburgh, c.1775

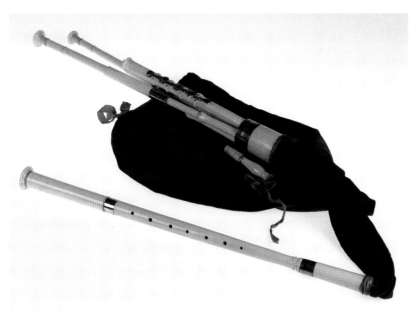

v. Art Collection

The University of Edinburgh Art Collection contains
over 8,000 works of art and consists of a wide variety of
styles, mediums and periods. In terms of sculpture alone,
this ranges from the 1st-century Gandharan fragments,
through 16th-century Italian Renaissance bronzes to
contemporary pieces. With the recent inclusion of
the Edinburgh College of Art Collection, the overall
University Art Collection is now more than four times
larger than it was before 2011 and is one of the most
important collections of its type in Scotland.

Blue Vase
Leslie Hunter
© The University of Edinburgh

University of Edinburgh Art Collection

The University holds more than 8,000 works of art, through a merger of the University of Edinburgh's original Fine Art Collection, which spans some 400 years of collecting, and the Edinburgh College of Art Collection of prints, drawings, paintings and sculpture. Some works in the Art Collection have been commissioned, some purchased, while others were acquired to decorate University rooms and certain collections came to the University as bequests. As a result, the collection has its own unique character.

Particularly with the addition of the Edinburgh College Art Collection, the University Art Collection is notable for an emphasis on Scottish art. This includes an extensive collection of historical and contemporary Scottish portraits featuring major historical figures and past principals and professors of the University. Modern Scottish art is also well represented with pieces by Joan Eardley, Francis Cadell, William MacTaggart and featuring a significant collection of works by William Johnstone.

A large percentage of the University Art Collection is on display throughout the campus, enhancing the public, staff and student spaces. A number of works from the Torrie Collection of Dutch and Flemish masters are on long-term loan to the National Galleries of Scotland where they are seen by upwards of one million people per year. The principal areas of display on campus include the Talbot Rice Gallery, Edinburgh College of Art, Old College, Playfair Library, Raeburn Room, Edinburgh University Library, New College, McEwan Hall and the Royal (Dick) School of Veterinary Studies.

The Art Collection is vital as a teaching resource and is actively used in seminars and lecture programmes. New interpretations and collaborations are sought so that collections are displayed in different and

Untitled (1959)
William Gear
© The Artist's Estate

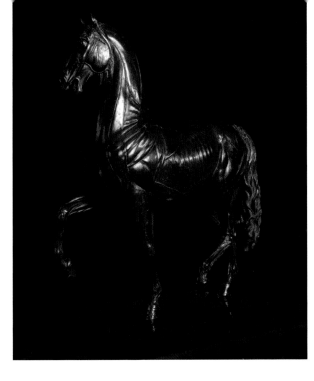

exciting ways, introducing contemporary insights to constantly reinvigorate debate, with the University community central to those conversations.

The University has been fortunate to have received many bequests of significant art works throughout its history. The size and circumstances of these gifts vary greatly and these stories add further richness to the overall history of the Art Collection; consequently, the collection itself is subdivided to retain the provenance of the collections. In 2013, two new collections were added – the Modern & Contemporary Art Collection and the Contemporary Art Research Collection. With the Contemporary Art Research Collection, still in its infancy, the development of the Art Collection will be linked clearly to academic teaching and research.

Individual iconic items from the Art Collection include:

Anatomical Figure of a Horse (ecorché) (1585), circle of Giovanni da Bologna (Jean de Boulogne) known as Giambologna (1529–1608)

A fine Mannerist bronze, the centrepiece of the Torrie Collection, bequeathed to the University by Sir James Erskine, 3rd Baronet of Torrie, in 1825.

Flemish-born artist Giambologna was the greatest sculptor in the 16th century and was second only in reputation in Italy to Michelangelo. He was court sculptor to three successive Medici Grand Dukes, and his influence on European sculpture was immense. This piece is a version of a flayed (ecorché or skinned) horse formerly in the Villa Mattei, Rome. Traditionally, it has always been connected with Giambologna's equestrian statue of Duke Cosimo I (1594), which stands in the Piazza della Signoria in Florence.

Cain and Abel (1612), Adrian de Vries

One of only three works by Adrian de Vries (1555/6–1626) in Britain and one of the most important in the Art Collection. After the death of Giambologna, de Vries was the most celebrated sculptor in Europe.

De Vries spent much of his career in Prague and, in 1601, became King's Sculptor to Emperor Rudolf II. It was during this period that *Cain and Abel* was commissioned. Rudolf's personal circumstances give an insight into the commissioning of the sculpture. He was involved in a bitter dispute with his brother Matthias that lasted until Rudolf's death in 1612. The significance of a commission depicting fratricide is clearly indicative of Rudolf's struggle for power.

Banks of a River (1649), Jacob van Ruisdael

An important early work by Jacob van Ruisdael (1628/9–1682), which is one of the finest by the artist in a British public collection. This sweeping river scene is based on various studies of nature and is an adaptation of another painting made two years earlier – *River Landscape with a High Sandy Bank* (Hague Collection, Denmark). The town in the distance is derived from drawings Ruisdael made of the town of Rhenen, on the Rhine. As with Rhenen, *Banks of a River* includes the distinctive tower of the church of St Cunera and the twin towers of the watergate. The figures in the scene were probably painted by Ruisdael's friend Nicolaes Berchem or by Philips Wouwerman.

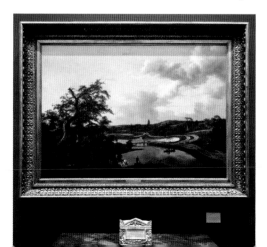

Going to the Fair **(1900), Pablo Picasso**

Bequeathed to the University in the 1980s by Hope Scott, *Going to the Fair* is one of only seven pre-1906 works by Picasso (1881–1973) on paper in British public collections. Most of the pieces from this period are in collections in Europe and America.

Created when he was 19 years old, *Going to the Fair* was made for display in formative exhibitions in Picasso's native Barcelona, before his move to Paris.

It is thought that the signature was added by the artist long after the work was completed. This was perhaps at the request of a private collector to further authenticate and add value to the piece as Picasso's fame soared.

....

Named Art Collections

Torrie Collection

Although the Art Collection truly begins in the 17th century, it is the Torrie Collection that signifies the core of the collection. Bequeathed by Sir James Erskine, 3rd Baronet of Torrie, the body of work consists of 46 paintings, 27 pieces of sculpture and three bronze vases. The main emphasis of this collection is on 17th century Dutch, Flemish and Italian art, including three iconic items

mentioned earlier: *Anatomical Figure of a Horse* by Giambologna (1585), Adrian de Vries' *Cain and Abel* (1612) and Jacob van Ruisdael's *Banks of a River* (1649).

James Erskine was born at Torrie House, Fife, in 1772 and, as well as an accomplished art collector, was a highly successful career soldier. Rising to the rank of Lieutenant General, he served with Wellington and it was through Erskine's military service that some of the works that now form the Torrie Collection would have been acquired. It was common for high-ranking military men to collect antiques and works of art to populate their residences and Dutch art was the emerging fashion of the time.

After the French Revolution and Napoleon's subsequent invasion of Holland, Dutch art entered the London art market for the first time. As well as Wellington himself, many of the people in Erskine's social and professional circles were keen art collectors. Between 1802 and 1804 Erskine was aide-de-camp to King George III and also a friend of the Prince Regent, who himself was a major collector of Dutch landscapes.

As well as being displayed extensively within the University and at the National Gallery of Scotland, works from the Torrie Collection have been loaned for exhibitions all over the world, including London, Vienna, Los Angeles and Madrid.

For further information, see:
The Torrie Collection. *An Exhibition to Mark the Quatercentenary of the University of Edinburgh* (Edinburgh, 1983).
Duncan Macmillan, *A Catalogue of the Torrie Collection* (Edinburgh, 2004)

Hope Scott Collection

Hope Scott was the only daughter of Henry Johnston Younger of Harmeny, near Balerno, of the long-established brewing dynasty. A large part of the art collection that she built was bequeathed to the University in 1989 and comprises three groups of pictures, totalling 99 works in all. Primarily, the collection consists of a group by the Scottish abstract artist William Johnstone, a close friend of Scott's.

In all, the Hope Scott Collection contains 59 pieces by Johnstone and, when combined with other work held by the University, this constitutes a major group of the later work of one of the most important and influential Scottish artists of the 20th century.

The collection also contains pieces by some illustrious artists, including *Going to the Fair* (1900) by Pablo Picasso, mentioned earlier. Other important works include paintings by

S J Peploe, Pierre Bonnard and Max Ernst and works on paper by Alan Davie, Francis Cadell and Sir William Gillies. The collection shows Scott's varied tastes and also – particularly in the case of Picasso, Ernst and Johnstone – a keen eye for Modernism and abstraction.

For further information, see:
Duncan MacMillan, *The Hope Scott Collection* (Edinburgh, 1991).

Portrait Collection

The University holds one of the largest collections of portraits in Scotland, second only to the National Galleries of Scotland. This area includes more than 400 portraits collected over the four centuries of the University's history. Most of these represent prominent figures connected with the University, including the philosopher Adam Ferguson, musician Sir Donald Francis Tovey, mathematician John Playfair, and medical pioneers Sir James Young Simpson and Sir Joseph Lister. Artists represented include Henry Raeburn, John Watson Gordon, Anne Redpath and Stanley Cursiter.

Sitters represented in the collection include King James VI, Queen Catherine of Braganza, Edward VII as Prince of Wales, Robert Burns and George Mackay Brown. Taken together, the portraits provide a fascinating reflection on the history of learning and culture in Scotland. More recent acquisitions include Ken Currie's 2008 portrait of the

Terra Rosso
William Johnstone
© The estate of William Johnstone

Peter Higgs (2008)
Ken Currie
© The artist / Courtesy
Flowers Gallery,
London and New York.

Nobel Prize-winning physicist Peter Higgs and a bust of the philanthropist Andrew Grant by Kenny Hunter.

Key to the portrait collection are half a dozen works by Sir Henry Raeburn, the leading Scottish portrait painter during the late 18th and early 19th centuries. Born in Edinburgh, Raeburn returned to the city in 1787 after spending time in Italy and began painting portraits of many of the notable figures of the Scottish Enlightenment.

The earliest Raeburn in the collection, from around 1790, is of Adam Ferguson and is a good example of his middle period. The portrait of William Robertson, Principal of the University from 1762 to 1793, is signed and dated 1792; this is reputed to be the only known signature of Raeburn. A portrait of Thomas Elder, Lord Provost of Edinburgh, was painted for the University in 1797 and shows an advance in development of the artist's style, but is not as striking as the 1798 portrait of John Robison, Professor of Natural Philosophy. This is an outstanding work and has been described as one of Raeburn's finest portraits.

For further information, see:
David Talbot Rice, *The University Portraits* (Edinburgh, 1957).
J H Burnett, David Howarth and Sheila D Fletcher, *The University Portraits, Second Series* (Edinburgh, 1986).

William Robertson (1792)
Henry Raeburn
© The University of Edinburgh

Modern and Contemporary Art Collection

The Modern and Contemporary Art Collection was formed in 2013 to build on existing holdings, particularly in the Hope Scott Collection, and also to bring the collection into the 21st century. Particularly after the merger between the University and the Edinburgh College of Art, it is important for the collection to reflect the burgeoning artistic output that the University now enjoys.

This is achieved through the acquisition of works from the ECA degree shows and also from artists who have worked with the University, either as staff or as students. The process of collecting from the ECA degree show was revived in 2013 through the ECA Art Collection Purchase Prize, which is awarded annually to final-year students of outstanding quality. In return for the prize, a work by the artist is collected. In addition, the collection contains works by artists who have exhibited at the Talbot Rice Gallery. Recent acquisitions include Callum Innes, David Batchelor and Katie Paterson.

Contemporary Art Research Collection

The Contemporary Art Research Collection is the newest addition to the University Art Collection. In contrast to the rest of the collection, which is linked in one form or another to the University either by artist, sitter or collector, the Contemporary Art Research Collection focuses on research and teaching.

The Collections Development Group was set up in 2013 to oversee the rationale of this collection; this is a group made up of academics, curators and, crucially, students. As well as signalling a new direction more generally, the Contemporary Art Research Collection offers a unique learning experience for students. As the collection evolves, students will be involved at every stage – including research, development and the acquisition process itself.

This collection was inspired by a piece that was discovered in the Edinburgh College of Art Collection. This work by Barbara

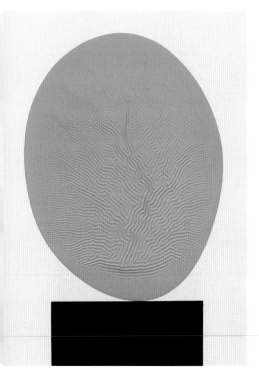

Colour Chart 5 (blue) (2011)
David Batchelor
© David Batchelor

Hepworth was purchased in 1952 for the purposes of teaching, and is part of a group of works by artists such as John Piper, Vanessa Bell, Augustus John and Ben Nicholson. It was this ethos of acquiring work to support teaching and research that has inspired this new direction.

....

Talbot Rice Memorial Collection

Consisting of some 20 oil and watercolour paintings, this collection was created to commemorate the late Professor of Fine Arts, David Talbot Rice. A number of his friends and former pupils presented the University with works of art either from their own collections or, in the case of practising artists, examples of their own work. This idea was conceived by Dr Harold Fletcher, who began the collection with the donation of a picture by John Houston, which Professor Rice had once said he wished he could have bought for the University. Other artists featured in this collection include Elizabeth Blackadder, William MacTaggart, Mardi Barrie, Sam Bough and Anne Redpath.

David Talbot Rice CBE was born in Gloucestershire in 1903. He attended Eton before studying archaeology and anthropology at Christ Church, Oxford, graduating in 1925. In 1932, Rice was appointed Lecturer in Byzantine and Near Eastern Art at the newly founded Courtauld Institute of Art in London. In 1934, he was appointed to the Watson Gordon Chair of Fine Art at the University of Edinburgh, which he held almost until his death in 1972. During the Second World War, Rice worked with the Intelligence Directorate

Timepieces (Solar System) (2014)
Katie Paterson
Nine modified clocks
© John Bryden

For the Edinburgh College of Art

Eduardo Paolozzi '71

SILKSCREEN: HISTORY OF A MEDIUM   PHILADELPHIA MUSEUM OF ART   DECEMBER 17, 1971 · FEBRUARY 27, 1

of the War Office. After the war he continued to build up the Department of Fine Art at the University, where he established an honours degree that combined art history and studio art – a degree which continues to this day.

Following his death, the University's newly established Talbot Rice Art Centre, now Talbot Rice Gallery, was named in his honour.

....

Eduardo Paolozzi Collection

By numbers of works alone, Eduardo Paolozzi is the most represented artist in the University Art Collection. Including prints, maquettes, sculptures and mosaics, the University has a wide representation of Paolozzi's career.

To coincide with the opening of the Swann Building in 1997, the University commissioned two pieces by Eduardo Paolozzi. The large bronze sculptures, *Parthenope* and *Egeria*, found on the site at King's Buildings campus were designed to represent the notion that knowledge can be formed only through use of the imagination, in particular in relation to the fields of science and human biology.

After Paolozzi's death in 2005, the University received a major bequest from his estate. It included a set of Paolozzi's Alan Turing series of prints, together with four large sculptures in chrome and bronze, and more than 120 small plaster maquettes. The

larger works are currently on display in the Informatics Forum, home of the University's School of Informatics.

In 2015, the University negotiated the donation of major sections of Paolozzi's mosaic installations at Tottenham Court Road underground station in London. These sections, which formed the arches over the escalators, were part of a major commission that Paolozzi undertook in the mid-1980s and is considered to be one of his most important works.

....

John Munro Collection

Bequeathed by the late Dr John Munro (1933–2013), this collection of some 40 works came to the University in 2016. Munro graduated from the University in 1960, studying medicine, and enjoyed a long career of clinical excellence over 40 years. Munro was consultant physician at the Eastern General and Edenhall Hospitals and, upon retirement, the University made him an Honorary Fellow and then a Clinical Teaching Fellow, with his teaching career spanning until 2002.

Outside his profession, Munro had a long-standing love of art. He amassed a large collection that included some of the most respected names in 20th-century Scottish art, including John Bellany, Peter Howson, Ian Hughes and Barbara Rae. However, it was Munro's support of emerging artists that makes his collection all the more impressive. John, along with his wife Jeanie, would often collect from art college degree shows in a direct attempt to offer opportunities

Head V
Peter Howson
© Peter Howson, Courtesy
of Flowers Gallery London

for emerging Scottish artists. Indeed, on occasion, this even extended to studio space – allowing young artists the use of the attic of their home.

Thomson-Walker Collection

Sir John William Thomson-Walker (1871–1937), surgeon and print-collector, formed an outstanding collection of engraved portraits of medical men. Born in Newport, Fife, Thomson-Walker was educated at the Edinburgh Institution and the University of Edinburgh, graduating in 1894, before going to postgraduate study in Vienna. He set up in Harley Street as a consultant at King's College and St Peter's Hospitals, becoming one of the leading urologists of his day. In 1907 he was appointed a Hunterian Professor of the Royal College of Surgeons of England, and was knighted in 1922. He held a number of visiting lectureships, and was elected President of the Medical Society of London in 1933.

Print collecting was his lifelong passion. In his will, Thomson-Walker bequeathed his prints to the University, '…in the hope of encouraging the study of the history of medicine on which this great medical school has had such a profound and lasting influence'. This collection includes more than 2,500 prints and a number of books on the art and technique of engraving. The collection came to the University in 1939.

Moray House Art Collection

Contained within the Moray House Art Collection is a core of work by some of Scotland's most illustrious artists; Alan Davie, James Cowie, Anne Redpath, Robin Philipson and Robert Colquhoun are all represented. This part of the collection was brought together by Morris Grassie, former Head of the Department of Fine Art and then of the Faculty of Aesthetic Studies. Grassie collected works of the highest quality for Moray House, often through conversations with the artists themselves.

Grassie was brought up in Arbroath and, as a child, was taught to draw by James Cowie, then Warden of nearby Hospitalfield. Cowie had a profound influence on Grassie and, when it came to the formation of this collection, he was the first artist collected.

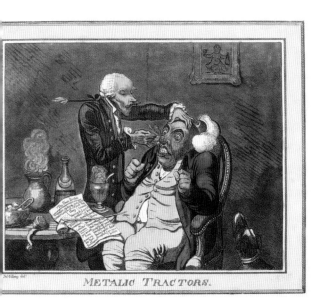

When Grassie retired, he donated one of his own paintings, *The Rehearsal*, to the collection.

The Moray House Art Collection also contains the Newington Collection and works collected from ECA degree shows, particularly from the 1990s.

....

The Gandharan Fragments

These sculptural fragments were donated to the University in 1872 by Colonel H C Johnstone. A year earlier, he donated a similar collection to the India Museum, which was later transferred to the British Museum in London.

Gandhara was located in the northern regions of modern Pakistan and eastern Afghanistan. The Kingdom of Gandhara lasted from around the 1st century BC to the 11th century AD.

The collection held by the University numbers around 27 individual pieces.

Gandharan sculpture fragments: Head of Buddha
c.1st century AD
© The University of Edinburgh

Edinburgh College of Art Collection

The ECA Collection consists of a diverse range of subjects and genres, including painting, sculpture, film, animation, textiles and jewellery. The largest of the collections is the Drawing & Painting Collection which contains approximately 2,000 items, largely consisting of graduate work.

The ECA Collection provides a fascinating insight into art education in Scotland in the 20th century. Due to its size and scope, it has been divided into sections relating to the relevant subject area; these areas are a mix of centrally managed collections, such as Drawing & Painting and the Cast Collection, and those that remain in their relevant departments due to their use in teaching, such as Textiles.

ECA Drawing & Painting Collection

The ECA Drawing & Painting Collection is composed primarily of work by ex-students and staff. Establishing such a collection was an institutional objective when ECA was founded, but collecting student work on a regular basis did not really occur until the 1914–1915 session. Although work was collected from this date onwards, the majority of works are from the second half of the 20th century. The collection contains a number of significant formative works by leading Scottish artists such as John Bellany, Elizabeth Blackadder, John Houston, Anne Redpath and David Michie. The collection also contains works by ECA staff, such as Sir William Gillies and James Cumming.

Smugglerius (1854)
Photograph by John K McGregor

ECA Cast Collection

The ECA Cast Collection contains 265 plaster casts of Antique, Renaissance and Gothic statues, bas reliefs and architectural passages. The casts are displayed in the ECA Main Building on Lauriston Place, which contains the beautiful neoclassical sculpture court specifically designed to house the casts of the Parthenon frieze.

The collection of plaster casts of the former Trustees' Academy in Edinburgh – the first public school of art in Britain, founded in 1760 – was acquired in the late 18th and early 19th centuries for the training of artists in Scotland. The collection was eventually transferred to ECA in 1911, with the first printed catalogue dating from 1837.

The casts are used less for direct drawing instruction today, but remain a key source of inspiration for wide ranging and innovative projects by staff, students and visiting artists.

ECA Print Collection

The ECA Print Collection has been built up by donation and by staff collecting student prints that are of particularly high quality or demonstrate specific techniques in an exemplary or unusual manner.

The collection is extensively used for teaching purposes in order to help students understand the potential of each technique available in the Print Workshop at ECA.

The works in the collection cover all techniques: intaglio, lithography, screenprinting and relief printing. Some of the largest prints were made on an offset press that had a bed measuring approximately 130cm x 100cm, which the workshop no longer has; these prints are of particular value.

The oldest prints date back to the early 20th century but the majority represent the period from around 1970 to 1995. The collection consists of more than 330 individual prints plus a series of folios.

ECA Artists' Books Collection

The ECA Library began actively collecting artists' books in the 1980s. The earliest books in the collection date back to the 1960s, for example Ed Ruscha's *Twenty-Six Gasoline Stations*, a now iconic paperback book. The collection is situated in the ECA Library at Evolution House, where there are also regular displays featuring the collection.

The collection consists of just over 500 artists' books. It is a working and handling collection, and is used regularly in group tutorials. Students and staff can also request individual artist's books for reference in the Library.

The collection is strong on Scottish artists such as Ian Hamilton Finlay, Helen Douglas, Jane Hyslop, Jenny Smith, Susie Wilson and Susie Leiper, but is also international in scope, including works by Hans Waanders, Maddy Rosenberg, and the works of Redfoxpress (featuring European contributors in the *C'est mon dada* series, and the works of Francis van Maele and Franticham). Recent acquisitions include Callum Innes and Garry

Fabian Miller. The collection also includes book-works by ECA students acquired from the annual ECA degree shows.

....

ECA Textile Collection

The ECA Textile Collection primarily comprises embroidery samples created through the Needlework Development Scheme (NDS). Originally established in Scotland in 1934, the NDS was a collaborative project aimed at encouraging embroidery, raising the standard of design in Britain and collecting historical and contemporary examples of embroidery design to serve as an educational resource. Financed by Paisley-based thread manufacturers J&P Coats, the scheme was organised by the four Scottish art schools: Gray's, Duncan of Jordanstone, ECA and Glasgow School of Art. With mills all over the world, Coats had international connections that greatly benefited this collection. During the 1930s the scheme concentrated on modern European design and, by 1939, some 900 embroideries had been acquired for use by art colleges, schools, training colleges, women's institutes and other organisations across Scotland.

When the scheme was re-established after the Second World War, its aims were retained, but the remit was expanded to include other arts schools in the UK where embroidery was taught. This expansion involved the Ministry of Education and the V&A Museum, and the recruitment of internationally celebrated textile designers as expert advisers. In the years following the war, the scheme became centralised and staffed with a qualified embroidery expert, a secretary and several practitioners.

The NDS was disbanded in 1961, although it was recognised that it had achieved its aims. More than 3,000 textile items had been amassed by this time, which were divided and distributed around universities, museums and other organisations. Of these, 64 items were donated to ECA.

There are also important items such as the paisley shawl designs which are held as part of the ECA Rare Books Collection.

....

ECA Jewellery & Silversmithing Collection

This collection consists of three diverse groups of work.

Silverware

Silverware including work designed and made by BA Hons students between 1974 and 1983. This collection includes prize-winning pieces entered for the Johnson and Matthey competitions from this period. It is notable that the majority of this work is by female students, which was not nationally typical for this time. A prime example of this collection is a cylindrical jug by Wendy Rae from 1977, with three matching beakers, all with waved moulded girdles.

Other objects in this collection were made for ECA as trophies or ceremonial tableware or are mixed pieces purchased or donated to the College.

Artist in Residency Collection

Started in 2010 by Programme Director Stephen Bottomley and made up of a piece of contemporary jewellery or silversmithing made by each successive artist in residence. The successful applicant spends a year in the School of Design as an incubator scheme, developing their own practice with the department's facilities and support. Artists in residence have been graduates of ECA or of other national and international schools such as the Royal College of Art. Each has donated a piece to this growing collection.

Sketchbooks, portfolio work and design sheets

A large open collection of donated student sketchbooks and portfolio work primarily from the mid-1980s onwards. These are used as teaching aids and are accessible by students for design and development.

The collection includes many original design boards to competitions including the RSA Awards, Craftsmanship and Design Council Awards and the Goldsmiths' Hall precious metal bursaries and Silversmithing and Design Awards.

ECA Film and TV Collection

The Film and TV Collection holds tape masters of all degree show compilations from 1991 to the present day. Holdings consist of a variety of formats; for the first ten years (1991–2001) films are in DVCPro format. Masters of degree show compilations from 1992 to 2009 are in DVCAM format and DVD. Holdings from 2010 until the present are in high definition video (HDV) format.

The collection contains work of students in third year and upwards from 2008 onwards.

ECA Animation Collection

The collection comprises animations produced by students from the 1970s to the present day, representing a complete record of all student work produced in this period. All the animations are stored on the original recording format, including analogue (16mm optical prints, 16mm separate Mag sountracks/Pic, Low Band Umatic Video, High Band Umatic Video, VHS, SVHS) and digital (DVC Pro, Mini DV, DV Cam, DVD (pal) SD). Viewing equipment for these formats is also held in the department.

ECA is the only art school in Scotland with an animation collection of this size. The historical depth of the collection is significant, as is the amount of foreign film. The collection is also particularly strong in satire and current affairs.

ECA Glass Collection

Stained glass, alongside embroidery and plaster work, has the longest history of subjects taught in the School of Design. This dates back to 1908, when Douglas Strachan, a celebrated glass artist, shared the role of Head of School of Design with William Small Black. Emphasis remains on the theory and practice of art, rather than the assembling of a collection of student work. However, works have been collected via the ECA Art Collections Purchase Prize and sit within the Modern and Contemporary Art Collection.

Edinburgh.

Section of Upper Museum. with Plan of part of Ceiling.

W.H. Playfair. Arch.t

August. 9.th 1817.

vi. Museum Collections

The Museum Collections, formed over four centuries, tell the story of the University of Edinburgh within Europe and the wider world. In the 19th century the University's natural history collections formed the basis for the new Scottish national museum collections. The object collections of individual professors have now grown into major collections which support the research, teaching and public engagement of the University.

Transverse section of the Upper Museum, University of Edinburgh, looking south (detail)

Dermatome Man

Anatomical Museum, University of Edinburgh

The Anatomy Collection at the University of Edinburgh dates from 1798 when Professor Alexander Monro *secundus* (1733–1817) donated his private collection, and that of his father Alexander Monro *primus* (1697–1767), to the Department of Anatomy. Over the 19th and first half of the 20th century, the collection increased in size and scope. In 1884 a purpose-built Anatomical Museum at the heart of the new medical school was opened to display this growing collection. The museum was designed by Robert Rowand Anderson as a three-storey, top-lit galleried hall, with skeletons of whales and dolphins suspended from the ceiling and a wide range of historical and anatomical specimens presented on display round about them. The museum continued to flourish under Sir William Turner, Professor of Anatomy (1867–1903) and Principal of the University from 1903 to 1916. In the 1950s the museum was reduced to a single upper storey, the site of the present museum. Many of the non-human specimens were transferred to other institutions; some of the whales were moved to the National Museum of Scotland. The lobby of the Anatomical Museum still contains elephant skeletons and other exhibits from the original museum.

The Anatomy Collection is currently subject to a detailed inventory project and is thought to consist of about 12,000 objects, including medical models, specimens and preparations, anatomical and phrenological casts, statues, original anatomical illustrations and prints, photographs,

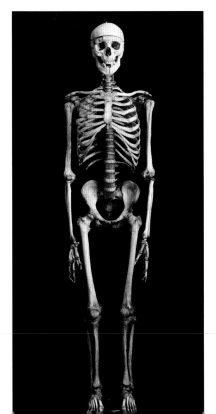

Burke's skeleton

Silver mask, 1832

Archaeology Collection

The collection is named after V Gordon Childe, Abercromby Professor of Prehistoric Archaeology at the University from 1927 to 1946 and the excavator of Skara Brae.

Traveller, linguist and lifelong Marxist, Childe was born in Sydney, studied there and at Oxford, was professor at Edinburgh 1927–1946 and finally Director of the University of London Institute of Archaeology. He recognised that prehistoric European culture and economy were derived from discoveries and inventions which had filtered from the Ancient East. Childe also showed that the prehistory of Britain is meaningless unless it is considered as part of Europe. In this, and other advances, Childe left an indelible mark on archaeological theory, in particular in his ability to see archaeological sites and artefacts as fossil remains of human behaviour.

Since Childe's initial contribution to the Reference Collection, additions were made by his successors, Stuart Piggott and Dennis Harding, as well as by outside donations. The collection now houses artefacts from the Indus Valley, the Near East including Egypt, Mediterranean regions and Europe north of the Alps, in addition to ethnographic items. The wide range of materials includes textile fragments from Neolithic Swiss Lake Villages.

lantern slides and departmental archives. One of the museum's most important, if infamous, specimens is the skeleton of William Burke, the Irish murderer who was hanged in 1829 for his part (with William Hare) in supplying freshly suffocated corpses for dissection by the anatomist Dr Robert Knox. Following his hanging, Burke was dissected by Professor Alexander Monro *tertius* in the University and his skeleton became part of the Anatomy Collection, subsequently being displayed at the museum.

Another renowned item is the silver mask made to disguise facial injuries in 1832. At the siege of Antwerp a young French gunner, Alphonse Louis, was badly injured, shrapnel removing his left cheek, soft palate and most of his lower jaw. A silver mask was constructed from a plaster cast of his face and was then painted with oils and adorned with a moustache and whiskers. It was attached to his head with straps and had a spring which opened the jaw.

Early Neolithic ground stone axe, collected by V G Childe

Chemistry Collection

The Chemistry Collection consists of several hundred items reflecting the history of chemistry research and teaching at the University of Edinburgh. Items include historical scientific instruments, samples of chemicals and crystals, three-dimensional models, notebooks, documents, photographs, prints and busts.

These items are distributed around various locations within the University. The School of Chemistry's museum has an extensive collection of exhibits; some others are on display in the department and some are on loan to various collections. The nucleus of the departmental museum is a collection of chemicals used by Lyon Playfair in illustrating his lectures and presented to the University on his resignation from the Chair of Chemistry in 1869. The collection was added to and largely preserved as a collection by Dr C Arnold Beevers, Reader Emeritus in Crystallography at the University of Edinburgh.

Among the numerous items of interest held in the museum is Professor Alexander Crum Brown's model of the crystal lattice structure of sodium chloride, dating from 1883. Brown (1838–1922) was a pioneering chemist whose models helped people to visualise his complex and challenging ideas. This model of the structure of sodium chloride (NaCl) was made from knitting needles and alternate balls of red and blue wool.

The museum collection also contains other Crum Brown artefacts such as complicated pieces of knitting in illustration of his mathematical work on interpenetrating surfaces. Other items of note include:

- a sample of strontia, isolated by Thomas Charles Hope in 1791 from mineral samples mined at Strontian
- a sample of arsenic from the internationally famous trial of Madeline Smith in 1897
- original Beevers-Lipson strips devised by Arnold Beevers of the University's School of Chemistry and as used by Watson and Crick in the determination of the structure of DNA
- a photograph from 1894 of the first and oldest chemistry society in the world
- a press cuttings book from 1925 detailing the international mix of Edinburgh's chemistry students at that time.

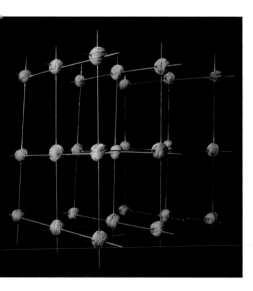

Model of rock salt,
by Alexander Crum Brown, 1883

Items currently on loan to other University collections include an original glass phial of carbon dioxide – one of only three remaining produced by Joseph Black – and the sovereign balance used by a chemistry professor to check the gold content of coins paid by students for their tuition.

....

Classics Teaching Collection and Cast Collection

Classics at the University of Edinburgh possesses a fine study collection of ancient objects – mostly terracotta vases – from Egypt, Cyprus, Greece and the Roman world, spanning from the prehistoric period to the Roman era. The complete state of the vases suggests that they come from a funerary context. Especially interesting are the Cypriot examples of white slip ware, proto-white painted and Cypriot-geometric vases. They offer a good sample of different materials and shapes from the Bronze Age to the Iron Age. The same can be claimed for the Corinthian *aryballoi* which, together with the Attic black-figure *lekythoi*, illustrate the variety of techniques employed to decorate funerary offerings at Athens and Corinth.

Our substantial collection of plaster casts of ancient works of sculpture is also on display. There are examples of three-dimensional statues, reliefs and portraits dated from the Archaic and Classical periods to the Hellenistic and Roman periods. The casts are used in courses on the study and dissemination of classical antiquity in the post-antique period.

....

Cockburn Museum of Geology Collections

The Cockburn Museum, housed in the Grant Institute, King's Buildings holds an extensive collection of geological specimens and historical objects which reflect Edinburgh's prominent position within the geological sciences since the time of James Hutton (1726–1797). The collections reflect the whole spectrum of earth science materials – minerals, rocks, fossils – as well as maps, photographs and archives of activity by famous earth scientists dating back as far as the late 18th century.

Many of the collections were donated to the museum in the late 19th and early 20th centuries. The mineral collection contains approximately 30,000 mineral specimens from all over the world and includes material from the Currie, Davidson and Brown of Lanfine Collections. These collections provide a unique insight into the historical practice of collecting. They include minerals found only in Scotland and some unique to the Cockburn Museum.

The Lyell collection was donated to the University by the Lyell family. Charles Lyell (1797–1875) is regarded as the intellectual successor of James Hutton. Most of the material was collected by Lyell himself, or given to him on his many geological excursions. Some of the specimens are especially significant because they were used to illustrate his books and were collected at a time when important geological theories were being developed.

The geological experiments of Sir James Hall of Dunglass (1761–1832), recorded

No. 16.
Nucula nucleus Linn.
Recent.

No. 32.
Leda ovum. (Sow)
Lias.
Robin

No. 100.
Leda

Septarian concretion from the Geology teaching collection

Polish School of Medicine Historical Collection

The establishment of the Polish School of Medicine in March 1941 was a unique wartime academic initiative.

Although originally intended to meet the needs of students and doctors in the Polish armed forces, the School opened its doors to civilians from the outset. Students followed a Polish curriculum, were taught mainly in Polish, and were awarded a Polish degree. By the time the school closed in 1949, more than 336 students had matriculated, of whom 227 had graduated with a medical diploma (MBChB) and 19 obtained a doctorate or MD.

The Polish School of Medicine Historical Collection was established in 1986 on its 45th anniversary. It was founded by Dr Wiktor Tomaszewski, a former member of staff at the Polish School and Edinburgh general medical practitioner. The Chancellor's Building at Little France has been home to the collection since 2004.

Many of the artefacts in the collection were gifted to the University of Edinburgh or to the collection by Polish Medical Academies, grateful former students, staff and graduates of the Polish School.

The collection is eclectic in nature and encompasses more than 100 medals, including the military medals and awards of the late Professor Antoni Jurasz, the first Dean of the School and of one of its graduates, Dr Stanley Kryszek. Also included are wartime memorabilia, books about the Polish School of Medicine, photographs, paintings, pen and ink drawings of key

in the collection, mark the foundation of experimental geology. Hall, a baronet from East Lothian and an alumnus, set out to prove James Hutton's theory that the interior of the Earth was hot. He carried out more than 500 experiments, many at some personal risk. He melted basalt in an iron furnace and proved that it resumed its original form on cooling. By heating limestone in a sealed gun barrel he showed that it did not decompose if heated under pressure. He also investigated folding in rocks, and simulated tidal waves – such as those caused by earthquakes – with charges of gunpowder.

The total holding of the Cockburn Museum exceeds 130,000 items. The breadth of the collection means that it is of considerable research and teaching value.

Shells collected by Charles Darwin, 1830s Lyell Collection

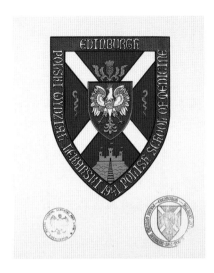

Polish School of Medicine, coat of arms

University and Edinburgh buildings with medical links by Polish artist Josef Młynarski.

Also part of the collection is a hand-gilded porcelain coffee/tea service, also the work of Josef Młynarski and his wife, which was presented to the University of Edinburgh in 1996. Of particular note are the sculptures by Professor Jakub Rostowski, the third and last Dean of the School, which tell the story of the Polish School from its beginnings.

Zoology – Natural History Collection

The Natural History Collection contains several thousand zoological specimens. Its national importance is that it remains one of the few university natural history collections still largely intact (particularly with respect to the invertebrate material and much vertebrate skeletal material). The collection

still forms an integral part of the teaching of biological sciences in the University.

In 1697 Robert Sibbald, Edinburgh's first Professor of Medicine, presented to the College a collection of natural history specimens gathered by himself and his recently deceased colleague, Andrew Balfour. The collection was placed on display in the original University buildings on the site of the present Old College. This was one of the first museums in Britain, created 60 years before the British Museum. The collection's reputation spread throughout Europe.

Professor Robert Jameson took over the Chair of Natural History in 1804 and revitalised the collection.

In the 50 years that Jameson held the chair, some 74,000 specimens were amassed for the collection. In 1812, the collection was given the title of 'Royal Museum of the University'.

As well as making purchases, Jameson compiled what he called a 'Set of Instructions for Collectors', which was distributed among the different ministers and public servants abroad in the hope that they would collect specimens and send them to the University. He issued his instructions to those he knew were about to travel, one of whom was William Scoresby (junior) who collected among other things a live polar bear.

Jameson re-housed the collection twice in better, larger premises. In 1826 the museum moved into what is now the Talbot Rice Gallery. In 1852, Jameson suggested that the collection should be placed in the hands of the nation and should be housed in a new national museum to be built in Chambers Street. Work began in 1854, the year of

Jameson's death. This 'new museum' was initially called the Museum of Science and Art, subsequently the Royal Scottish Museum and is now the National Museum of Scotland.

The University now set about acquiring a new collection for its own use, under James Cossar Ewart, Professor of Natural History from 1882. James Hartley Ashworth became first Professor of Zoology in 1919 and succeeded Ewart in 1927. Under Ashworth a new building at the King's Buildings was erected to house the Department of Zoology and the Natural History Collections. The building now known as the Ashworth Laboratories was completed in 1929 and currently houses the collection.

The Ashworth Laboratories are decorated with sculptures of animals made by Phyllis Bone, who was the first female Royal Scottish Academician. She made three sculptures – a dung beetle, an octopus and a crab – to represent the invertebrates. The animals were first modelled in clay and the models then cast in artificial stone to make the 17 plaques which decorate the exterior of the building. Phyllis Bone also made the sculptures which decorate the National War Memorial in Edinburgh Castle.

The collection was enlarged continuously from 1928 onwards and now holds many historically and scientifically important specimens. Most prominent among these is the collection of corals donated by Sir Maurice Yonge. Other items include:

- two large sea shells, the sole article of dress of the inhabitants of the Admiralty Isles, which had never been visited by scientists until HMS *Challenger* went there in 1874
- jellyfish and sea-spiders from one of the 'Discovery' voyages
- giant Australian earthworms
- emperor penguin eggs brought back from Scott's ill-fated quest for the South Pole
- an incredible selection of finely crafted papier-mâché models ranging from sea urchins to a life-size human figure
- a squid brought back from Port Seton in a bucket by Mrs Ashworth, the Professor's wife.

Morpho peleides
(Blue Morpho butterfly)

Conclusion and Future Directions

With Zoology this survey of the collections of the University of Edinburgh, as they stand in 2016, comes to an end. However, the story of the collections, which we steward for the University and the wider world, will continue. At the time of writing we are starting to digitise the University's thesis collection, which dates back to the early 17th century and includes about 25,000 volumes. This is the largely unpublished story of student research at the University, including the arrival of the first Chinese student in the 1850s and the admission of women to the University from the late 19th century. As these collections become available online they will be accessible across the world, for enjoyment as well as study. However, the rise of the digital presents us with new challenges: how to store, preserve and make accessible this content. We have kept safe Clement Litill's books from their arrival in 1580; we intend that our digital photographs and emails will still be viewable four hundred years from now.

While tackling these new challenges, we also need to ensure that our still-growing physical collections can still be seen and used. Increasingly our objects will be displayed in exhibitions at the University or on loan to museums and libraries across the world. However, we also need to allow them to be touched and handled in classes or the reading room, thereby fulfilling their original purpose to help people understand their world and history. To preserve the vast range of items described in this book, some dating back to the 1st century, a great deal of skilled work is required, ranging from archival cataloguing to musical instrument conservation. New kinds of physical collections are arriving as the collections expand into new areas, particularly in the visual arts. These collections will require specialist skills and resource so they can be stewarded for future generations. The University and its collections came into being through the generosity and support of countless individuals; it is a continuing story of people. The names of the collectors and donors recorded in this Directory are hopefully only the first in a list that will grow with the collections in centuries to come.

Detail of *Mesostic Interleaved*, Alec Finlay, 2010

Index

Numbers in *italic* refer to illustrations.

Index